DIY

I-Ching
& Modern
Feng Shui

易經與現代風水

Roger Wu 吳治逸

English Version

自 序

　　無極生太極，太極生兩儀，兩儀生四象，四象生八卦。無極是陰陽未分的混沌狀態，沒有開始也沒有結束，無限久遠，永續恆遠；太極乃無止境的空間，陰陽靜動確立，萬物生長。兩儀生四象，四象乃少陽(春分)、少陰(秋分)、太陽(夏至)與太陰(冬至)，農作之生長收藏即是配合春夏秋冬四季(四象)之氣候。聖人伏羲作先天八卦，大禹推演後天八卦重疊成六十四卦。易經是中國古聖人之集體創作，它的哲學包含變易、不易與簡易(容易)三大意涵。變易是宇宙萬物無時無刻都在變動與變化，從而產生新事象；不易則是在宇宙萬物之變化中，仍有永恆不變的真理法則存在；而簡易(容易)是吾人經歷變動，變化後產生新的事象，適應並與之和平共存，進而使之變成簡易、容易。學易經可預知事物變化之始末，若事物不失中正得宜就是不變。人生起伏不定，驟變不已就是變易；易經教導如何逢凶化吉使得事情順利容易，就是簡易、容易。古今不論有無生命之成長過程與循環皆不出其右。能夠透過易經之學習而博古通今，就是知難行易。本書嘗試詮釋翻譯易經64卦，384爻與建言，共448則，使易經簡單易懂與成語化；而易經具有預言，卜噬功能，人們對於未來之不確定性與期待，都可透過卜卦得到釋疑。

　　第二篇現代風水，乃是研究如何能提供最佳生活環境品質的一門學問，它能提供風水相關知識，改善住家格局，使全家安和樂利。本人曾受邀赴美幫一家新設銀行看風水，從建址到開幕都給與改進意見。有些人認為風水是迷信，但人體血液中含有鐵質，因其受到地球磁場的影響，個性與健康均會有所關連。另外，每間屋子會有一條鬼門線，即東北與西南之中間連線，如果把貓或狗甚至老鼠用籠子把它放在鬼門線上，它一定會移開，因它受到磁場的干擾。又最近幾年世界各地常出現人性偏離的怪事，這可能與地球軸心偏離有關，造成部分人性的乖違。一般勘查居家風水首先對居住者之生辰與屋內之格局勘查外，也要對屋外之環境與家人作評估。坊間有幾種職業，為了要提供更好的服務，需要懂居家風水，例如：建築師、地理師、房屋仲介、殯葬業與命理師等。我年輕時坎坷，但自從學風水，且自我改善居家格局後，一路順遂，平步青雲，這是我學習風水後老天對我的眷顧。

　　本書易經與現代風水以英文為主、中文為輔詮釋，再再希望有興趣之海內外人士亦能分享中國人之先聖智慧。共享福祿壽喜的人生。

　　拙才疏學淺，殷盼諸先進前輩們指教，謝謝。

Preface

The Infinity (Endless Ultimate) gives rise to the Supreme Ultimate, the Supreme Ultimate gives rise to the Duality (Yin and Yang), the Duality generates four emblematic symbols and the four emblematic symbols engender eight basics Ba-Gua. The Infinity, which is boundless and eternal, signifies Yin and Yang in the primal order less chaos, without beginning and end. The Supreme Ultimate refers to endless space. The harmony of Human beings and the nature depends upon the seamless coordination of Yin and Yang. Four emblematic symbols are the spring equinox, the summer solstice, the autumn equinox and the winter solstice. Farmers in ancient times planned the farm work according to the four seasons. They sowed in spring, planted in summer, reaped in autumn and stored in winter. The Sage Fu-Xi applied Yin and Yang symbols (duality) to create primordial Ba-Gua. Xia-Yu later reinterpreted it to become the "Manifested Ba-Gua". King Wen of Zhou state overlapped the Ba-Gua (Eight Trigrams) and developed it into the current 64 Gua (64 Trigrams). I-Ching is one of the oldest Chinese classic texts. It was created collectively by the Sages in ancient China. "Variability"," Persistency" and "Simplicity" are the philosophy of I-Ching. Variability signifies that all creatures in the cosmos are constantly changing, which result in new phenomena. Persistency means although all creatures are changing constantly, there is still a universal truth, or so-called "law of being", governing everything. Simplicity means that after all creatures experienced changes, new situations occurred, but the creatures became adapted and everything co-existed peacefully once again. At the end, they live prosperously and successfully. Learning I-Ching will enable you to foresee the ins and outs of things. If a thing is handled according to the doctrine of the mean, it then complies with the "Persistency". Life is full of ups and downs. The uncertainty and changeability of life is "Variability". I-Ching teaches you to turn bad luck into good fortunes and help things go smoothly. This is called "Simplicity". From ancient times to the present day, all matter on earth and the life cycles of all living beings never fall outside of the scope of "Variability", "Persistency" and "Simplicity". Learning I-Ching will educate and inform you about the past and the present, which is exactly what the proverb "To know is difficult, to do is easy!" preaches. This book is attempting to interpret the 64 hexagrams and 384 yaos (lines on a trigram), providing 448 suggestions in total, allowing 64 hexagrams and 384 yaos be idiomized and easily understandable. I-Ching is also a book of divination, used as a tool to predict the future to relieve people's doubts.

The second part of the book– Modern Feng Shui provides readers with related knowledge of Feng Shui to improve the design and layout of a house to help the family live in harmony and prosperity. I was once invited to the US to do a Feng Shui consultation for a new bank. The consultation ranged from the choice of address, office layouts to grand opening. Many people in the West do not believe in Feng Shui. They tend to see it as a superstition. However, I always take the chance to explain to them. For example, the blood vessels in human bodies are influenced by the magnetic fields because there is iron in the vessels. Also, many people experience a sudden change of character as they are influenced by the axial tilt of the earth. In addition, there is a line between the center of northeast and southwest of a house. In feng shui, the line is called "the ghost gate line ". If a cat, a dog, or a mouse kept in a cage is placed on the ghost gate line, it will become agitated and try to move away immediately. To provide valid Feng Shui consultation for a house, I have to carefully study the layout, outside environment and zodiac signs of the families. I think some occupations, architects, Feng Sui masters, real estate agents, funeral service workers and fortunetellers in particular, need to know Feng Shui to provide better services to customers. When I was young, life was full of frustrations. Since I studied Feng Shui, my career has prospered rapidly and smoothly. It is perhaps due to the blessing from the God, but could it also be due to the results of studying Fend Sui?

This book is mainly written in English. I hope everyone in the world can learn and appreciate the wisdom of the sages in ancient China and have blessings, lucks, happiness, fortunes and longevity from I-Ching and Feng Shui.

Your kind advice is highly appreciated! Happy reading!

Roger Wu in Taipei

目　錄　　Contents

第二篇　現代風水　Part Two：Modern Feng Shui

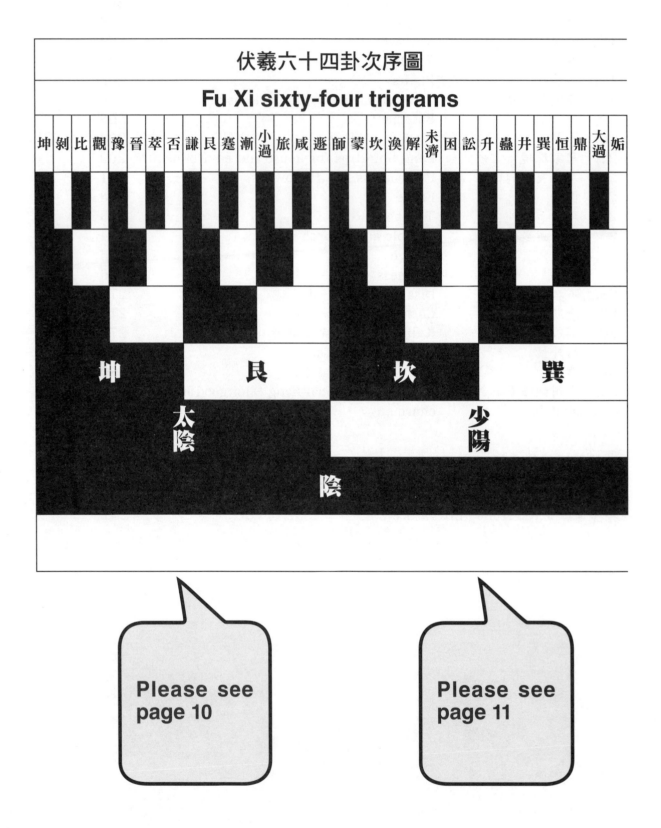

伏羲六十四卦次序圖
Fu Xi sixty-four trigrams

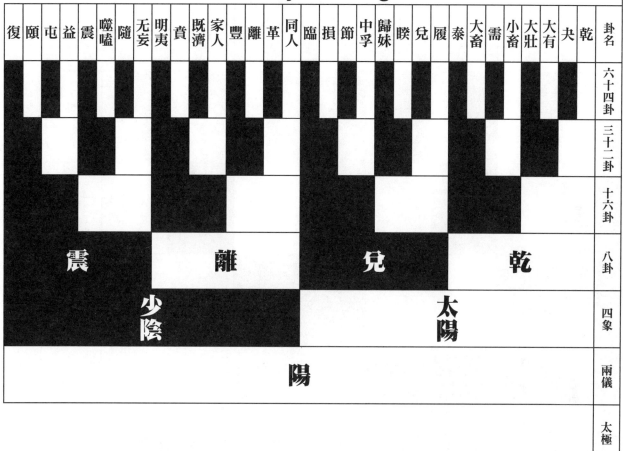

復	頤	屯	益	震	噬嗑	隨	无妄	明夷	賁	既濟	家人	豐	離	革	同人	臨	損	節	中孚	歸妹	睽	兌	履	泰	大畜	需	小畜	大壯	大有	夬	乾	卦名

六十四卦

三十二卦

十六卦

| 震 | 離 | 兌 | 乾 | 八卦 |

| 少陰 | 太陽 | 四象 |

| 陽 | 兩儀 |

太極

Please see page 12

Please see page 13

伏羲六十四卦次序圖
Fu Xi sixty-four trigrams

2	23	8	20	16	35	45	12	15	52	39	53	62	56	31	33	序號 No.
坤 Kun	剝 Bo	比 Bi	觀 Guan	豫 Yu	晉 Jin	萃 Tsui	否 Pi	謙 Qian	艮 Gen	蹇 Jian	漸 Jiang	小過 Xiao-Guo	旅 Lu	咸 Shian	遯 Duen	卦名 Gua Name

六十四卦 / 64 Gua (64 Trigrams)

三十二卦 / 32 Gua

十六卦 / 16 Gua

坤 Kun — 艮 Gen / 八卦 8 Gua

太陰 Taiyin / 四象 Four emblematic symbols

陰 Yin / 兩儀 Duality

太極 Infinity (Endless Ultimate) / 太極 Infinity (Endless Ultimate)

伏羲六十四卦次序圖

Fu Xi sixty-four trigrams

7	4	29	59	40	64	47	6	46	18	48	57	32	50	28	44	序號 No.
師 Shi	蒙 Meng	坎 Kaan	渙 Huan	解 Jie	未濟 Weih-Jih	困 Kuen	訟 Soong	升 Shen	蠱 Gu	井 Jing	巽 Xun	恒 Heng	鼎 Ding	大過 Da-Guo	姤 Guo	卦名 Gua Name

六十四卦 / 64 Gua (64 Trigrams)

三十二卦 / 32 Gua

十六卦 / 16 Gua

坎 Kaan　　　巽 Xun — 八卦 / 8 Gua

少陽 Shaoyang — 四象 Four emblematic symbols

陰 Yin — 兩儀 Duality

太極 Infinity (Endless Ultimate) — 太極 Infinity (Endless Ultimate)

伏羲六十四卦次序圖
Fu Xi sixty-four trigrams

24	27	3	42	51	21	17	25	36	22	63	37	55	30	49	13	序號 No.
復 Fuh	頤 Yi	屯 Tuen	益 Yih	震 Jehn	噬嗑 Shi-He	隨 Sui	无妄 Wuh-Whang	明夷 Ming-Yi	賁 Bih	既濟 Jih-Jih	家人 Jia-Ren	豐 Feng	離 Li	革 Ger	同人 Tong-Ren	卦名 Gua Name

六十四卦 64 Gua (64 Trigrams)

三十二卦 32 Gua

十六卦 16 Gua

震 Jehn　　離 Li — 八卦 8 Gua

少陰 Shaoyin — 四象 Four emblematic symbols

陽 Yang — 兩儀 Duality

太極 Infinity (Endless Ultimate) — 太極 Infinity (Endless Ultimate)

伏羲六十四卦次序圖
Fu Xi sixty-four trigrams

19	41	60	61	54	38	58	10	11	26	5	9	34	14	43	1	序號 No.
臨 Lirn	損 Suen	節 Jier	中孚 Zhong-Fu	歸妹 Gui-Mei	睽 Kui	兌 Duei	履 Lyu	泰 Thai	大畜 Da-Shiu	需 Shiu	小畜 Shiao-Shiu	大壯 Da-Juang	大有 Ta-Yu	夬 Guai	乾 Chian	卦名 Gua Name

六十四卦
64 Gua (64 Trigrams)

三十二卦
32 Gua

十六卦
16 Gua

兌 Duei **乾 Chian**
八卦
8 Gua

太陽 Taiyang
四象 Four emblematic symbols

陽 Yang
兩儀 Duality

太極 Infinity (Endless Ultimate)
太極 Infinity (Endless Ultimate)

六十四卦名中英對照表 (64 Gua Table in Chinese & English)

								上卦 Upper Gua / 下卦 Low Gua
坤（地）Kun 8	艮（山）Gen 7	坎（水）Kaan 6	巽（風）Xun 5	震（雷）Jehn 4	離（火）Li 3	兌（澤）Duei 2	乾（天）Chian 1	上卦 Upper Gua 下卦 Low Gua
地天泰 Thai 11	山天大畜 Da-Shiu 26	水天需 Shiu 5	風天小畜 Shiao-Shiu 9	雷天大壯 Da-Juang 34	火天大有 Da-Yu 14	澤天夬 Guai 43	乾為天 Chian 1	乾（天）Chian 1
地澤臨 Lirn 19	山澤損 Suen 41	水澤節 Jier 60	風澤中孚 Zhong-Fu 61	雷澤歸妹 Gui-Mei 54	火澤睽 Kui 38	兌為澤 Duei 58	天澤履 Lyu 10	兌（澤）Duei 2
地火明夷 Ming-Yi 36	山火賁 Bih 22	水火既濟 Jih-Jih 63	風火家人 Jia-Ren 37	雷火豐 Feng 55	離為火 Li 30	澤火革 Ger 49	天火同人 Tong-Ren 13	離（火）Li 3
地雷復 Fuh 24	山雷頤 Yi 27	水雷屯 Tuen 3	風雷益 Yih 42	震為雷 Jehn 51	火雷噬嗑 Shi-He 21	澤雷隨 Sui 17	天雷無妄 Wuh-Whang 25	震（雷）Jehn 4
地風升 Shen 46	山風蠱 Gu 18	水風井 Jing 48	巽為風 Xun 57	雷風恆 Heng 32	火風鼎 Ding 50	澤風大過 Da-Guo 28	天風姤 Guo 44	巽（風）Xun 5
地水師 Shi 7	山水蒙 Meng 4	坎為水 Kaan 29	風水渙 Huan 59	雷水解 Jie 40	火水未濟 Weih-Jih 64	澤水困 Kuen 47	天水訟 Soong 6	坎（水）Kaan 6
地山謙 Qian 15	艮為山 Gen 52	水山蹇 Jian 39	風山漸 Jiang 53	雷山小過 Xiao-Guo 62	火山旅 Lu 56	澤山咸 Shian 31	天山遯 Duen 33	艮（山）Gen 7
坤為地 Kun 2	山地剝 Bo 23	水地比 Bi 8	風地觀 Guan 20	雷地豫 Yu 16	火地晉 Jin 35	澤地萃 Tsui 45	天地否 Pi 12	坤（地）Kun 8

鑫富樂文教編輯部繪製

第一篇 Part One

易經
I-Ching

第一章 易經卜卦步驟、實例與基礎

Chapter 1 I-Ching divination, examples and basic concepts

1. 易經形成：

易經是伏羲觀察天象，以天、地、雷、風、水、火、山、澤應用在陰陽符號作先天八卦，到夏朝，大禹因為治水而悟出後天八卦。經周文王把八卦重疊成八八六十四卦，且每卦演繹六爻，成為三百八十四爻。易經是本文與傳構成的，本文即周易經文，而傳是易傳，用來解釋經文的。迄今有十篇傳亦稱十翼，即彖傳、象傳、繫辭傳各兩篇，加上序卦傳、說卦傳、雜卦傳、文言傳共十篇。

2. 學易經的好處：

(1) 人生指引：人生禍福無常，無法守善無過。誰都想要榮華富貴，趨吉避凶，但人生十之八九不如意。學易經能引領您寡過避禍，尤其當身處逆境時更要低調行事。

(2) 提升解析應變能力：人往往會面臨難以抉擇的窘境，如果學易而懂陰陽二元之應用道理，凡事不離正反兩面，例如上下、日月、天地、冷熱、寒暑、夫妻、高低、水火、好壞、順逆等，就不會無所適從，還能免災。

(3) 預知先機，掌握未來：透過卜卦察覺事象的發展，提前作好準備或防患，更可藉此造福人群，提升個人層次。

1. The origins of I-Ching

I-Ching was initially created by Fu-Xi, who carefully observed the patterns of the world and applied Yin and Yang to create the eight trigrams (Ba-Gua). Later Xia Yu, a legendary ruler in ancient China, created the "Manifested Ba-Gua" from "Primordial Ba-Gua" inspired by his experiences in implementing flood control. King Wen of Zhou state later updated the Ba-Gua (Eight Trigrams) and developed it into the current 64 Gua (64 Trigrams).

I-Ching consists of "Zhou Yi" and "I Chuan" — the main text and the commentaries. Part of the canonization of the Zhou Yi bound it to a set of ten commentaries called the "Ten Wings". The ten Wings include two chapters of Tuan Chuan, Xiang Chuan and Si Cih Chuan. The 4 others are called Syu Gua Chuan, Shuo Gua Chuan, Za Gua Chuan and Wen Yen Chuan.

2. The benefits of learning I-Ching

(1) Life guide.

Life has ups and downs. Nobody can live a life without adversity. Although everyone likes to have all the splendor in the world, life cannot always be smooth. Through the study of I-Ching, you can reduce the chance of making mistakes and avoid misfortune. Especially when things turn sour, always keep a low-profile.

(2) To improve your analytical skills and your ability to adapt.

Predicaments are common in life. If you know duality and apply it in life, you will know that everything is within the scope of "duality", meaning it's either positive or negative. You will know what course to take to avoid disasters. Examples of duality : high and low, young and old, sun and moon, top and bottom, cold and hot, husband and wife, water and fire, good and bad, smoothness and adversity, etc.

(3) Predict the future and seize the opportunities.

I-Ching serves as an ancient Chinese method of divination. It can foresee the developing situation and guide you in preparing your contingency plans. Moreover, you will take your life to the next level through learning I-Ching.

3.卜卦 DIY

3-1.骰子卜卦法

(1)卜卦時應虔誠，空間安靜且心情平靜，問題單一且明確，不是選擇題。每事一日一問，勿反覆卜卦或變更字句，但同樣地重複詢問與卜卦；儘量在白天卜卦。

(2)卜卦程序：

a.請示卦神的事，要先擬定，才不至於混亂。盡量用是非題方式詢問，而不是選擇題。

(註：卜卦祈禱文，有人拜請四聖，即伏羲、文王、周公、孔子；也有版本以「卦神」稱呼。這裡以「卦神」稱呼，取其方便性，實質無異。)

b.準備一顆骰子、筆、紙與玻璃杯。

c.念誦祈禱文 (只需念誦1次)

我是 xxx，今年xx 歲，住在xxxxxxxxxxx。 今日有一事，………。

請卦神透過易經64卦，變爻指示。謝謝。

d.念完祈禱文即擲骰子七次於玻璃杯中，每次的點數「自下而上」，依序記錄。前三次為下卦，後三次為上卦，第七次是變爻，記錄在最下方。

3. Divination DIY

3-1. Dice method

(1) To use I-Ching for divination, one should be sincere and respectful. The place for divination should be quiet and calm. Ask clear and simple questions and avoid multiple-choice questions or questions with multiple answers. Do not consult I-Ching late at night or in the early hours. Also avoid being impatient and rushed.

(2) Divination Sequence

a.Prepare the question in your head before the divination. Ask yes or no questions instead of multiple-choice questions. (Note: While addressing the universe before asking a question, some versions call for certain Saints for help, i.e. Fu-Xi, Wen Wang, Chou-Gong, Confucius. In this edition, "Gua-Shen" or "the God of Divination" is used for simplification and convenience in praying. It makes no difference in their nature.)

b.Prepare a dice, a pen, a piece of paper and a glass.

c.Phrasing a question (only recite one time)
I am Mr. Xxx. I am xx years of age. My address is ⋯⋯⋯⋯⋯. Today I sincerely pray for an answer to my question through casting the I-Ching hexagrams. Thank you.

d.After the prayer, cast the dice seven times. Record each number on the dice on a piece of paper from bottom to the top. The first three casts are regarded as the "Low-Gua". The second three casts are regarded as the "Upper-Gua." The seventh cast is considered as the yao which is recorded on the very bottom.

自下而上↑	後三次	上卦	第6次
			第5次
			第4次
	前三次	下卦	第3次
			第2次
			第1次
	最下方	變爻	第7次

from bottom to the top ↑	the second three casts	Upper-Gua	6th
			5th
			4th
	the first three casts	Low-Gua	3rd
			2nd
			1st
	the very bottom	Variable yao	7th

e. 前六次的點數，如果是奇數屬陽▬▬，偶數屬陰▬ ▬；下卦加上卦，可算出屬於64卦的哪一卦。

e. If the total of the six casts is an odd number, it belongs to Yang ▬▬ . If it is an even number, it belongs to Yin ▬ ▬ . Low gua plus upper gua make the hexagram.

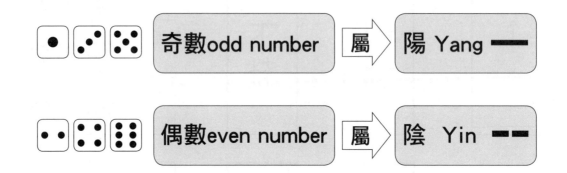

奇數 屬陽 符號 「▬▬」
偶數 屬陰 符號 「▬ ▬」
odd number belongs to Yang ▬▬
even number belongs to Yin ▬ ▬

f. 可透過查表(表1.1)查出其屬於64卦的哪一卦，查到後就可翻閱到本書的64卦所屬頁數，進一步查詢該卦的內容。

f. Table 1.1 shows you which "gua" you get among 64 hexagrams. Then find out the meaning corresponding to each hexagram.

g. 最後一次(第7次擲骰子)的數字，為變爻，每一卦都有6爻。第7次擲骰子的數字，為1，代表第1爻；為6，代表第6爻。

g. The number of the last cast (seventh) is defined for Yao. There are six yaos in a hexagram. If the seventh cast number is 1, it is the 1st yao. If the cast number is 6, it is the 6th yao.

(3) 範例：

　　a. 骰子前三次之點數，依序記錄為：「4—2—2」，偶數屬陰，符號為「▬ ▬」，作為下卦；

　　b. 後三次點數，依序記錄為：「5—3—1」，奇數屬陽，符號為「▬▬」，作為上卦；

　　c. 第七次點數為：「2」，為變爻。

(3) Example:

　　a. The first three numbers of the dice cast are "4,2,2". They are even numbers or "Yin numbers" that are indicated with the symbol of Yin "▬ ▬". The first three Yin numbers are regarded as low gua.

　　b. For instance, the second three casts have the numbers of "5,3,1". They are odd numbers or Yang numbers that are indicated with the symbol of "▬▬". The second three Yang numbers are regarded as upper gua.

　　c. The 7th cast of the dice has the number "2", meaning the 2nd yao of the hexagram is your answer to the divination. Record it below the first cast.

　　上卦：乾 1
　　(三個陽 – 乾卦 1)
　　◆ ▬ 第6次
　　◆ ▬ 第5 次
　　◆ ▬ 第4次
　　下卦： 坤 8
　　(三個陰 – 坤卦 8)
　　◆ ▬ ▬ 第3 次
　　◆ ▬ ▬ 第2 次
　　◆ ▬ ▬ 第1次
　　變爻：
　　◆ 2 變爻 第7次

1 —— 6th cast

3 —— 5th cast

5 —— 4th cast (Upper Gua) 3 Yang symbols belong to "NO.1, Chian".

2 - - 3rd cast

2 - - 2nd cast

4 - - 1st cast (Low Gua) 3 Yin symbol belong to "NO.8, Kun".

2 - 7th cast

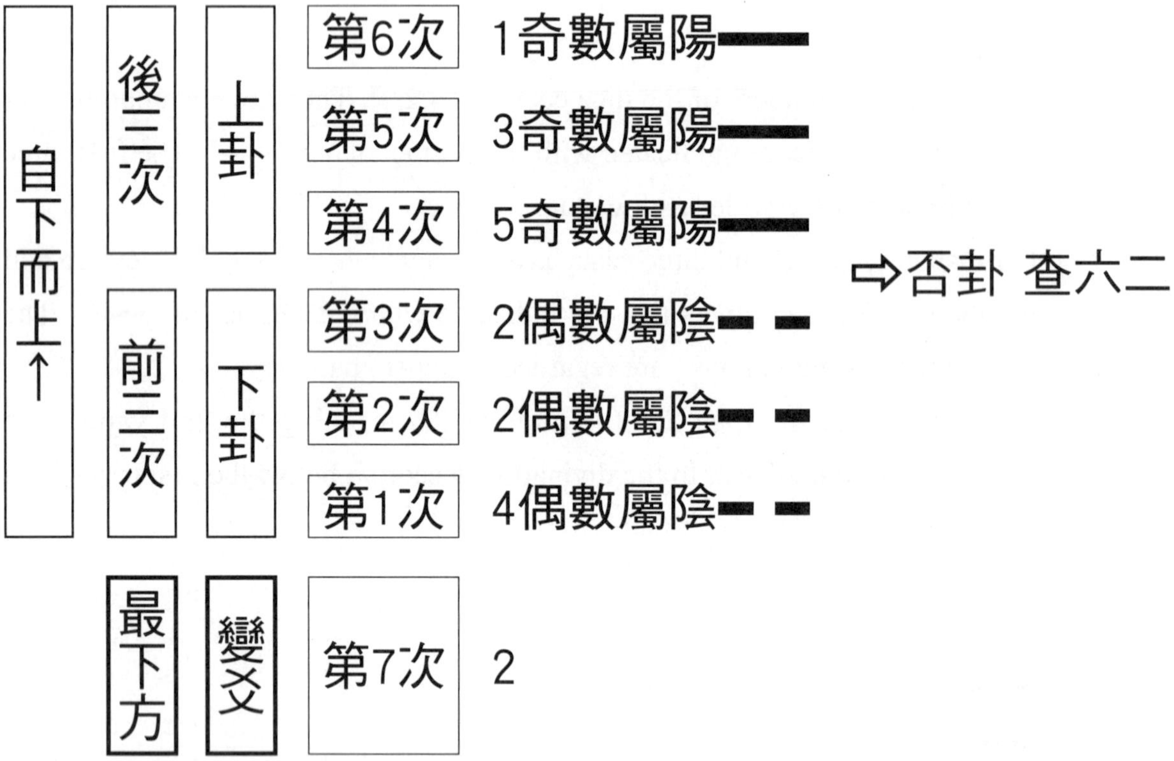
自下而上↑
後三次
上卦
第6次
1奇數屬陽
第5次
3奇數屬陽
第4次
5奇數屬陽
前三次
下卦
第3次
2偶數屬陰
第2次
2偶數屬陰
第1次
4偶數屬陰
⇨否卦 查六二
最下方
變爻
第7次
2

按下表得 8×1= 12 否卦 （×：表示查表對照，非乘法)

☆否卦 2 爻 即為所求之卦爻。

8&1→12 Pi Gua (the 7th cast, gets number 2. The seventh cast decides what yao in this hexagram.)

According to the table of 64 hexagrams below, you can get 12th hexagram of Pi, 2nd yao.

表 1.1

卦象 Gua symbols	☰	☱	☲	☳	☴	☵	☶	☷
卦名 Name	乾 Chian	兌 Duei	離 Li	震 Jehn	巽 Xun	坎 Kaan	艮 Gen	坤 Kun
序號 No.	1	2	3	4	5	6	7	8
口訣	乾三連	兌上缺	離中虛	震仰盂	巽下斷	坎中滿	艮覆碗	坤六斷

下卦	×	上卦	=	64	卦
1	×	1	=	1	乾
1	×	2	=	43	夬
1	×	3	=	14	大有
1	×	4	=	34	大壯
1	×	5	=	9	小畜
1	×	6	=	5	需
1	×	7	=	26	大畜
1	×	8	=	11	泰

Low Gua & Upper Gua → Hexagram		
1 & 1 →	1st	Chian
1 & 2 →	43rd	Guai
1 & 3 →	14th	Ta-Yu
1 & 4 →	34th	Da-Juang
1 & 5 →	9th	Shiao-Shiu
1 & 6 →	5th	Shiu
1 & 7 →	26th	Da-Shiu
1 & 8 →	11th	Thai

下卦	×	上卦	=	64	卦
3	×	1	=	13	同人
3	×	2	=	49	革
3	×	3	=	30	離
3	×	4	=	55	豐
3	×	5	=	37	家人
3	×	6	=	63	既濟
3	×	7	=	22	賁
3	×	8	=	36	明夷

Low Gua & Upper Gua → Hexagram		
3 & 1 →	13th	Tong- Ren
3 & 2 →	49th	Ger
3 & 3 →	30th	Li
3 & 4 →	55th	Feng
3 & 5 →	37th	Jia- Ren
3 & 6 →	63rd	Jih-Jih
3 & 7 →	22nd	Bih
3 & 8 →	36th	Ming-Yi

下卦	×	上卦	=	64	卦
5	×	1	=	44	姤
5	×	2	=	28	大過
5	×	3	=	50	鼎
5	×	4	=	32	恆
5	×	5	=	57	巽
5	×	6	=	48	井
5	×	7	=	18	蠱
5	×	8	=	46	升

Low Gua & Upper Gua → Hexagram		
5 & 1 →	44th	Guo
5 & 2 →	28th	Da-Duo
5 & 3 →	50th	Ding
5 & 4 →	32nd	Heng
5 & 5 →	57th	Xun
5 & 6 →	48th	Jing
5 & 7 →	18th	Gu
5 & 8 →	46th	Shen

下卦	×	上卦	=	64	卦
7	×	1	=	33	遯
7	×	2	=	31	咸
7	×	3	=	56	旅
7	×	4	=	62	小過
7	×	5	=	53	漸
7	×	6	=	39	蹇
7	×	7	=	52	艮
7	×	8	=	15	謙

Low Gua & Upper Gua → Hexagram		
7 & 1 →	33rd	Duen
7 & 2 →	31st	Shian
7 & 3 →	56th	Lu
7 & 4 →	62nd	Xiao-Guo
7 & 5 →	53rd	Jiang
7 & 6 →	39th	Jian
7 & 7 →	52nd	Gen
7 & 8 →	15th	Qian

下卦 × 上卦 = 64 卦					Low Gua & Upper Gua → Hexagram		
2	×	1	=	10 履	2 & 1 →	10th	Lyu
2	×	2	=	58 兌	2 & 2 →	58th	Duei
2	×	3	=	38 睽	2 & 3 →	38th	Kui
2	×	4	=	54 歸妹	2 & 4 →	54th	Gui- Mei
2	×	5	=	61 中孚	2 & 5 →	61st	Zhong- Fu
2	×	6	=	60 節	2 & 6 →	60th	Jier
2	×	7	=	41 損	2 & 7 →	41st	Suen
2	×	8	=	19 臨	2 & 8 →	19th	Lirn

下卦 × 上卦 = 64 卦					Low Gua & Upper Gua → Hexagram		
4	×	1	=	25 無妄	4 & 1 →	25th	Wuh-Whang
4	×	2	=	17 隨	4 & 2 →	17th	Sui
4	×	3	=	21 噬嗑	4 & 3 →	21st	Shi-He
4	×	4	=	51 震	4 & 4 →	51st	Jehn
4	×	5	=	42 益	4 & 5 →	42nd	Yih
4	×	6	=	3 屯	4 & 6 →	3rd	Tuen
4	×	7	=	27 頤	4 & 7 →	27th	Yi
4	×	8	=	24 復	4 & 8 →	24th	Fuh

下卦 × 上卦 = 64 卦					Low Gua & Upper Gua → Hexagram		
6	×	1	=	6 訟	6 & 1 →	6th	Soong
6	×	2	=	47 困	6 & 2 →	47th	Kuen
6	×	3	=	64 未濟	6 & 3 →	64th	Wieh-Jih
6	×	4	=	40 解	6 & 4 →	40th	Jie
6	×	5	=	59 渙	6 & 5 →	59th	Huan
6	×	6	=	29 坎	6 & 6 →	29th	Kaan
6	×	7	=	4 蒙	6 & 7 →	4th	Meng
6	×	8	=	7 師	6 & 8 →	7th	Shi

下卦 × 上卦 = 64 卦					Low Gua & Upper Gua → Hexagram		
8	×	1	=	12 否	8 & 1 →	12th	Pi
8	×	2	=	45 萃	8 & 2 →	45th	Tsui
8	×	3	=	35 晉	8 & 3 →	35th	Jin
8	×	4	=	16 豫	8 & 4 →	16th	Yu
8	×	5	=	20 觀	8 & 5 →	20th	Guan
8	×	6	=	8 比	8 & 6 →	8th	Bi
8	×	7	=	23 剝	8 & 7 →	23rd	Bo
8	×	8	=	2 坤	8 & 8 →	2nd	Kun

3-2.錢幣卜卦法

通常錢幣也適用於卜卦。

(1)卜卦時應虔誠，空間安靜且心情平靜，問題單一且明確，不是選擇題。每事一日一問，勿反覆卜卦或變更字句，但仍同樣地重複詢問與卜卦；儘量在白天卜卦。

(2)卜卦程序

　a.請示卦神的事，要先擬定，才不至於混亂，盡量用是非題方式詢問，而不是選擇題。

　b.準備一枚錢幣、筆、紙；一枚硬幣常應用於卜卦，取其便利。

　c.念誦祈禱文 (只需念誦1次)

　　我是 xxx , 今年xx 歲，住在xxxxxxxxxxx。今日有一事，………。

　　請卦神透過易經64卦，變爻指示。謝謝。

　d.念完祈禱文即擲錢幣六次於桌上，每次的正反面「自下而上」，依序記錄。前三次為下卦，後三次為上卦，無需擲第七次。

3-2.The Coin Method

The coin method is popular in consulting I-Ching.

(1) One should be respectful while doing a divination. Do it in a quiet place. Ask simple and clear questions, not multiple-choice questions. Do not ask the same question over and over again within a day. Avoid consulting I-Ching late at night or in the early hours.

(2) Process of Divination

a. Prepare your question before the divination to avoid confusion. The question should be limited to yes or no questions, not multiple-choice questions.

b. Prepare a coin, a pen and a piece of paper.

c. Phrasing a prayer (only recite one time)

I am Mr. Xxx, xx years of old. My address is ……………. Today I sincerely pray to have the answer to my question ………through the 64 hexagrams and yao. Thank you.

d. After praying, a coin will be cast for six times on the table. The coin will have its head side or tail side. The casts will be recorded on the paper from bottom to the top in sequence. The records of the first three casts will be seen as the low gua, the records of the second three casts will be used as the upper gua. There is no need for the seventh cast.

			第6次
			第5次
自下而上↑	後三次	上卦	第4次
			第3次
	前三次	下卦	第2次
			第1次
	最下方	變爻	第7次

			6th
			5th
from bottom to the top	the second three casts	Upper-Gua	4th
			3rd
	the first three casts	Low-Gua	2nd
			1st
	the very bottom	The change of yao	7th

e.六次的正反，如果是反面屬陰「━ ━」，正面屬陽「━━」；下卦加上卦，可算出屬於64卦的哪一卦。

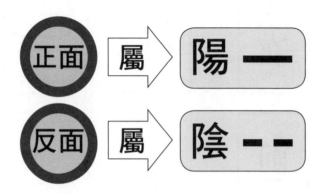

e. If the cast result is the head side, record it as Yang number, which is indicated as"＿＿". If the cast result is tail side, consider it as Yin number which is indicated as" ▃ ▃". The low gua plus upper gua make a hexagram. (圖表B)

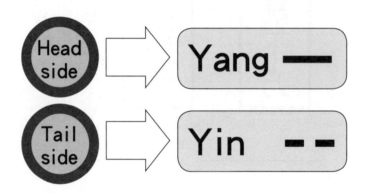

f.可透過查表(表1.2)查出其屬於64卦的哪一卦，查到後就可翻閱到本書的64卦所屬頁數，進一步查詢該卦的內容。

g.計算爻卦：每一卦都有6爻，計算方式如下：

●總數：上卦序號+下卦序號+卜卦時程序號(查表1.3)。

●總數除上6計算餘數。餘數為3，代表第3爻；餘數為6，代表第6爻。依此類推。

f. Table 1.2 shows you which "gua" you get among 64 hexagrams. Then find out the meaning corresponding to each hexagram.

g. There are six yaos in a hexagram. The method to figure out the yao is as follows:

The total =No. of Upper Gua + No. of Low Gua + No. of earthly branch.

The total= No. is divided by six (yao), the remainder is the yao you obtain.

If the remainder is 3, it is 3rd yao of the hexagram. If the remainder is 6, it is 6th yao.

(3) 範例：

第一次至第六次之擲幣順序為：「反－反－反，正－正－正」。前三次屬下卦，後三次屬上卦。卜卦時間為上午9：30。

上卦　乾，序號1（後三次）

◆ ━━ 第6次

◆ ━━ 第5次

◆ ━━ 第4次

下卦　坤，序號8（前三次）

◆ ▬ ▬ 第３次

◆ ▬ ▬ 第２次

◆ ▬ ▬ 第１次

下卦坤，序號8；上卦乾，序號1，依 64卦表（如表1.2- 64 卦）得序號12，否卦。

Chian:

In the 1st NINE：the *dragon* is still hidden

In the 2nd NINE：the *dragons* appear in the fields

In the 3rd NINE：the vigilant *dragons* work hard in the day and stay alert all the time.

In the 4th NINE：the *dragon* leaps up in the sky or is hidden in the deep

In the 5th NINE：a *dragon* flies in the sky

In the topmost NINE：the arrogant *dragons* that flies too high will reach its limits and plunge into sorrows.

(3) Example:

The cast of the coin appears 6 times as "1st tail, 2nd tail, 3rd tail. 4th head, 5th head, 6th head." The first 3 times are defined as low gua; the second 3 times are defined as upper gua. The time of divination is 9：30 in the morning. (the No. of traditional sexagenary cycle is 6)

The six casts of the coin are recorded as followings:

━━
━━ Chian NO. 1 (Upper Gua)
━━

━ ━
━ ━ Kun NO. 8 (Low Gua)
━ ━

According to the table of 64 hexagrams shown below, you'll get the 12th gua, Pi. (hexagram).

表 1.2
基本卦 Eight Basic Guas：

卦象 Trigram Figure	☰	☱	☲	☳	☴	☵	☶	☷
卦名 Gua Name	乾 Chian	兌 Duei	離 Li	震 Jehn	巽 Xun	坎 Kaan	艮 Gen	坤 Kun
序號 Serial NO.	1	2	3	4	5	6	7	8

64 卦表

坤 8	艮 7	坎 6	巽 5	震 4	離 3	兌 2	乾 1	上卦／下卦
11卦 泰	26卦 大畜	5卦 需	9卦 小畜	34卦 大壯	14卦 大有	43卦 夬	1卦 乾	1 乾
19卦 臨	41卦 損	60卦 節	61卦 中孚	54卦 歸妹	38卦 睽	58卦 兌	10卦 履	2 兌
36卦 明夷	22卦 賁	63卦 既濟	37卦 家人	55卦 豐	30卦 離	49卦 革	13卦 同人	3 離
24卦 復	27卦 頤	3卦 屯	42卦 益	51卦 震	21卦 噬嗑	17卦 隨	25卦 無妄	4 震
46卦 升	18卦 蠱	48卦 井	57卦 巽	32卦 恆	50卦 鼎	28卦 大過	44卦 姤	5 巽
7卦 師	4卦 蒙	29卦 坎	59卦 渙	40卦 解	64卦 未濟	47卦 困	6卦 訟	6 坎
15卦 謙	52卦 艮	39卦 蹇	53卦 漸	62卦 小過	56卦 旅	31卦 咸	33卦 遯	7 艮
2卦 坤	23卦 剝	8卦 比	20卦 觀	16卦 豫	35卦 晉	45卦 萃	12卦 否	8 坤

Table of 64 Hexagrams

8 Kun	7 Gen	6 Kaan	5 Xun	4 Jehn	3 Li	2 Duei	1 Chian	Upper／Low
11st Thai	26th Da-Shiu	5th Shiu	9th Shiao-Shiu	34th Da-Juang	14th Da-Yu	43rd Guai	1st Chian	1 Chian
19th Lirn	41st Suen	60th Jier	61st Zhong-Fu	54th Gui-Mei	38th Kui	58th Duei	10th Lyu	2 Kun
36th Ming-Yi	22nd Bih	63rd Jih-Jih	37th Jia-Ren	55th Feng	30th Li	49th Ger	13rd Tong-Ren	3 Li
24th Fuh	27th Yi	3rd Tuen	42nd Yih	51st Jehn	21st Shi-He	17th Sui	25th Wuh-Whang	4 Jehn
46th Shen	18th Gu	48th Jing	57th Xun	32nd Heng	50th Ding	28th Da-Guo	44th Guo	5 Xun
7th Shi	4th Meng	29th Kaan	59th Huan	40th Jie	64th Weih-Jih	47th Kuen	6th Soong	6 Kaan
15th Qian	52nd Gen	39th Jian	53rd Jiang	62nd Xiao-Guo	56th Lu	31st Shian	33rd Duen	7 Gen
2nd Kun	23rd Bo	8th Bi	20th Guan	16th Yu	35th Jin	45th Tsui	12nd Pi	8 Kun

古代中國把一日24小時劃分成12等份，每一等份為2小時，序數為 1~12。

Figure out which yao in the hexagram (six yaos in a hexagram).

The ancient Chinese divided 24 hours into 12 sections; each section (two hours) was an earthly branch. The numbers are from 1 to 12.

The 12 earthly branches and numbers are shown in the table.

表 1.3

序數 No.	1	2	3	4	5	6	7	8	9	10	11	12
時間 Hour	23-1	1-3	3-5	5-7	7-9	9-11	11-13	13-15	15-17	17-19	19-21	21-23
地支 Earthly Branch	子 Zi	丑 Chou	寅 Yin	卯 Mao	辰 Chen	巳 Si	午 Wuu	未 Wei	申 Shen	酉 You	戌 Xu	亥 Hai

以否卦為例　☰ 乾　　序號1　（上卦）
　　　　　　　Chain　No.1 (Upper Gua)

　　　　　　　☷ 坤　　序號8　（下卦）
　　　　　　　Kun　　No.8 (Low Gua)

卜卦時間上午9：30，時間序數為6。

變爻 為 (1+8+6)=15　15/6【固定數】＝ 2…3，變爻 3 。【6為固定數,因每卦有6爻】

否卦第3爻則是所求。

Example：

The time of divination is 9:30 AM (Sih), the earthly branch No. in the table is 6.

The change of yao in the hexagram is found to be 3.

The upper gua is Chian NO. 1, low gua is Kun NO.8. The time (9:30AM) is defined as No. 6

$$(1+ 8 + 6) /6 \text{ (yao)} = 2 \cdots\cdots 3 \text{ (remainder)}$$

You have the 3rd yao of the 12th Pi Gua (hexagram).

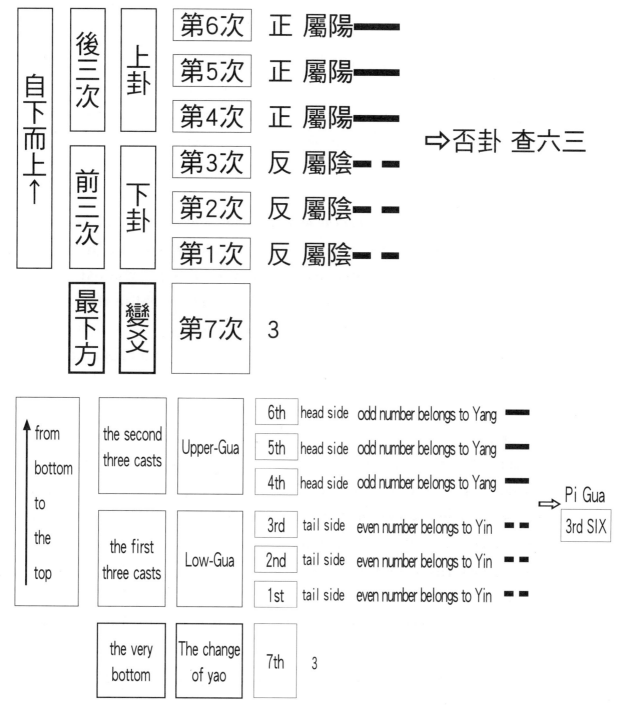

4. Examples of divination.

(1) Example 1

There was a news story that happened in December of 2013. The story was about the largest provider of semi-conductor packing and testing services in Kaohsiung accused of dumping polluted waste into the rivers. Since it was a serious offense, the company should certainly be fined.

We consulted the I-Ching for the company and got 21st hexagram and 5th yao which descriptions were provided below.

In the fifth SIX : The law enforcement may not be smooth as the criminal is a big elephant with power and money. The enforcement is just like biting a piece of meat made with wax, it takes enormous courage and determination to execute. In the end, the enforcement was done properly, thus justice was served.

Xiang Chuan : The law enforcer comes across a big shot criminal. He needs to be righteous and determined to deal with the case properly.

Suggestion : Through persistence and determination, criminal charges against the company in question will be established.

That means "The evil can never prevail over good".

From the results of divination, don't you think it fits what happened in real life?

(2) Example 2

In June, 2003, a woman named Chen Qiao Ming from Changhua, who was the founder of a cult called "Sun Moon Gong", was trying to recruit new members for her cult to practice spirituality. A woman member asked her son, then a high school student, to take sick leave to practice Sun-Moon Gong. Unfortunately, the son died. His mother submitted a written claim to the police that the son died of drug abuse, but the police wouldn't drop the investigation. Six months later, the mother finally confessed that her son died in the cult place instead of at home.

The event was mysterious. While consulting the I-Ching, we got 24th hexagram and 1st yao.

In the first NINE :

Despite being lost, you are not too far away and you know your way back. There is neither remorse nor disaster. Very positive. Overall the divination means

that even if you do something wrong, if you can fix it in time, there will be no downsides.

Xiang Chuan：While going astray, it is of great value to right your wrongs in time. Behave morally and properly. Do not be tempted by evil.

Suggestion：Repentance is salvation.

☯ Our kind reminder~

1. Life is full of problems. Do not depend on divinations every time you run into problems. Otherwise you'll lose self-judgment and the ability to develop your wisdom. That being said, there are still situations that will put you between a rock and a hard place, therefore divinations still serve as a good tool to help you in the decision making process.

2. All the situations in our lives are within the scope of I-Ching. If we can understand the moral of each of the hexagrams, face up to life's challenges using the wisdom provided by the I-Ching, we'll have a broad and generous outlook on life.

☯ Q&A~

Q: What are the meanings of "in the first Nine, in the second Nine, in the third Nine, in the fourth Nine, in the fifth Nine, in the sixth Nine, All yaos are Nines" in the Gua?

A:

If the lowest Yao of a Gua is Yang(▬), we call it Nine. If you look at it from the lowest Yao to the upper ones, they are the first Yao, the second Yao, the third Yao, the fourth Yao, the fifth Yao and the sixth Yao etc. Therefore; in the first Nine, the second Nine, the third Nine, the fourth Nine, the fifth Nine and the sixth Yao will replace them in the Guas. On the contrary, the lowest Yao of a Gua is Yin (▬ ▬), in the first Six, the second Six, the third Six, the fourth Six, the fifth Six, the sixth Six, all yaos that are Sixes replace their six Yaos.

All yaos of Nines represent lunar months that has 30 days. All Yaos of Sixes belong to Yin gua. They indicate lunar months that have 29 days. The Yaos of Sixes indicate that it is an intercalary month.

☯ 陰陽六爻對照
6 yaos of Yin & Yang

陽 稱九 (—)	陰 稱六 (– –)
Yang (—), we call it Nine	Yin (– –), we call it Six

六爻⇨ 上九	六爻⇨ 上六
6th yao ⇨ In the topmost NINE	6th yao ⇨ In the topmost SIX
五爻⇨ 九五	五爻⇨ 六五
5th yao ⇨ In the fifth NINE	5th yao ⇨ In the fifth SIX
四爻⇨ 九四	四爻⇨ 六四
4th yao ⇨ In the fourth NINE	4th yao ⇨ In the fourth SIX
三爻⇨ 九三	三爻⇨ 六三
3rd yao ⇨ In the third NINE	3rd yao ⇨ In the third SIX
二爻⇨ 九二	二爻⇨ 六二
2nd yao ⇨ In the second NINE	2nd yao ⇨ In the second SIX
初爻⇨ 初九	初爻⇨ 初六
1st yao ⇨ In the first NINE	1st yao ⇨ In the first SIX

from bottom to the top

第二章 六十四卦精要與建言

Chapter Two I-Ching Contents and Suggestions

1. 乾⟨⟩ Chian

 乾上 乾下
乾為天

乾：元、亨、利、貞。

象傳：天行健，君子以自強不息。

乾：開創，健。 乾乃萬物之根元。

Chian：Creative initiation and invigoration, the essence of all creatures. It consists of four virtues; these are：

a. Creation, vastness and comprehensiveness.

b. Prosperity.

c. Harmony, smoothness, advantage.

d. Righteousness, perseverance and perpetuity.

Xiang Chuan：Things keep changing and nothing ever seems to stay the same. A man of noble character should make continuous efforts to progress.

Suggestion：One should learn from the invigoration of astronomical phenomena to strive continuously and make progress.

初九：潛龍勿用。

象傳：潛龍勿用，陽在下也。

In the first NINE：The dragon (the talent) is still hidden. You should not act at this time as all the things are still in the beginning stage. It is premature. You have to downplay your talents at present. It is premature to show your talent to have results.

Xiang Chuan：The hidden dragon (the talent) means that you should not act right now as things need time to develop and you need to accumulate your energies. Wait for opportunities to act. If you act prematurely, things will be against your interests.

Suggestion：To save energy and to build on your strength. A wise man would not fight against the wind.

九二：見龍在田，利見大人。
象傳：見龍在田，德施普也。

In the second NINE: The dragons appear in the fields. It increases opportunities to meet men of great importance.

Xiang Chuan：The dragons appearing in the fields means the people are going to benefit from the virtues of great men. Local officials may be promoted to utilize their talents for the greater good, which brings hope to the public.

Suggestion：The timing is mature and it is sure that one can shoulder important tasks.

九三：君子終日乾乾，夕惕若，厲無咎。
象傳：終日乾乾，反復道也。

In the third NINE: When one achieves all his goals, one should not get dizzy with the success. One should still work hard during the day, stay alert and reflect on future improvements at night. Then there will be no disasters.

Xiang Chuan：The man of noble character works hard all day and always makes the moral choice.

Suggestion：Perseverance and caution make progress.

九四：或躍在淵，無咎。
象傳：或躍在淵，進無咎也。

In the fourth NINE: The dragon leaps up in the sky or is hidden in the deep, meaning that one makes his decision according to the situation. There will be no blame.

Xiang Chuan：Advancement or regression depends upon one's core value. If he does not deviate from the right course, there will be no blame.

Suggestion：Act according to the circumstances and decide promptly.

九五：飛龍在天，利見大人。

象傳：飛龍在天，大人造也。

In the fifth NINE : The country is prosperous and the people live in safety due to a virtuous and wise sovereignty that empowers talents as if a dragon flies in the sky, bringing luck to benefit the people. In this situation, the man of noble character has the opportunity to meet with the great men to utilize his talents.

Xiang Chuan：The virtuous emperor is like a dragon flying in the sky to bring luck to benefit the people. The grandeur is brought by the great man.

Suggestion：At the peak of one's career, avoid the situation where there is nowhere to go but down.

上九：亢龍有悔。

象傳：亢龍有悔，盈不可久也。

In the topmost NINE : The emperor is placed highly and acts arrogantly as if the dragon flies too high in the sky, forgetting about its limits which will eventually bring sorrow. This means that a man of noble character needs to realize that if ones career is at its peak, the only direction to go is down. Things always reverse themselves after reaching an extreme.

Xiang Chuan：A man of noble character reaches his peak without practicing temperance. This will eventually attract failures because one's career cannot always be on the top.

Suggestion: Be prepared for danger in times of peace.

用九：見群龍無首，吉。

象傳：用九，天德不可為首也。

All yaos are NINES : In the situation, he is generally acknowledged as a powerful chief of an area. He is highly regarded and can become arrogant, yet he is still very humble in facing these rising independent warlords. He is very humble and unassuming to communicate and coordinate with these opinion leaders. It is commendable and brings good fortune.

Xiang Chuan：All yaos are Nines. They represent a combination of virtues that show strength and flexibility at the same time. Therefore, he will not be obstinate and inflexible to get along with people and he won't consider himself to be the chief.

Suggestion：Being in a leading position, he is positive and agreeable. He is flexible in handling things while staying humble. He does not act rashly and always seeks peaceful solution.

2. 坤 Kun

 坤上 坤下
坤為地

坤：元亨，利牝*馬之貞。君子有攸往，先迷，後得，主利。西南得朋，東北喪朋，安貞吉。

象傳：地勢坤；君子以厚德載物。

Kun：Bearing is the origin of everything in nature. Practice obedience, perseverance and tolerance just like a mare or like the earth moves around the sun without fail. If the man of noble character fights to be the first to get advanced, he is very likely to go astray, but if he respects the order, he will benefit. Similarly, the southwest is easy to walk on, meaning one can easily have good company with the same goal. On the contrary, the northeast is mountainous, which is difficult to pass, meaning one will not find company. So long as one is perseverant and always makes the moral choice, luck will always follow him.

Xiang Chuan：The subject should be respectful and obedient. His great ability to tolerate is like the Mother Earth holds every creature.

Suggestion：All creatures have their own ways to survive.

＊註１：牝ㄆㄧㄣˋ，雌牛。

初六：履霜，堅冰至。
象傳：履霜堅冰，陰始凝也；馴致其道，至堅冰也。

In the first SIX : Treading on frost, strong ice is soon to come. Early symptoms indicate future developments. One should take precautions to deal with them. Neglecting symptoms at the beginning may cause uncorrectable mistakes.

Xiang Chuan：Treading on frost, strong ice is soon to come. Chilly air keeps blowing and one knows that winter is coming.

Suggestion：A stitch in time saves nine.

六二：直、方、大，不習，無不利。
象傳：六二之動，直以方也；不習無不利，地道光也。

In the second SIX : The Earth is limitless. It bears all the creatures in the world. So long as one possesses the virtues of integrity, tolerance and good manners, even if one does not learn, there will be no harm.

Xiang Chuan：If one follows the law of nature, even if he does not learn, there will be no harm. This is because he respects the wisdom of nature.

Suggestion：Have a big heart. Treat people with sincerity and honesty. Luck will follow you everywhere.

六三：含章可貞，或從王事，無成有終。
象傳：含章可貞，以時發也；或從王事，知光大也。

In the third SIX : The man with noble character speaks and behaves in a modest fashion. He neither exaggerates his virtues nor takes credit serving the government.

Xiang Chuan：Possess the virtue of modesty. Wait for opportunities to come. When the time comes that one can finally serve the government, this is because he follows this wisdom.

Suggestion：Keeping a low-profile and having modesty wins trust.

六四：括囊，無咎無譽。

象傳：括囊無咎，慎不害也。

In the fourth SIX: Tie up one's bag carefully. There will be neither blame nor praise. This means that despite being in a dangerous situation, if one keeps his mouth shut, there will be no harm.

Xiang Chuan：Keep one's mouth shut. Avoid thoughtless comments to prevent disasters.

Suggestion：A closed mouth catches no flies. With no ambition at all.

六五：黃裳，元吉。

象傳：黃裳元吉，文在中也。

In the fifth SIX: Yellow garments bring fortune. This means that despite being in a noble position, if one can still treat people with humility, this will bring great luck.

Xiang Chuan：Despite being in a noble position, one still remains humble and modest to other people, which reflects his inner grace.

Suggestion：One should treat people with sincerity instead of hypocrisy.

上六：龍戰于野，其血玄黃。

象傳：龍戰于野，其道窮也。

In the topmost SIX: Dragons are arrogant and are reluctant to yield to others. They scramble for power and profit. They fight violently in the fields. Both suffer from severe injuries. Their blood is blue and yellow. If the serious situation continues, it will cause destruction to both sides. The metaphor is that the emperor is facing serious threats due to arrogant and power hungry subordinates. If the subordinates still remain arrogant and do not respect the hierarchy, the fall will begin.

Xiang Chuan：Dragons fight severely in the fields, both suffer from injuries. There is no way out. Nobody wins.

Suggestion：Going too far is as bad as not going far enough.

用六，利永貞。

象傳：用六永貞，以大終也。

All yaos are Sixes : They stand for virtues of "genuine and lasting sincerity." If he is in an inferior position, he tries hard to perform his duty honestly. It can be regarded as the virtue of the element "Earth".

Xiang Chuan：All yaos are Sixes. The virtues of the element "Earth" are genuine and lasting sincerity. It is also the law of existence.

Suggestion：Being in an inferior position, one should be very humble, gentle and submissive to his superior from the beginning to the end.

3. 屯 Tuen

水雷屯   坎上 震下

水雷屯

屯：元、亨、利、貞。勿用有攸往，利建侯。

象傳：雲雷，屯；君子以經綸。

Tuen : Initiation, germination. "Tuen" implies that beginning is difficult. It's still a long way from success. All living creatures on earth are still in their beginning stage. They are still weak but full of vitality. One should insist on four virtues : Creation, prosperity, harmony and righteousness. If you do not act rashly, it will help you to build the foundation of success in the future.

Xiang Chuan：Dark clouds are seen and thunder strikes. Thunderstorms are coming. It is the hexagram of Tuen. The man of noble character realizes the process of thinking is just like that of gathering threads to knit with silk fabrics. One should organize his thoughts and fully exploit his talents to contribute to society.

Suggestion：Beginning is difficult, but perseverance enables you to broaden your vision.

初九：磐桓利居貞。利建侯。

象傳：雖磐桓，志行正也；以貴下賤，大得民也。

In the first NINE: In the initial stage, inevitably one has to deal with pressure from all sides as if one is in between a rock and a hard place. Under the circumstances, he had better stay put and always make the moral choice. Do not try to show one's capabilities. Thus he can use this free time to build trust with others and use that as the foundation to succeed in the future.

Xiang Chuan：Although one cannot show his capabilities, one does not deviate from the right course. He can even descend from his level of superiority to work with the masses. This way he will win more support and confidence from people.

Suggestion：A just cause wins much support and an unjust one finds little.

六二：屯如，邅*如，乘馬班如。匪寇，婚媾。女子貞不字，十年乃字。

象傳：六二之難，乘剛也；十年乃字，反常也。

In the second SIX: Initiation is difficult. Hesitation. Lingering with no progress. The bridegroom accompanied by his horse-riding team arrives in the evening to marry his bride only to find that they are treated as bandits by mistake. Later, the identity of the bridegroom is finally confirmed. The young lady who rejected marriage proposals for ten years is still waiting for the best husband to come.

Xiang Chuan：It is against the norm that the young lady rejects all the marriage proposals for the past ten years.

Suggestion：Neither threats nor force can bend you.

六三：即鹿無虞，惟入於林中，君子幾，不如舍。往吝。

象傳：即鹿無虞，以從禽也；君子舍之，往吝窮也。

In the third SIX: Chasing after a deer in the forest without a guide is dangerous. Firstly, one should know the circumstance he is in without blindly chasing after the

---

＊註2：邅 ㄓㄢ，難以進行的樣子。

prey. The man of noble character would give up the pursuit to avoid danger.

Xiang Chuan : The man of noble character would rather give up chasing the deer blindly in the forest than chase after prey and put himself in a dangerous situation.

Suggestion : Eagerness for quick success and instant benefits will possibly lead to misfortune. One does not commit to a goal without confidence. Opinionated.

六四：乘馬班如，求婚媾；往吉，無不利。

象傳：求而往，明也。

In the fourth SIX : The bridegroom with his horse-riding team comes to marry his bride, which complies with the Chinese saying "a man should take a wife and a woman should take a husband." It signifies auspicious development.

Xiang Chuan : A prompt agreement for a marriage is wise.

Suggestion : If the target is clear and definite, then opportunity never knocks twice at any man's door. When the rain is over, the sky clears up.

九五：屯其膏。小，貞吉；大，貞凶。

象傳：屯其膏，施未光也。

In the fifth NINE : When one is in the beginning stage of developing his talents, he should value all the limited resources available. It is auspicious when he does not reach beyond his capabilities and only takes advantage of the reachable resources. If he violates this rule, he would attract misfortune and criticism. This implies that even when a country is in serious financial difficulties, a small tax increase won't hurt but heavy taxes are going to hurt people and would result in revolt.

Xiang Chuan : Without sufficient resources at the beginning stage, even if one has ambition, his outlook won't be bright.

Suggestion : A slow fire makes sweet malt. The road to happiness is strewn with setbacks.

上六：乘馬班如，泣血漣ㄌㄧㄢ如。

象傳：泣血漣如，何可長也？

In the topmost SIX : In a difficult situation, the horse riders hesitate and split up. They are in a dilemma and they linger around. Instead of helping, they block one other, which makes people feel hurt and tearful.

Xiang Chuan：The scenario makes people feel hurt and weepy. How can such a sorrowful situation go on?

Suggestion：Don't focus excessively on personal gains and losses.

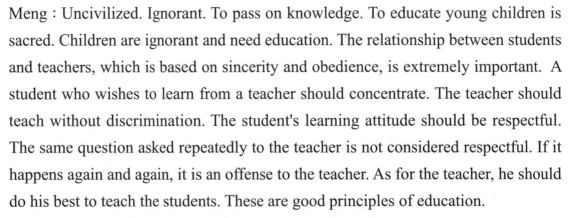

4. 蒙 Meng

山水蒙　艮上 坎下

蒙：亨。匪我求童蒙，童蒙求我。初筮ㄕˋ告，再三瀆，瀆則不告。利貞。

象傳：山下出泉，蒙；君子以果行育德。

Meng：Uncivilized. Ignorant. To pass on knowledge. To educate young children is sacred. Children are ignorant and need education. The relationship between students and teachers, which is based on sincerity and obedience, is extremely important. A student who wishes to learn from a teacher should concentrate. The teacher should teach without discrimination. The student's learning attitude should be respectful. The same question asked repeatedly to the teacher is not considered respectful. If it happens again and again, it is an offense to the teacher. As for the teacher, he should do his best to teach the students. These are good principles of education.

Xiang Chuan：Spring water trickles slowly from the mountains to form rivers to nourish all creatures. It means that the elementary education should not be discontinued. It is the meaning of Meng. The man of noble character should be determined to be engaged in education and cultivate virtues.

Suggestion：The teacher passes on knowledge to the students without

discrimination. To teach students according to their aptitude.

初六：發蒙，利用刑人，用說桎梏，以往吝。
象傳：利用刑人，以正法也。

In the first SIX: During the period of enlightening the young students, the teacher sets up rules to discipline students to prevent them from going astray. It is like putting chains and shackles on criminals to direct them on the right track. However, permanent punishment is not recommended.

Xiang Chuan：Penalizing criminals is the best way to help them to give up evil and return to good.

Suggestion：Strict discipline is still a must for education.

九二：包蒙，吉。納婦，吉。子克家。
象傳：子克家，剛柔接也。

In the second NINE: It is auspicious of educating all the ignorant without sex discrimination according to their aptitude with extreme tolerance. Educating with the most patience and giving systematic guidance. Practice empathy to educate our descendants. The next generation will receive good education and will be capable of supporting their families. It brings good fortunes.

Xiang Chuan：A son grows up to inherit the family properties. This is called the succession of generations.

Suggestion：To teach with patience, without discrimination and to give systematic guidance are the important thoughts of Confucius education.

六三：勿用取女，見金夫，不有躬。無攸利。
象傳：勿用取女，行不順也。

In the third SIX: The biggest taboo for beginning learners is to learn too fast since

"Haste makes waste." This is just like a material woman who has a tendency to be tempted by rich men. Do not marry such a woman. By the same token, if one is half-hearted in learning, it hinders the learning results.

Xiang Chuan : Do not take a material woman as wife because her behaviors may violate the middle way.

Suggestion : Do not forget honor at the sight of money. Do not be a rolling stone.

六四：困蒙，吝。
象傳：困蒙之吝，獨遠實也。

In the fourth SIX : Illiterate people may easily encounter hardships in life due to the lack of basic education. They can not make positive contributions to the society.

Xiang Chuan : Illiterate people may easily encounter hardships in life. They have a tendency to be lonely and are secluded from the world.

Suggestion : Being unrealistic and half-hearted in learning are taboos of education.

六五：童蒙，吉。
象傳：童蒙之吉，順以巽也。

In the fifth SIX : Children are innocent and pure as blank papers. They receive education with open hearts because they are easily moldable.

Xiang Chuan : The smoothness of educating children owes to their innocence, humbleness and obedience.

Suggestion : Education is just like the growth of children. It requires nourishing and caring. Either one is indispensable.

上九：擊蒙，不利為寇，利禦寇。
象傳：利用禦寇，上下順也。

In the topmost NINE : Education is to develop wisdom. Cramming is not helpful in gaining wisdom. Severe punishments on students are just like beating up criminals. It is prohibited. However, for the stubborn ones, some level of punishment is appropriate. Inductive teaching is preferred because children will be brought up well and perfectly educated, which enhances social harmony.

Xiang Chuan : If severe discipline on students improves learning attitude, it is due to mutual respect between the teacher and the students.

Suggestion : **In formative education, it is better to use strict rules than violence.**

5. 需 Shiu

坎上 乾下

水天需

需：有孚，光亨。貞吉，利涉大川。

象傳：雲上於天，需；君子以飲食宴樂。

Shiu : Waiting and expectation. The timing is not mature yet. For now, one should develop social networking and patiently wait for opportunities. Waiting and expectation are based on the foundation of sincerity. Sincerity makes one selfless, honest and prosperous. Sincerity also allows one to be realistic about the outcome and helps him to succeed.

Xiang Chuan : The sky is cloudy. It is going to rain. This means it is necessary to wait as if the virtues of the emperor take time to trickle down to benefit people, allowing people to live in prosperity and peace.

Suggestion : **Haste makes waste. It is a good principle to conserve energy and build up one's strength.**

初九: 需於郊，利用恆；無咎。

象傳：需於郊，不犯難行也；利用恆，無咎，未失常也。

In the first NINE : A man of great talents and ambition always laments that it is not his time to shine. There are no opportunities for him to showcase his talents. He can do nothing but wait patiently for the opportunities. Although there are difficulties in front of him, he has to keep a distance from danger to secure his life. In a word, he should take the bad with the good.

Xiang Chuan：On some occasions, it is not appropriate to advance. One should wait patiently for opportunities. This decision can help you to avoid making mistakes.

Suggestion：Do not act rashly. Abide by the rules.

九二 ：需於沙，小有言，終吉。
象傳：需於沙，衍在中也；雖有小言，以終吉也。

In the second NINE : As the timing is not mature yet, one should patiently wait on the sandbank. On this occasion, many people have different opinions on how to cross the river. They are still unable to reach an agreement.

However, eventually, the leader will come up with constructive solutions and bring satisfying results.

Xiang Chuan：As the timing is not mature yet, one should patiently wait on the sandbank. Although gossip may hurt, if one always makes the moral choice, he can turn peril into safety.

Suggestion：Gossip hurts; keep your mind in perfect peace. With generosity and tolerance, one can overcome all the difficulties.

九三 ：需於泥，致寇至。
象傳：需於泥，災在外也；自我致寇，敬慎不敗也。

In the third NINE : If one is not aware of the risks, he could encounter difficulties and have to wait for rescue. It is as if a person falls into the mud, waiting to be rescued. If bandits come, a disaster is inevitable.

Xiang Chuan：When one falls into the mud, it seems that the misfortune comes from the outside, but actually it comes from improper judgment on the situation. One should be more cautious to avoid failures.

Suggestion：Good advice may sound harsh to the ears.

六四: 需于血，出自穴。

象傳：需于血，順以聽也。

In the fourth SIX : When one is in difficulty, he is eager to climb out of the hole, but it is just like lying in blood looking for rescue, it takes perseverance to crawl out of the cave.

Xiang Chuan：One is now in danger. He must be calm and composed to wait for opportunities and follow the instructions to escape from the dangers.

Suggestion： When falling into difficulty stay calm and never stretch yourself too far.

九五: 需于酒食，貞吉。

象傳：酒食貞吉，以中正也。

In the fifth NINE : Although one is in peril, he is still content with his fate. He enjoys the feast as if nothing had happened. The underlying meaning is that the virtuous emperor should share his delicious wine and food with people because this is the right thing to do.

Xiang Chuan：Despite being in peril, he is composed and enjoys the feast as if nothing had happened. He waits at ease for the enemy to be exhausted while staying on the moral course.

Suggestion：To face danger fearlessly.

上六: 入于穴，有不速之客三人來，敬之終吉。

象傳：不速之客來，敬之終吉，雖不當位，未大失也。

In the topmost SIX : One is in difficulty. Three guests arrive without invitation. Although they are low-status people, remain composed and treat them with respect. There is a saying that goes, "Since they have come, let them stay and enjoy it." To treat these uninvited guests with sincerity, let them be tipsy and merry. Then both the host and the guests are happy. It attracts good fortune in the end.

Xiang Chuan：Be composed and treat people with respect, which will attract good fortune in the end and can avoid great loss.

Suggestion：It is not wise to fight for temporary superiority.

6. 訟 Soong

 乾上 坎下
天水訟

訟：有孚窒＊，惕，中吉，終凶。利見大人。不利涉大川。

象傳：天與水違行，訟；君子以作事謀始。

Soong：A lawsuit always arises because the interests are not distributed fairly and thus one's integrity or credit is brought into question. To stop the legal action in the middle is good. On the contrary, if the lawsuit continues, it will become a disaster. It is advantageous to have an important mediator to settle the disputes. If the disputes are not settled, it will result in catastrophe.

Xiang Chuan：Sky and water go in opposite directions. The man with noble character should have detailed planning in the beginning to avoid any legal conflicts.

Suggestion：Even if one finally wins a lawsuit, it is not worthy of praise.

初六：不永所事，小有言，終吉。

象傳：不永所事，訟不可長也；雖小有言，其辯明也。

In the first SIX : Lawsuits can drag on for a long time. Do not get entangled in a

long-lasting lawsuit. If one is weak and unable to continue the lawsuit, it is better to end it as soon as possible. It will bring positive outcome.

Xiang Chuan：Do not get entangled in a long-lasting lawsuit. Even though there are still disputes, you could settle them through debates, clearly presenting the rights or wrongs.

Suggestion：Present one's case clearly to prevent the lawsuit from getting out of hand.

九二：不克訟，歸而逋ㄅㄨ*，其邑人三百戶，無眚ㄕㄥ。
象傳：不克訟，歸逋竄也；自下訟上，患至掇ㄉㄨㄛ*也。

In the second NINE：If one is not sure of winning a lawsuit, it is better to compromise and head home. Thus, the three hundred residents in his hometown will not suffer from collective punishment.

Xiang Chuan：If the lawsuit is in an unfavorable situation, it is wise to patch up the lawsuit and compromise. One has to free the community from anxieties. It is fortunate to stop the lawsuit where a socially inferior person accuses the socially superior one.

Suggestion：Don't let your efforts go down the drain.

六三：食舊德，貞厲，終吉；或從王事，無成。
象傳：食舊德，從上吉也。

In the third SIX：One is incompetent to accuse. He can only rely on the shelter provided by his ancestors and live a life standing aloof from worldly affairs. He is lucky to be given an unimportant government job, but he will not have great achievements.

Xiang Chuan：While one is in difficult situation, he is forced to be sheltered by his ancestors and live a peaceful life. It is better for him follow people with high social

---

＊註3：逋ㄅㄨ，逃亡。
＊註4：掇ㄉㄨㄛˊ，摘取。

status.

Suggestion：To be content with one's lot. Do not flaunt one's ability on litigation.

九四：不克訟，復即命，渝, 安貞吉。

象傳：復即命，渝，安貞不失也。

[In the fourth NINE]: If one is not sure of winning the lawsuit, he would rather make concessions and return to the moral course. Change the original intention and make the moral choice. There will be no blame and things will be auspicious.

Xiang Chuan：If one is not certain of winning the lawsuit, he would rather make concessions, patch up the disputes and return to the moral course. If he can change the original intention and follow the moral course, he will not have any loss.

Suggestion：When the water subsides, the rocks emerge.

九五：訟，元吉。

象傳：訟，元吉，以中正也。

[In the fifth NINE]: Lawsuits can be fairly and impartially judged, which brings great fortunes as the results are well received by the public.

Xiang Chuan：Lawsuits can be fairly and impartially judged, which brings great fortunes as the results reflect justice.

Suggestion：Fair judgment. Feeling at ease and justified.

上九：或錫之以鞶*帶，終朝三褫之。

象傳：以訟受服，亦不足敬也。

[In the topmost NINE]: One obtains a high power position by winning legal disputes, but he could also be demoted three times in a day due to mistakes.

＊註5：鞶ㄆㄢˊ，束衣帶（鞶帶：官服）。

Xiang Chuan：Using litigation as a means to obtain a high power position is not worthy of respect. On the contrary, people despise it.

Suggestion：He who is too self-assured and who uses endless litigation to gain personal interests will bring negative consequences to himself.

7. 師 Shi

地水師　　坤上 坎下

師：貞，丈人吉，無咎。

象傳：地中有水，師；君子以容民畜眾。

Shi：Armed force, fighting. A war is fought for political purposes. In general, political intention outmaneuvers other factors. The reasons for conflicts never go beyond the interests of resources, the differences on religious belief, nationalism and frontier territory. If conflicts are inevitable, an experienced, professional, composed general is needed. A war certainly causes damage and hurts people, but if the war is waged in the name of justice, it will win full support from the people. It will not be blamed. In a word, the principles of a war consist of：

1) A good and competent general.

2) Justified cause to wage a war.

Xiang Chuan：Water is found in the ground, meaning soldiers are recruited from people. During the time of peace, people have their own businesses as if water is buried underground. As soon as the war is started, people will come out to fight for the nation which is the meaning of hexagram Shi. The man of noble character understands that treating people generously eventually pays off by a well-maintained army.

Suggestion：The appointment of the general determines the success of a war.

初六：師出以律，否臧凶。
象傳：師出以律，失律凶也。

In the first SIX : The very top priority of a military expedition is strict discipline. If the military orders are not completely implemented, it is destined to fail.

Xiang Chuan：The top priority of a military expedition is strict discipline. Without them, the expedition is destined to fail.

Suggestion：Military discipline is the soul of an army.

九二：在師中，吉，無咎，王三錫命。
象傳：在師中吉，承天寵也；王三錫命，懷萬邦也。

In the second NINE : A competent marshal does not only lead troops to fight and win every battle but also wins the soldiers' hearts. It is certainly fortunate. Nothing to blame. His great track record wins trust from the emperor. He also repeatedly receives awards and praise from the emperor.

Xiang Chuan：The track record and army support of a great marshal are recognized by the emperor. The emperor repeatedly awards and praises him as he contributes to the peace of many nations.

Suggestion：To win over through conciliation. Do not solve problems only by military aggression.

六三：師或輿尸，凶。
象傳：師或輿尸，大無功也。

In the third SIX : An incompetent marshal, whose lack of leadership and stubbornness in the battlefield, causes the troops to suffer heavy casualties. The military expedition suffers complete defeat, the only thing that returns are corpses of the soldiers.

Xiang Chuan：The troops suffer heavy casualties and many corpses of the soldiers are returned. Obviously the expedition has been a complete failure.

Suggestion：Bragging and showing off.

六四：師左次，無咎。

象傳：左次無咎，未失常也。

In the fourth SIX ： Stationing the troops temporarily in lowlands in front of the left side makes it convenient to attack the enemy. It is a military strategy. Nothing wrong.

Xiang Chuan：Stationing the troops temporarily in lowlands in front of the left side makes it convenient to attack the enemy. It does not violate general principles of commanding the troops.

Suggestion：It is appropriate to use the art of war. There is no blame.

六五：田有禽，利執言，無咎。長子帥師，弟子輿尸。貞凶。

象傳：長子帥師，以中行也；弟子輿尸，使不當也。

In the fifth SIX ： The enemy invades our territory as if birds and beasts ravage our farms. A competent marshal fights back as a self-defense to the invasion. He is not to blame. However, if the expedition is led by an incompetent marshal, whose failure would result in corpses of soldiers. It is a misfortune.

Xiang Chuan：A competent marshal with great integrity leads troops to go to wars frequently and wins every battle whereas the only things that an incompetent marshal brings back are corpses of soldiers. The root cause for the failure is inappropriate appointments.

Suggestion：Careful deliberation on appointments.

上六：大君有命，開國承家，小人勿用。

象傳：大君有命，以正功也；小人勿用，必亂邦也。

In the topmost SIX ： The prime minister obeys the decree from the emperor who announces that those with great achievements at war will be awarded but those without will be relieved from duty and won't be trusted with important tasks.

Xiang Chuan：The prime minister obeys the decree from the emperor who announces that people should be awarded based on their merits. Otherwise, it will lead to social unrest.

Suggestion: Fair rewards and punishments win people's hearts.

8.　比　Bi

 坎上 坤下
水地比

比：吉。原筮，元永貞，無咎。不寧方來，後夫凶。

象傳：地上有水，比；先王以建萬國，親諸侯。

Bi：Closeness. Relying on one another. It is a good omen. The hexagram Bi is particularly about the closeness and mutual reliance among countries. If allies are faithful and stick to the right path, they will not be blamed. Only insecure and unstable countries will seek to join allies hoping the attachment will bring benefits. Those that sit on the fence and come late shouldn't be trusted. They will bring misfortune.

Xiang Chuan：Water flows to all sides on the ground. It symbolizes that water and earth are mutually reliant. Earth turns wet because of water permeating into the ground. It dawns on the emperors that the law of mutual reliance also prevails in the relationship between the emperor and his ministers. Close relationship is built when ministers are rewarded based on their merits.

Suggestion：To make friends from all over the world.

初六：有孚比之，無咎。有孚盈缶，終來有它吉。

象傳：比之初六，有它吉也。

In the first SIX: It is not wrong to make friends with sincerity as if a pot is full of delicious wine to greet the guests. An unexpected good fortune is coming.

Xiang Chuan：If the attachment is based on sincerity, there will be an unexpected fortune.

Suggestion：More sincerity, more happiness.

六二：比之自內，貞吉。
象傳：比之自內，不自失也。

In the second SIX: To attach oneself to a great man shall be originated from his heart and free will. His insistence on always choosing the moral path will bring fortune.

Xiang Chuan：If one's attachment to a great man is coming from his heart, he will not be confused and lose his viewpoint.

Suggestion：Attaching to a great man should originate from one's heart instead of evil intentions.

六三：比之匪人。
象傳：比之匪人，不亦傷乎？

In the third SIX: Be careful not to attach to a crooked man.

Xiang Chuan：Attaching to an evil man. Isn't it sad?

Suggestion：Mixing with wrong people is equal to playing fire, you eventually get burned.

六四：外比之，貞吉。
象傳：外比於賢，以從上也。

In the fourth SIX: To expand one's scope to attach to the people with great virtues and stick to the moral path make good fortunes.

Xiang Chuan：If one expands his scope to attach to the people with great virtues, he will find it easy to be associated with respectable people, which leads to self-improvement.

Suggestion：He who handles vermilion will be reddened and he who touches ink will be blackened.

九五：顯比，王用三驅，失前禽，邑人不誡，吉。
象傳：顯比之吉，位正中也；舍逆取順，失前禽也。邑人不誡，上使中也。

In the fifth NINE：An emperor has a big heart and high moral standards. All the neighboring countries are willing to attach to him. It is as if an emperor goes hunting but only attacks from three sides（rear, right and left）. He leaves one side open to let prey escape. This gesture disarms people because the emperor has a big heart and is kind even to those who make mistakes. It is a great omen.

Xiang Chuan：Because of the virtues of kindness and integrity, the powerful and the influential as well as the neighboring countries all become attached to the emperor. It is a great omen. When going hunting, the emperor would rather let the prey escape than capture them all. This kind gesture will disarm the people because the emperor follows the moral path.

Suggestion：Do not be ruthless.

上六：比之無首，凶。
象傳：比之無首，無所終也。

In the topmost SIX：He who has an intention to attach to a great man but does it in an indecisive manner is as unpredictable as a homeless person.

Timing is important; missing the opportunity will only bring regrets. Therefore, one should seize the opportunity to attach to a great man without hesitation. If one does not do it from the very beginning, his indecisiveness only backfires. He will be left with no one to rely on.

Xiang Chuan：Attaching to a great man should be done in a timely manner.

Indecisiveness only results in poor outcome, leaving one with nobody to rely on.

Suggestion：To regret that things haven't been done the other way.

9.　小畜　Shiao-Shiu

 巽上 乾下

風天小畜

小畜：亨。密雲不雨，自我西郊。

象傳：風行天上，小畜；君子以懿文德。

Shiao-Shiu：Little savings. Little savings make good fortune. Dense and floating clouds are coming over from suburban areas on the West, but no rain is seen. It represents that one's ability is falling short of expectation, meaning people are disappointed by the emperor's ability to accomplish.

Xiang Chuan：The wind is blowing. All creatures on earth are eager to have winds blow to spread the seeds to procreate, which is the meaning of this hexagram. The man with noble character realizes that he needs to improve his cultural sense and increase his virtues for unforeseen events.

Suggestion：Virtuous achievements come to their successful conclusion.

初九：復自道，何其咎？吉。

象傳：復自道，其義吉也。

In the first NINE：Accepting people's advice and reflecting on one's behavior to look for problems. Using self-examination as a way to return to the right path. It is no blame. It is a great omen.

Xiang Chuan：It is auspicious to restrain oneself and look at oneself first to find problems and then correct them.

Suggestion：To restrain self and to observe the proprieties.

九二：牽復，吉。
象傳：牽復在中，亦不自失也。

In the second NINE: Uniting with comrades and following the moral path brings good fortune. It means that one is encouraged to cooperate with comrades who share the same goals and visions to overcome the difficulties.

Xiang Chuan：He who works with comrades and sticks to the moral path will not go astray.

Suggestion：A break through in a difficult situation.

九三：輿說輻。夫妻反目。
象傳：夫妻反目，不能正室也。

In the third NINE: In times of difficulties, couples tend to have arguments just like a wagon disconnected from its shafts. It is hard to restore to the original status.

Xiang Chuan：Couples stop living in harmony and behave like strangers. The husband can neither settle the disagreements nor restore harmony in the family.

Suggestion：If the family lives in harmony, all affairs will prosper.

六四：有孚，血去惕出，無咎。
象傳：有孚惕出，上合志也。

In the fourth SIX: Treating people with sincerity prevents disasters and fear. Complete sincerity can never do harm.

Xiang Chuan：Sincerity prevents disasters and fear. He who is sincere wins trust from the emperor.

Suggestion：Mental communications reduce misunderstanding.

九五：有孚攣如，富以其鄰。
象傳：有孚攣如，不獨富也。

In the fifth NINE : He who is able to get rid of greed and cooperate sincerely with comrades can not only enrich himself and enjoy social status but also make his neighbors rich.

Xiang Chuan：Advancing hand in hand with comrades not only enriches himself but also his neighbors.

Suggestion：Working together with one heart maximizes fortunes.

上九：既雨既處，尚德載ㄗ；婦貞厲，月幾望；君子征凶。

象傳：既雨既處，德積載ㄗ也；君子征凶，有所疑也。

In the topmost NINE : When the rainfall is accumulated to a certain extent, it should be properly dredged or reserved. It means that people should not be insatiably greedy. Focus more on developing one's virtues. A wife shouldn't keep her husband on a tight leash because this will hurt his self-esteem. It is the law of nature just like the moon changes from full moon to a crescent. A man with noble character should exercise self-control to avoid disasters.

Xiang Chuan：When the rainfall is accumulated to a certain extent, it should be properly dredged or reserved. Focus more on developing one's virtues. If one doesn't have the sense to stop before going too far, his future is full of doubts.

Suggestion：To stop before going too far.

10. 履 Lyu

天澤履　　乾上 兌下

履：履虎尾，不咥人，亨。

象傳：上天下澤，履；君子以辨上下，定民志。

Lyu：To implement. One treads after the tail of a tiger but doesn't get bitten. It is good luck. It reflects that the moral standards in this world are going down and people's hearts are not as pure as they used to be. It seems that the world we live in is full of danger. Therefore, dealing with people requires extreme cautions as if you are treading on thin ice to avoid disasters.

Xiang Chuan：Sky is above the lake, which represents the difference between a superior and a subordinate. A man with noble character should behave like a model citizen to influence normal people to respect the social norms.

Suggestion：One's words and behaviors should not go against the social norms. Respect the norms and people will live in peace and prosperity.

初九：素履，往無咎。

象傳：素履之往，獨行願也。

In the first NINE：Leading a simple and frugal life. There is nothing to blame.

Xiang Chuan：Leading a simple and frugal life. Treating people without pretense. This will help to fulfill one's wishes.

Suggestion：Treating people with sincerity and living in simplicity and frugality causes no harm. To refuse to be contaminated by evil influence.

九二：履道坦坦，幽人貞吉。

象傳：幽人貞吉，中不自亂也。

In the second NINE : It is auspicious to lead a life as if walking on the flat road, living in seclusion freely and not be tempted by worldly affaires.

Xiang Chuan：It is auspicious to lead a moral life, live in carefree seclusion and not be tempted by worldly affaires.

Suggestion：East is East, West is West and never the twain shall meet. At peace with everyone.

六三：眇能視，跛能履，履虎尾，咥人，凶。武人為于大君。

象傳：眇能視，不足以有明也。跛能履，不足以與行也。咥人之凶，位不當也。武人為於大君，志剛也。

In the third SIX : A one-eyed man who doesn't see well but is convinced that he has good eyesight. A cripple can't walk but thinks he can move freely. The level of ignorance is just like a man playing with a tiger without good self-judgment, he will step on the tiger's tail and get bitten. It is also like a warrior thinking he can declare independence and become a king himself. Overestimating one's strength is very dangerous.

Xiang Chuan：A one-eyed man who doesn't see well but is convinced that he has a good eyesight. A cripple fails to walk but thinks he can move freely. Their irrational thoughts are just like a man playing with a tiger without good self-judgement, he will step on the tiger's tail and get bitten. It is also like a warrior thinking he can declare independence and becoming a king himself. Overestimating one's strength is dangerous.

Suggestion：Overestimating one's strength is very dangerous.

九四：履虎尾，愬*愬，終吉。

象傳：愬愬終吉。志行也。

In the fourth NINE : If one is cautious as if he is skating on thin ice, he can avoid stepping on the tail of a tiger and turn a crisis into an opportunity. Eventually, he

---

＊註6：愬 ㄙㄨㄟ，驚恐。

can turn things around.

Xiang Chuan：It is auspicious to be cautious and avoid stepping on the tail of a tiger. He who does things cautiously and stays within his guidelines can fulfill his dreams.

Suggestion：One should always have a sense of crisis.

九五：夬履，貞厲。
象傳：夬履貞厲，位正當也。

In the fifth NINE : It is not necessarily bad to come up with a quick response to handle things. However, if one handles a situation in a dictatorial and rude manner, even if he follows the moral choice, it is very dangerous.

Xiang Chuan：One cannot be rude and irrational just because he has great talents and position. It is dangerous.

Suggestion：Too assertive in making decisions is dangerous.

上九：視履考祥，其旋元吉。
象傳：元吉在上，大有慶也。

In the topmost NINE : Whether one is fortunate or not in life depends upon his level of virtues and merits.

After reviewing all the things one has done in the past, if the conclusion is positive, it is surely a great omen.

Xiang Chuan：The fortune and lucks in a person's life depends on whether he has high level of virtues and merits.

Suggestion：Value one's past so that one can be motivated for the future.

11. 泰 Thai

地天泰　坤上 乾下

泰：小往大來，吉，亨。

象傳：天地交，泰；后以財成天地之道，輔相天地之宜，以左右民。

Thai：Prosperity. Little gone, big comes. Hexagram – Thai represents January in lunar calendar.

The vital energy becomes stronger in the first month of the year. The weather is getting warmer at this time and all the creatures are full of vitality. It means that a man of noble character is gaining power, whereas the villains are losing power. It is a great omen.

Xiang Chuan：Heaven interacts with earth. All the creatures thrive and prosper. It is a great omen. The emperor realizes that he should help people to keep regular hours and make rules according to the laws of nature so that people can live peacefully and safely.

Suggestion：Follow the laws of nature, all creatures live in prosperity.

初九：拔茅茹，以其彙。征吉。

象傳：拔茅征吉，志在外也。

In the first NINE：Concentrating all the efforts to uproot a couch grass is as if working with comrades to create a new dimension. It brings good fortunes.

Xiang Chuan：Concentrating all the efforts to uproot a couch grass as if working with comrades to create a new dimension. It is auspicious because people are united towards their goals.

Suggestion：Unity of will is an impregnable stronghold.

九二：包荒，用馮河；不遐遺，朋亡，得尚于中行。

象傳：包荒，得尚于中行，以光大也。

In the second NINE : One is generous and open-minded to tolerate those who hold opposite opinions. He even has the audacity to cross the river by foot. He will not turn his back on decent people who come all the way from afar. The subjects will not gather together to plot against him. Everything will follow the moral path.

Xiang Chuan：Be generous and open-minded. The reason that everything will follow the moral path is because he is just and honorable.

Suggestion：To forgive and do not hold grudges.

九三：無平不陂，無往不復；艱貞無咎；勿恤其孚，于食有福。
象傳：無往不復，天地際也。

In the third NINE : There is not a flat road without a ramp and there is not a straight road without a turn. Despite difficulties, if one can stay on the moral course there will be no disasters. If one is honest and trustworthy, he need not worry about the lack of clothing and foods because Karma will make sure he is blessed.

Xiang Chuan：There is not a straight road without a turn. Everything follows a natural cycle.

Suggestion：Complete sincerity brings blessing.

六四：翩翩，不富以其鄰，不戒以孚。
象傳：翩翩，不富，皆失實也。不戒以孚，中心願也。

In the fourth SIX : A frivolous man will not make solid efforts to get things done. He is destined to be poor in life. He even has a negative impact on his neighbors. He never learned the lesson that sincerity is the best policy.

Xiang Chuan：A frivolous man is destined to be poor in life because he is spendy and wasteful. Moreover, he never learned that sincerity is the best policy. He will go down in the end.

Suggestion：Having altruistic motivation is easy to reach consensus.

Self-destruction.

六五：帝乙歸妹，以祉*元吉。

象傳：以祉*元吉，中以行願也。

In the fifth SIX : The emperor agrees to let his daughter marry a subject of virtues in an ordinary wedding. It is a great fortune.

Xiang Chuan：The emperor is so humble to treat his people. He deserves to be blessed because of his humility and compassion.

Suggestion：It is rare and commendable to break the belief that says "Couples of equal social standing are well matched".

上六：城復于隍，勿用師，自邑告命。貞吝。

象傳：城復于隍，其命亂也。

In the topmost SIX : The city walls collapse into the moat. It signals that the situation is getting worse. It's not the right timing to launch a war, the armies need to rest and build up their strength. The emperor should abolish unfit rules to avoid future regrets.

Xiang Chuan：The city walls collapse into the moat, which symbolizes that the country is declining.

Suggestion：When in prosperity, one should be humble and cautious to maximize the staying power.

12. 否 Pi

 乾上 坤下
天地否

否：否之匪人，不利君子貞，大往小來。

象傳：天地不交，否；君子以儉德辟²難，不可榮以祿。

Pi：Blockage. The world is going downhill. Manners and morals are non-existent. The villains are gaining power, the man of noble character should keep a low profile to avoid disasters.

Xiang Chuan：The world is blocked. There is no communication. The man with noble character should neither show off his talents nor pursue power and money to avoid disasters.

Suggestion：To rise above the difficulties and enjoy good fortune. When you hit rock bottom, there is nowhere to go but up.

初六：拔茅茹，以其彙，貞吉，亨。

象傳：拔茅貞吉，志在君也。

In the first SIX：In the times of uncertainty, the villains are gaining power and they form groups to pursue selfish interests. The man with noble character should be united to kick out villains just like uprooting a couch grass. It brings good luck.

Xiang Chuan：The man with noble character should concentrate all the efforts to get rid of villains just like uprooting a couch grass.

Suggestion：Solidarity drives out villains.

六二：包承。小人吉，大人否。亨。

象傳：大人否亨，不亂群也。

In the second SIX : In times of uncertainty, the villains prefer ass-kissing. They enjoy wealth and power. On the contrary, the man with noble character doesn't. He has morality and will not be surrounded by the villains. It is a good omen.

Xiang Chuan：The more difficult a situation is, the more perseverant he will be to stay on the moral path. He will never hang out with villains.

Suggestion：To improve oneself.

六三：包羞。

象傳：包羞，位不當也。

In the third SIX : The situation is still uncertain. The villains are ruthless in disregard of laws and morality. They are not ashamed of what they've done.

Xiang Chuan：The villains are ruthless in disregard of laws and morality. They are not ashamed of what they've done. Their wrongdoings deserve to be condemned.

Suggestion: Overlooking is the same as helping to commit a crime.

九四：有命，無咎，疇離祉。

象傳：有命無咎，志行也。

In the fourth NINE : After a period of uncertainty, the situation is going to change. One should have the ambition and mission to help those in danger and relieve those in distress. There is nothing to be blamed. Many comrades will come to attach to share the fortunes.

Xiang Chuan：After a period of certainty, the situation is going to change. One should have the ambition and mission to help those in danger and relieve those in distress. There is nothing to be blamed. Many people sharing the same ideology will come to join and their wishes will come true.

Suggestion：Collective wisdom and efforts will turn things around.

九五：休否，大人吉。 其亡其亡，繫於苞桑。

象傳：大人之吉，位正當也。

In the fifth NINE : The uncertain situation is going to an end. It will be a good omen. Although the situation is going better, the man of noble character still has a strong commitment to national safety, whose loyalty is deeply rooted in him just like the white mulberry is deep-rooted to the earth.

Xiang Chuan：The uncertainty is going to an end. Peaceful days are coming back. It is a good sign. The positive development is due to the fact that the great man always makes the moral choice.

Suggestion：To be circumspect and farsighted. To be prepared for danger in times of peace.

上九：傾否，先否後喜。

象傳：否終則傾，何可長也。

In the topmost NINE : The bad times are over. When one hits rock bottom, there is nowhere to go but up.

Xiang Chuan：The times when villains prevail are over. It is worthy of celebration. The villains shouldn't be given room for survival.

Suggestion：Evil can never prevail over good.

13. 同人　Tong-Ren

 乾上　離下

天火同人

同人：于野，亨。利涉大川，利君子貞。

象傳：天與火，同人；君子以類族辨物。

Tong-Ren：Working together with one heart will bring fortune. The comrades

gathering together in the fields are above-board, honest and selfless. It is helpful for them to overcome difficulties. It is also great luck for a man with noble character to stay on the moral course.

Xiang Chuan：Air and fire are mutually dependent just like people indicated by Tong-Ren. The man with noble character realizes human beings need to reach consensus despite their vastly different backgrounds.

Suggestion：To seek common ground while reserving differences.

初九：同人于門，無咎。
象傳：出門同人，又誰咎也？

In the first NINE ：Even while just stepping outside of the door, a man with noble character can make friends with all walks of lives. He regards a passerby as a member of his family and nobody will blame him.

Xiang Chuan：The man with noble character can go out and actively look for comrades to fulfill their common goals. Nobody will blame him.

Suggestion：To break the "parochial prejudice".

六二：同人于宗，吝。
象傳：同人于宗，吝道也。

In the second SIX ：Only cooperating with kin group is narrow-minded. This choice will bring regrets.

Xiang Chuan：Only cooperating with kin group leaves room for corruption.

Suggestion：Being far-sighted is a prerequisite of success.

九三：伏戎于莽，升其高陵，三歲不興。
象傳：伏戎于莽，敵剛也；三歲不興，安行也。

In the third NINE ：Set up the troops for an ambush. Climb up to the hills to monitor the enemy's movements. Since three years, all the concerns on enemies' surprise attacks have not been realized.

Xiang Chuan：Because of the enemy's strong forces, one's troops remain inactive for three years. Nobody expects a victory. Everyone is happy with the status-quo.

Suggestion：You can't achieve anything with reckless courage.

九四：乘其墉，弗克攻，吉。

象傳：乘其墉，義弗克也；其吉，則困而反則也。

In the fourth NINE : Climb up to the city walls to find a chance to attack. However, after much deliberation, one still withdraws the armies since there is big uncertainty about the outcome. Caution brings luck.

Xiang Chuan：Climb up to the city walls to find a chance to attack. However, because there is no chance of winning, the attack is stopped. It is auspicious to examine oneself in difficulties and do the right thing.

Suggestion：To have a thorough knowledge of oneself. To rein in at the edge of the precipice.

九五：同人先號咷而後笑，大師克相遇。

象傳：同人之先，以中直也；大師相遇，言相克也。

In the fifth NINE : An ally is suffering in an invasion. He is immediately looking for back-up from the leader of the alliance. At the beginning, he cried out loud because he suffered from the attack, but soon burst into laughter when the back-up arrived and saved the day.

Xiang Chuan：If he is sincere and makes the moral choice, he certainly has the capability to ask for back-up to defeat the enemy.

Suggestion：When the rain is over, the sky clears up.

上九：同人于郊，無悔。

象傳：同人于郊，志未得也。

In the topmost NINE : Join the comrades in the suburban areas. One will not have regrets.

Xiang Chuan：Join the comrades in the suburban areas. However, he has not reached his goals.

Suggestion：One has not fulfilled his ambition.

14. 大有 Ta-yu

離上 乾下
火天大有

大有：元亨。
象傳：火在天上，大有；君子以遏惡揚善，順天休命。

Ta-yu：Greatest harvest. Treat people with modesty. Distribute favors widely to the people. Ta-yu means that abundant harvests win people.

Xiang Chuan：Fire energy is from the sky because sunshine that brightens every corner of the world also comes from the sky. It means greatest harvest. Under the blessing of a kind emperor, the man with noble character should promote good deeds, discourage evil activities and follow natural laws and he will have good luck.

Suggestion：Unselfish contributions help one to feel the richest!

初九：無交害，匪咎，艱則無咎。
象傳：大有初九，無交害也。

In the first NINE : There will be no disasters if one gets along with people and avoids having conflicts of interest. However, one should always remain prudent, avoid being arrogant, then he is sure to overcome difficulties.

Xiang Chuan：It is disadvantageous not to interact with people.

Suggestion：Starting a business is difficult but worldly wisdom and human interests should never be overlooked. Harmony is the key to long-lasting generations.

九二：大車以載，有攸往，无咎。

象傳：大車以載，積中不敗也。

In the second NINE : The man with noble character not only seeks to better himself, but also to set a moral example for the world. He is full of goals and ambitions just like a fully-loaded wagon charging towards the destination. There is no blame. It implies that objectives and continuous progress assure great results.

Xiang Chuan：If the driver follows the rules and drives safely, the fully-loaded wagon is sure to reach the destination timely and safely. It implies that tolerance and forgiving are the greatest gifts.

Suggestion：To bear heavy responsibilities through a long struggle.

九三：公用享于天子，小人弗克。

象傳：公用享于天子，小人害也。

In the third NINE : When the dukes have great harvest, they regularly donate gifts to show their gratitude to the emperor but when the villains become rich, they are arrogant and skimp on donations.

Xiang Chuan：The dukes regularly donate gifts to the emperor to show their gratitude to the emperor. On the contrary, when the villains become rich, they are selfish and blinded by material desires. Eventually they become the heartless rich and are detrimental to the world.

Suggestion：When drinking water, think of its source.

九四：匪其彭，无咎。

象傳：匪其彭，无咎。明辨晢也。

In the fourth NINE : Be humble and repress one's desires. Do not show off one's wealth. There is no blame. The man with noble character will not show off his wealth because he knows this is the best way to protect himself.

Xiang Chuan：Be humble and repress one's desires. Do not show off one's wealth. There is no blame. One is wise to understand the benefits.

Suggestion：Pride leads to loss while modesty brings benefit.

六五：厥孚交如，威如，吉。
象傳：厥孚交如，信以發志也；威如之吉，易而無備也。

In the fifth SIX : Although being in a noble position, he still treats superiors and subordinates with humbleness and dignity. It is a great omen.

Xiang Chuan：Although being in a noble position, he still treats superiors and subordinates with complete honesty and sincerity. He inspires other people and establishes his prestige and popular trust not because of being fake, but because of his modest behavior.

Suggestion：To apply the carrot and stick sensibly.

上九：自天祐之，吉無不利。
象傳：大有上吉，自天祐也。

In the topmost NINE : As an emperor, it is right to cultivate virtues and to share his wealth and happiness with the people. His affluence comes from the blessing of Heaven. There are no downsides.

Xiang Chuan：The affluence comes from the blessing of Heaven. In fact, whether one's words and deeds are in accord with the ethics determines the blessing he gets.

Suggestion：The truth of long lasting affluence is to never show off one's riches and treat people with extreme modesty so that one's wealth can last from generation to generation.

15. 謙 Qian

地山謙　　坤上 艮下

謙：亨，君子有終。

象傳：地中有山，謙；君子以裒多益寡，稱物平施。

Qian：Unassuming. Humble. Being humble means never thinking highly of one's talents and achievements. Moreover, one can accept criticism.

Modesty makes one prosperous. The man with noble character is able to be modest from the beginning to the end of his life. It is the way of Qian.

Xiang Chuan：The mountain is rooted in the earth. This represents that overdoing is equally bad as not doing enough. Even though one is menial, one will not violate moral principles.

The man with noble character understands that he should "reduce the surplus to fill the shortage" to make things balanced and treat people fairly as well.

Suggestion：Not to be shaken or modified by one's poverty or destitution.

初六：謙謙君子，用涉大川，吉。

象傳：謙謙君子，卑以自牧也。

In the first SIX：A man with noble character is able to overcome difficulties because of his modesty. It brings good fortune.

Xiang Chuan：His modesty prevents him from reckless behavior as if a bull is controlled by the rope on its nose during the herding.

Suggestion：Modesty is not to concede passively but a positive attitude.

六二：鳴謙，貞吉。

象傳：鳴謙，貞吉，中心得也。

In the second SIX : One's modesty resonates with people and his reputation spreads far. It is auspicious if he can continue to make the moral choice.

Xiang Chuan：One's modesty resonates with people and his reputation spreads far. His modesty is coming from his true heart, not from faking.

Suggestion：Modesty coming from the true heart is pure and right.

九三：勞謙君子，有終，吉。

象傳：勞謙君子，萬民服也。

In the third NINE : A man with noble character is always humble and will never claim credit. His humbleness from the beginning to the end is worthy of praise.

Xiang Chuan：Despite his contributions, a man with noble character is always humble. His giving and reliance receive full support from people.

Suggestion：People who are modest and are bearing hardships without any complaints are rare and commendable.

六四：無不利，撝*謙。

象傳：無不利，撝謙，不違則也。

In the fourth SIX : It is very favorable for one to refuse to be excessively modest.

Xiang Chuan：It is very favorable for one to refuse to be excessively modest. It isn't against the principles.

Suggestion：Excessive modesty is equal to insincerity.

六五：不富以其鄰，利用侵伐，無不利。

象傳：利用侵伐，征不服也。

In the fifth SIX : The emperor will not enjoy wealth alone. He always shares the resources to the subjects with merits.

＊註7：撝ㄏㄨㄟ＝揮，把內在能力表現出來。

If his authority is challenged, the emperor will send an army to subdue the rebellion. The expedition is not disadvantageous.

Xiang Chuan：If his authority is challenged, the emperor will send an army to subdue the rebellion. The expedition is not disadvantageous.

Suggestion：It is not necessarily wrong to have to settle all the disputes by force.

上六：鳴謙，利用行師，征邑國。

象傳：鳴謙，志未得也；可用行師，征邑國也。

In the topmost SIX ：It is favorable to against rebellion or resisted rebellious neighbors by means of modest virtues resonance.

Xiang Chuan：If the goal of integrating neighboring countries peacefully has not been fulfilled, punitive action is inevitable. One has no choice but to resort to military force.

Suggestion：It takes not only a modest attitude but also deliberate action to complete the mission.

16. 豫 Yu

震上 坤下

雷地豫

豫：利建侯行師。

象傳：雷出地奮，豫；先王以作樂崇德，殷薦之上帝，以配祖考。

Yu：Joyful. The nation prospers and the people live in safety. It is favorable for the emperor to grant the title of duke or to send an army to crush the rebellions.

Xiang Chuan：The spring thunder claps and all the creatures are awakened. The late

emperors were inspired by this natural phenomenon and imitated the thunderclaps to compose music and drum beats to praise virtue and achievements. The music was played in religious ceremonies to worship to God and ancestors.

Suggestion：To thrive in difficulties and deteriorate in peace.

初六：鳴豫，凶。

象傳：初六鳴豫，志窮凶也。

In the first SIX：Bad reputation travels far when one is indulged in worldly pleasure and doesn't have any self-control. It is bad luck.

Xiang Chuan：Bad reputation travels far when one is indulged in worldly pleasure and doesn't have any self-control. He has no ambition and will not have any hope.

Suggestion：One gets carried away!

六二：介于石，不終日，貞吉。

象傳：不終日，貞吉，以中正也。

In the second SIX：It is auspicious for one to treat people with honesty and ethics as solid as a rock.

Although everyone else is lost in self-indulgence, he is able to exercise self-control.

Xiang Chuan：It is positive for one to be able to stop his indulgence in entertainment in a day. His good luck is coming from his moral choice.

Suggestion：More than enough is too much.

六三：盱*豫，悔；遲，有悔。

象傳：盱豫有悔，位不當也。

In the third SIX：One is selfish and only looks to maximize personal interests. He butters up his superiors only to benefit himself. His behavior will cause regrets. If

---

＊註8：盱ㄒㄩ，張眼看。

corrections are not done in time, it may incur more regrets.

Xiang Chuan：One is selfish and only looks to maximize personal interests. He butters up his superiors only to benefit himself. His behavior will cause regrets because they are not right.

Suggestion：Those who are smooth talkers and present smiley faces are seldom kind.

九四：由豫，大有得，勿疑。朋盍簪。

象傳：由豫，大有得，志大行也。

In the fourth NINE：One grows up in a well-off family. He always leads an optimistic and comfortable life. He is friendly and is willing to share happiness with them. Of course, he is going to receive a lot because of his good deeds. Maintaining a sincere and happy friendship without second guessing each other is just like hairpins holding the hair tightly.

Xiang Chuan：One grows up in a well-off family. He always leads an optimistic and comfortable life. He is going to receive a lot because his ambition and goals will be fulfilled.

Suggestion：A just cause attracts much support, an unjust one finds little.

六五：貞疾，恆不死。

象傳：六五貞疾，乘剛也；恆不死，中未亡也。

In the fifth SIX：The emperor is indulged in food, drinking and pleasure. He neglects political affairs for a long time. The villains take advantage of the situation to take control of the politics, which worsens the situation so much that it is beyond rescue. There are no ethics. The emperor does nothing as a patient with a serious illness can do nothing but lie on the bed for a long time.

Xiang Chuan：The emperor is indulged in pleasures and neglects political affairs. Although he is still in power, he is no longer in charge. His regime exists in name only.

Suggestion：Thrive with worries, perish in peace.

上六：冥豫成，有渝無咎。
象傳：冥豫在上，何可長也？

In the topmost SIX：The emperor neglects political affairs and indulges in pleasures to the extreme. He becomes muddle-headed and incompetent. His brain is dizzy and not functioning. If he can correct himself in time, the problem still can be solved.

Xiang Chuan：The emperor is lost in sensual pleasures to the extreme. How can he reverse the situation?

Suggestion：Extreme pleasure is followed by sorrow. Correct evil doings and return to good deeds.

17. 隨　Suei

 兌上 震下
澤雷隨

隨：元、亨、利、貞，無咎。
象傳：澤中有雷。隨；君子以嚮晦入宴息。

Suei：Follow. Easygoing. One is humble and kind to people so people are kind to him. "Suie" consists of four virtues：comprehensive, prosperous, harmonious and ethical. Therefore, it will attract no blame.

Xiang Chuan：Thunder claps in the lake. The man with noble character follows the natural cycle. He works hard during the day and rests in the evening.

Suggestion：Follow the natural cycles to make the best in life.

初九：官有渝，貞吉，出門交有功。

象傳：官有渝，從正吉也；出門交有功，不失也。

In the first NINE : One should not be unhappy about the personnel change because the circumstances may change and one's views may change too. If ethics are firmly respected, it will be positive. Furthermore, one should go out to connect with people and treat people with an easygoing attitude. It is healthy to broaden his views.

Xiang Chuan：It is favorable to view personnel changes positively. Going out to meet people and treat people with easygoing attitude won't attract any blame.

Suggestion：Don't judge a person by his social status. It shows ethics and open-mindedness.

六二：係小子，失丈夫。

象傳：係小子，弗兼與也。

In the second SIX : Getting closer to people with power and money because of instant benefit is at the same time distancing oneself away from ordinary people. You cannot eat your cake and have it too. It is impossible to benefit from both sides at the same time. You will suffer a big loss for a tiny gain. It means that blindly chasing after immediate gains results in big potential loss.

Xiang Chuan：Getting close to common people is equal to keeping distance from high power people. You cannot eat your cake and have it too.

Suggestion：Risk a big loss for a little gain.

六三：係丈夫，失小子，隨有求得，利居貞。

象傳：係丈夫，志舍下也。

In the third SIX : If you are close to bigshots, you will naturally keep distance from common folks. Although you will benefit from following the big shots, being ethical is the best policy.

Xiang Chuan：Being close to bigshots is to abandon common folks. It shows his

intention.

Suggestion：As long as the green mountains are there, one needs not worry about firewood. While there is life, there is hope.

九四：隨有獲，貞凶。有孚在道，以明，何咎？

象傳：隨有獲，其義凶也；有孚在道，明功也。

In the fourth NINE : It is beneficial to follow the bigshots. Even if this is done ethically, your intention inevitably attracts disaster. However, if you are sincere, honest and incorruptible, is there anything people could blame?

Xiang Chuan：It is beneficial to follow the bigshots. Even if this is done ethically, your intention inevitably attracts disaster. A wise man knows that one needs to be sincere, honest, and incorruptible. Wisdom is the best protection.

Suggestion：A blessing in disguise.

九五：孚于嘉，吉。

象傳：孚于嘉，吉，位正中也。

In the fifth NINE : One is trusted and praised as he sincerely follows the great man, which brings good fortune.

Xiang Chuan：He is trusted and relied on because he is morally upright in following the great men's good deeds.

Suggestion：Follow well-intentioned advice like water flowing smoothly downward.

上六：拘係之，乃從；維之，王用亨于西山。

象傳：拘繫之，上窮也。

In the topmost SIX : Although an emperor treats people with kindness, there will still be rebellions. The emperor cannot avoid using force to have them give their submission. The emperor is sincere to worship and reform them in the ancestral temple.

Xiang Chuan：The emperor cannot help but use force to have them give in their submission. There is no alternative.

Suggestion：Not to stop until one reaches one's goal.

18. 蠱 Gu

 艮上 巽下
山風蠱

蠱：元亨。利涉大川，先甲三日，後甲三日。

象傳：山下有風，蠱；君子以振民育德。

Gu：Reformation. Clean up the corruption and squash the rebellions in the beginning. It brings great luck. In order to have a clean government, the first priority is to launch a reform. It is just like crossing a big river, it needs make-or-break determination. At the beginning, new decrees should be constantly communicated to the people to avoid any unexpected happenings. Then supervision and corrective measures are followed.

Xiang Chuan：The winds blow to the bottom of the hill. It means to clean up corruption and squash rebellions. The man with noble character should inspire people and cultivate the virtues of people.

Suggestion：If the goal is to clean up corruption and squash the rebellions, it has to be done in a "nip in the bud" manner with firm execution.

初六：幹父之蠱，有子，考無咎，厲，終吉。

象傳：幹父之蠱，意承考也。

In the first SIX：It is fortunate to have a talented son who is able to correct the

problems his dead father has caused. In order to relieve the criticisms on his father, he took the responsibility of correcting his father's faults. The son doesn't only inherit the family fortunes but also the responsibilities.

Xiang Chuan：The son bears the responsibilities to correct his dead father's mistakes and to rebuild the family's reputation. He intends to carry out his father's will.

Suggestion： Merits offset faults. One should not blame others for all the problems or come up with an excuse to decline.

九二：幹母之蠱，不可貞。
象傳：幹母之蠱，得中道也。

In the second NINE : It is inappropriate for a son to correct the faults of his mother who took over the responsibilities from his dead father. Even if a son has to rebuild the family reputation, he has to do it without hurting the mother's feelings.

Xiang Chuan：When correcting the faults of one's mother, one has to respect the doctrine of the mean. Do it in a polite manner and don't hurt the mother's feelings.

Suggestion：Things have their order of priority.

九三：幹父之蠱，小有悔，無大咎。
象傳：幹父之蠱，終無咎也。

In the third NINE : The son is keen on correcting his fathers' mistakes but setbacks are inevitable. Even if there is a little regret, there will be no disasters because only by overcoming difficulties can one avoid big problems.

Xiang Chuan：The son corrects his dead father's faults. There will be no blame.

Suggestion：So long as one's action is well justified, one should carry it out without regrets.

六四：裕父之蠱，往，見吝。
象傳：裕父之蠱，往未得也。

In the fourth SIX : There will be disasters if a son is over tolerant of his dead father's mistakes. If it goes on like this, he will have regrets.

Xiang Chuan：If one continues to be over tolerant of his dead father's faults, we cannot expect him to launch any reforms.

Suggestion：Be strict with oneself and lenient towards others.

六五：幹父之蠱，用譽。

象傳：幹父用譽，承以德也。

In the fifth SIX : Correcting faults of one's dead father by the doctrine of means will get praises.

Xiang Chuan：Correcting faults of one's dead father by the doctrine of means is considered as honoring traditional morals and virtues.

Suggestion：Appoint talented people and people with virtue to clean up corruption and crush rebellions. This must be done in a "nip in the bud" manner and with firm execution.

上九：不事王侯，高尚其事。

象傳：不事王侯，志可則也。

In the topmost NINE : The purpose of cleaning up corruption is not to pursue fame, power and fortune. It is to show one's noble character and his indifference to fame and fortune.

Xiang Chuan：A man with noble character is indifferent to fame and fortune. He doesn't cling on to positions. His noble character serves as a great example for people.

Suggestion：Resignation after having made one's mark.

19. 臨 Lirn

坤上 兑下

地澤臨

臨：元、亨、利、貞。至於八月有凶。

象傳：澤上有地，臨；君子以教思無窮，容保民無疆。

Lirn：Leadership. The emperor descends to the world. It consists of four virtues：comprehensiveness, prosperity, harmony and ethics. It means that everything goes well in the beginning of the reform, but the reform should have consistent execution and should not be carried out half-heartedly. When August comes, things tend to change at this time. Thus important things need to be well taken care of.

Xiang Chuan：Earth is above the lake. It means that the emperor occupies a commanding position over his people.

The man with noble character realizes that he has responsibilities to educate, enlighten, tolerate, protect and defend people.

Suggestion：To carry out an undertaking from start to finish. Seize the opportunity because it is transient.

初九：咸臨，貞吉。

象傳：咸臨貞吉，志行正也。

In the first NINE：The humbleness of the newly throned emperor inspires and moves people. People are happy and obedient. The emperor descends the world. The nation is in propriety and people live in safety.

Xiang Chuan：The humbleness of the newly throned emperor inspires and moves people. It brings good luck because of his sincerity and ethical behavior.

Suggestion：Leadership involves sincere interactions and mutual echoing between the leader and the people.

九二：咸臨，吉，無不利。

象傳：咸臨，吉，無不利，未順命也。

In the second NINE : It's fortunate to lead people by inspiring them.

Xiang Chuan：It's fortunate to lead people by inspiring them. It has no disadvantages because he will not give in to circumstances.

Suggestion：Apply the carrot and stick judiciously.

六三：甘臨，無攸利；既憂之，無咎。

象傳：甘臨，位不當也；既憂之，咎不長也。

In the third SIX : A ruler always flatters people but never means it. He will eventually loses credibility and attract disapproval. If he is conscious of the wrongdoings and corrects it, there will be no disasters.

Xiang Chuan：If the ruler is conscious of his wrongdoings, the disaster will not last long.

Suggestion：Nothing is worse than losing one's credibility among people.

六四：至臨，無咎。

象傳：至臨，無咎，位當也。

In the fourth SIX : Care about people at the grass root level and communicate policies to people personally. His sincerity inspires people's morale. It is the right thing to do.

Xiang Chuan：Care about people at the grass root level and communicate policies to people personally. His sincerity inspires people's morale. It is the right thing to do. He occupies the right position to do the right things.

Suggestion：Sometimes it is not wrong to attend to thing personally, especially important matters.

六五：知臨，大君之宜，吉。

象傳：大君之宜，行中之謂也。

In the fifth SIX : A wise emperor understands his people comprehensively and descends to the world with wisdom. It is a great omen.

Xiang Chuan：A wise emperor understands his people comprehensively and descends to the world with wisdom. He just fulfills an unshakable duty and follows the moral path.

Suggestion：An excellent leadership trait is to appoint the virtuous and the talented for important positions and authorize them to solve problems of the people. He utilizes the collective wisdom from the talents and he doesn't have to attend to everything personally so that he can be close to people.

上六 : 敦臨，吉，無咎。
象傳：敦臨之吉，志在內也。

In the topmost SIX : An emperor descends the world with generosity and tolerance. It is a good omen.

Xiang Chuan：It is fortunate for an emperor to descend the world with generosity and tolerance. He tries hard to care about his people.

Suggestion：Being generous and tolerant. Always bear in mind the interests of others. Not to gloat over someone's misfortunes. No mocking words towards someone's sorrow. Never add insult to injury.

20. 觀　Guan

 巽上 坤下
風地觀

觀：盥而不薦，有孚顒若。

象傳：風行地上，觀；先王以省方，觀民社教。

Guan：Observation. Sharp observation. Even before the offerings are placed on the altar, we can clearly feel the devotion of a worshiper judging by the way he washes his hands.

Xiang Chuan：The wind blows to the ground, meaning that the official visit of the ancient emperor is like the wind touching the people. He takes everything about people into consideration and based on this understanding, he educates and inspires people.

Suggestion：Before trying to educate and inspire people, an emperor carefully and extensively observes the public opinion, which serves as the guidance for political policies.

初六：童觀，小人無咎，君子吝。

象傳：初六童觀，小人道也。

In the first SIX：The observation of a child is just like that of a villain. The superficial views of the two make no difference. It is acceptable for a child to have the same view as a villain, but for a man with noble character, he will be humiliated.

Xiang Chuan：The observation of a child is equal to the short sight of a villain.

Suggestion：One can not look at things just from the macro perspective, he needs to be far-sighted too.

六二：闚觀，利女貞。

象傳：闚觀，女貞，亦可醜也。

|In the second SIX|: Peeping through the crack of a door from outside only allows you to see part of the whole. It is acceptable for a woman to have a narrow view.

Xiang Chuan：Peeping through the crack of a door from outside only allows you to see part of the whole. It is acceptable for a woman to have a narrow view but it is shameful for a man with noble character.

Suggestion：Sharp observation requires open-mindedness.

六三：觀我生，進退。
象傳：觀我生進退，未失道也。

|In the third SIX|: Careful observation on yourself serves as a guidance for future behaviors.

Xiang Chuan：Careful observation on yourself serves as a guidance for future behaviors. Then you will not stray away from moral course.

Suggestion：Self-examination on one's conduct. Have a clear conscience and have nothing to be ashamed of.

六四：觀國之光，利用賓于王。
象傳：觀國之光，尚賓也。

|In the fourth SIX|: Careful observation of the customs, tradition, achievements and public opinions allows you to know right away the political and social climate of a country. It provides helpful information to the virtuous to contribute to the royal court.

Xiang Chuan：Careful observation of the customs, tradition, achievements and public opinions allows you to know right away the political and social climate of a country. It provides helpful information to the virtuous to decide whether he will be involved in politics.

Suggestion：Before starting one's career as a public servant, one should

observe what causes people to suffer.

九五：觀我生，君子無咎。
象傳：觀我生，觀民也。

In the fifth NINE : There will be no blame if a ruler examines himself on his performance and public opinions. In fact, public opinions are an index to show what people think of the government.

Xiang Chuan：Public opinions reflect one's political performance.

Suggestion：The self-examination of a statesman is positively correlated to the outcome of the poll.

上九：觀其生，君子無咎。
象傳：觀其生，志未平也。

In the topmost NINE : People all focus on the behaviors of high ranking officials. If they are ethical and are not lost in greed, they will not be blamed.

Xiang Chuan：The high ranking officials are always examined by the people. They should have high integrity, knowing when to advance and when to step back.

Suggestion：Officials should be under the supervision of the people.

21. 噬嗑 Shi-He

 離上 震下
火雷噬嗑

噬嗑：亨，利用獄。

象傳：雷電，噬嗑；先王以明罰勅法。

Shi-He：Crumping. Criminal penalty. While eating, you need to chew food to have better digestion. Any obstacles should be overcome before reaching the target. It is a good omen. It implies that disputes among people always come from bad communications. If the disputes are not settled, going to court is the only way out.

Xiang Chuan：Thunderclaps combine with the lightening. These two natural phenomena coexist and interact with each other. The emperor needs to make the laws more clear and court judges fairer.

Suggestion：Law enforcement needs to be fair to win people's trust.

初九：履校滅趾，無咎。

象傳：履校滅趾，不行也。

In the first NINE：A criminal's feet are shackled. His toes are hurt and he cannot move freely. Because the offense isn't a serious crime, the criminal is able to correct his fault. There is no blame.

Xiang Chuan：A criminal's feet are shackled. His toes are hurt and he cannot move freely. The shackles remind him that he shouldn't repeat the same mistake.

Suggestion：Light punishment and harsh admonishment prevent one from committing the same crime.

六二：噬膚，滅鼻，無咎。

象傳：噬膚滅鼻，乘剛也。

In the second SIX : Executing a criminal must be fast and determined. This is not wrong because this is just like biting a piece of tender meat.

Xiang Chuan：Severe punishment on an offender can discourage a die-hard criminal from committing the same crime again.

Suggestion：Severe punishments help to reduce crime.

六三：噬腊ㄒˊ肉，遇毒，小吝，無咎。
象傳：遇毒，位不當也。

In the third SIX : While facing complaints, the law enforcer is hesitant about the enforcement. It is as if eating a piece of cured meat that causes stomachache because the meat is contaminated during the long period of preservation. It is only a minor problem, you will recover soon. Although it is regretful, there is no need to blame. It means that the ruler may sometimes encounter tricky issues as if he is biting a piece of tough meat. However, the setbacks will be overcome soon if he does the right thing.

Xiang Chuan：The law enforcer will sometimes face a die-hard criminal and he cannot enforce the law fairly. The experience is like being poisoned by a piece of cured meat.

Suggestion：You should overcome all the frustrations of law enforcement.

九四：噬乾胏ㄗˇ*，得金矢。利艱貞，吉。
象傳：利艱貞，吉，未光也。

In the fourth NINE : Charging a powerful and wealthy criminal is like biting a piece of cured meat. It is not smooth. The law enforcers' attitude should be as firm as a copper arrow to complete the charging and the sentencing process.

Xiang Chuan：Despite running into difficulties, the law enforcer is still morally upright. Therefore, it is tough to charge a criminal. After all, the whole charging process is not so admirable.

＊註9：胏ㄗˇ，帶有骨頭的乾肉。

Suggestion：Enforce the law thoroughly and do not give up principles.

六五：噬乾肉，得黃金。貞厲，無咎。

象傳：貞厲，無咎，得當也。

In the fifth SIX：Charging a powerful and wealthy criminal is like eating a piece of hard cured meat. The law enforcer has to be bold and determined just like a copper arrow. Since the charging process is well carried out, there is no downside.

Xiang Chuan：The law enforcer comes across a big shot criminal, he is morally upright and enforces the law fairly.

Suggestion：Using perseverance to complete the criminal charges. Evil can never prevail over good.

上九：何校滅耳，凶。

象傳：何校滅耳，聰不明也。

In the topmost NINE：A criminal is wearing shackles on the neck and shoulders. The heavy shackles even hurt his ears. Apparently the criminal doesn't take the advice from others and committed a heavy crime. Of course, it is unfortunate.

Xiang Chuan：The criminal is wearing shackles so heavy to hurt his ears. He created his own misery.

Suggestion：It is not easy to reform a heinous criminal. Nothing can extenuate such an appalling crime.

22. 賁 Bih*

艮上 離下

山火賁

賁：亨，小利有攸往。

象傳：山下有火，賁；君子以明庶政，無敢折獄。

Bih：Embellishment. All objects need to be embellished to enhance their appearance, values and shine. Embellishment can also be applied to inner qualities. It is fortunate if one is elegant and refined in his manner. However, embellishment is like decoration and thus is not worthy of so much attention.

Xiang Chuan：There is fire on the bottom of the hill. The flames light up the mountain. It's the symbol of hexagram of Bih. The man of noble character realizes that embellishment is only superficial. He dares not recklessly get involved into lawsuits because he is afraid of misjudging the case.

Suggestion：Too much attention on formalities is equal to overlooking the fundamental nature.

初九：賁其趾，舍車而徒。

象傳：舍車而徒，義弗乘也。

In the first NINE：One decorates his toes to show off. He gives up the convenience of taking a carriage and chooses to walk. It is logical since he intends to show off his toes. It signifies that one would rather lead a plain and simple life than enjoy a comfortable living.

Xiang Chuan：One gives up the convenience of taking a carriage. Instead, he chooses to walk. In the sense, he would rather walk instead of taking a carriage.

Suggestion：Practical. No wishful thinking. Concentrate on details but forget the main purpose.

＊註10: 賁ㄅㄧˋ，裝飾。

六二：賁其須。

象傳：賁其須，與上興也。

In the second SIX : Beards help to improve your face shape. Beards are attached to the face as elegance is to a person.

Beards can cater to different preferences. Face and beards coexist. Beards symbolize prudence, maturity and thought fullness in handling things.

Xiang Chuan：Beards help to improve your face shape. Beards are attached to the face as elegance is to a person. Beards can cater to different preferences. Well-trimmed beards brighten a man's face. Beards and face coexist. It means that if he intends to achieve something, he should attach to a great man and learn from him.

Suggestion：Elegance and quality complement each other. They are inseparable.

九三：賁如，濡如，永貞吉。

象傳：永貞之吉，終莫之陵也。

In the third NINE : Embellishment on the appearance makes one look gorgeous, stand out and pleasant to look at. If he can maintain the appearance for a long time, it is fortunate. It indicates that inner beauty is mightier than appearance.

Xiang Chuan：Excessive embellishment makes one gorgeous and lost at the same time but if he follows the doctrine of the mean, he will realize that appearance can never outweigh inner quality.

Suggestion：Excessive embellishment makes one lost.

六四：賁如，皤如，白馬翰如；匪寇，婚媾。

象傳：六四，當位疑也；匪寇，婚媾，終無尤也。

In the fourth SIX : People in white clothes are fast approaching by horses. They are not bandits, but are people who come to propose. Because of too much embellishment of white clothes and white horses, they easily trigger suspicion.

Xiang Chuan：Fearful of the purpose of coming people. Uncertain whether they are proposing peacefully or by force. Despite the worries, the marriage is completed after all. There is no blame.

Suggestion：Do not give people the opportunities to have doubts on you.

六五：賁於丘園，束帛戔戔。吝，終吉。

象傳：六五之吉，有喜也。

In the fifth SIX : The emperor embellishes the hills and the gardens, showing that he emphasizes very much on the fundamental nature. It looks rather stingy for an emperor to pay only a small price to decorate. However, this is good evidence that he is a good emperor because he is not ostentatious and wasteful and he cherishes people's hard-earned money.

Xiang Chuan：The emperor strongly emphasizes essentials instead of appearance. He is not wasteful and ostentatious and values people's hard-earned money. It is undoubtedly a great omen for the nation.

Suggestion：Emphasis on fundamental nature instead of appearances.

上九：白賁，無咎。

象傳：白賁，無咎，上得志也。

In the topmost NINE : Without embellishment, there will be no blame as everything goes back to its pure state. It will be well received if one pursues wisdom and virtues. If one understands that everything is empty in nature, it is not wrong to return to simplicity.

Xiang Chuan：Without embellishment, there will be no blame as everything goes back to its pure and simple state.

Suggestion：All embellishments come to emptiness at the end, the state of purity and simplicity.

23. 剝　Bo

剝：不利有攸往。

象傳：山附於地，剝；上以厚下安宅。

Bo：Shedding. The situation falls into chaos. It is time for villains to gain power. The villains and the men with noble character can't coexist at the same time because the villains try to eradicate the men with noble character. Therefore, the men with noble character have to lay low and hide their talents to avoid oppression or being forced to cooperate with the villains. In such a situation, the men with noble character need to be patient and wait for things to change instead of acting prematurely.

Xiang Chuan：The mountains are grounded to the earth. Earth and rocks are the foundation of mountains. If earth and rocks are shedding, the mountains are sure to collapse. The emperor realizes that treating people with generosity is a sure way to guarantee the peace and stability of the country. Everybody knows that if the foundation of the State is stable, people will live in peace and prosperity.

Suggestion：People are the foundation of the state. If the people can't live in peace and safety, the regime is bound to collapse.

初六：剝床以足，蔑貞，凶。

象傳：剝床以足，以滅下也。

In the first SIX ：A bed starts to wobble because the legs are broken, as if a house collapses because the ridgepoles and beams start to deteriorate. Likewise, the collapse of a country starts from the time when the evil drives out the good.

Xiang Chuan：A wobbled bed is surely because of a broken leg. The collapse of a country is due to the fact that evil prevails over good.

Suggestion：Slow deterioration gradually threatens the foundation. Attention

to details.

六二：剝床以辨，蔑貞凶。

象傳：剝床以辨，未有與也。

In the second SIX : It is dangerous for the deterioration to spread to the frame of a bed. This is because the broken legs from the beginning are overlooked. It will be unfortunate as right things are not done in time.

Xiang Chuan：It is dangerous for the deterioration to spread to the frame of a bed. The situation is helpless.

Suggestion：Quickly fix the broken part so it won't spread.   Give him an inch and he will want a mile.

六三：剝之，無咎。

象傳：剝之，無咎，失上下也。

In the third SIX : Personal indulging is harmful, but if the indulging is limited to drinking, eating, or personal desire, because this doesn't concern public interests, this won't attract any blame.

Xiang Chuan：Personal indulging is harmful, but as long as it is limited to areas that don't concern public interests, the worst is that he will not be trusted and will lose credibility among the public.

Suggestion：Do not wallow with somebody in a mire and loot a burning house.

六四：剝床以膚，凶。

象傳：剝床以膚，切近災也。

In the fourth SIX : The shedding spreads to the bed, it threatens the safety of the sleepers. It implies that the political situation is worsening just like the rotting bed hurts the sleepers' skin.

Xiang Chuan：The shedding spreads to the bed, it threatens the safety of the sleepers. The disasters are coming. There is no way to avoid.

Suggestion：It takes determination and courage to fix an urgent problem.

六五：貫魚以宮人寵，無不利。

象傳：以宮人寵，終無尤也。

In the fifth SIX ： As a way for a wise emperor to avoid the concubines fighting for favors, he will put a service order among the concubines. Also, he will not allow the concubines to be involved in politics. This way, the villains will not drive out the virtuous. It means that the emperor is wise enough to prevent villains from interfering with public affairs, which is beneficial to the country.

Xiang Chuan：The emperor prevents villains from interfering with political affairs like the concubines are not permitted to be involved in politics. This will not cause any regrets.

Suggestion：There is no need to deal with villains openly. Brush them off whenever you can.

上九：碩果不食，君子得輿。小人剝廬。

象傳：君子得輿，民所載也；小人剝廬，終不可用也。

In the topmost NINE ： A virtuous man will not take credit from others. Therefore he receives full support from people. On the contrary, the villain is eager to use his privilege to take credit from others. If the villain can hurt the virtuous without being penalized, people will not feel secure.

Xiang Chuan：The man with noble character receives full support from people, but the villain deprives the people of shelter. In a word, the villains are despised by the people.

Suggestion：A man of virtue can never be isolated. He is sure to have like-minded companions.

24. 復 Fuh

地雷復 　坤上 震下

復：亨。出入無疾。朋來無咎。 反復其道，七日來復。利有攸往。

象傳：雷在地中，復；先王以至日閉關，商旅不行，后不省方。

Fuh：Rotation. Cycle. After winter solstice, spring is coming. All the creatures turn to life. Everything is prosperous and positive. Bad things are disappearing. Friends with the same goal gather together. There is nothing wrong about that. It is favorable for a man with noble character to be morally upright.

Xiang Chuan：The ancient Chinese used to believe that the thunderclaps originated from the earth. Everything comes back to life in spring. All things take on a new aspect. The late emperor closed all the mountain entrances and stopped all the business practices on the day of winter solstice (Dec. 21-22 or 23 on the lunar calendar). He even avoided conducting any official visits on this day.

Suggestion：In ancient times, all the activities such as farming needed to follow the lunar calendar to avoid natural disasters. Even people's daily routines should comply with the natural rhythm.

初九：不遠復，無祇悔，元吉。

象傳：不遠之復，以修身也。

In the first NINE：When going astray, if one doesn't go too far and can correct himself in time, there will be no disasters. It means that if one corrects his mistakes in time, there will be no regrets.

Xiang Chuan：It is precious for one to go astray but immediately return to the moral path. It is also very positive for one to cultivate his virtues and not to deviate from the moral path.

Suggestion：Repentance is salvation.

六二：休復，吉。

象傳：休復之吉，以下仁也。

[In the second SIX]: It is fortunate if one treats people with basic decency.

Xiang Chuan：It is fortunate if one treats people with basic decency. Decency draws people.

Suggestion：There is justice in this world.

六三：頻復，厲無咎。

象傳：頻復之厲，義無咎也。

[In the third SIX]: Because one is out of control, it is easy for him to make mistakes repeatedly. He regrets many times and corrects himself. Although it is dangerous to be out of control, there will be no disasters.

Xiang Chuan：Frequently make mistakes and repent afterwards. As long as one doesn't shun the responsibilities and revert to good deeds, he should not be blamed.

Suggestion：To correct evil doings and revert to good deeds.

六四：中行，獨復。

象傳：中行獨復，以從道也。

[In the fourth SIX]: Generally speaking, people think it's wise to follow the majority, but if one finds that his companions don't share the same goal, he is determined to drop out of the group and go separate ways.

Xiang Chuan：When one finds that his companions don't share the same goal, he is determined to leave and go separate ways. He returns alone to follow the moral path.

Suggestion：He would rather sacrifice benefits for justice.

六五：敦復，無悔。

象傳：敦復，無悔，中以自考也。

In the fifth SIX : One will not regret if he is generous and honest and always follows the moral choice.

Xiang Chuan：One is generous and honest and always follows the moral choice. One will not regret because he often examines himself.

Suggestion：One will not regret if he doesn't deviate from a moral path.

上六：迷復，凶，有災眚。用行師，終有大敗，以其國君凶。至於十年不克征。

象傳：迷復之凶，反君道也。

In the topmost SIX : It is dangerous for an emperor to lose himself and deviate from the moral path without knowing he is wrong.

Natural disasters and wars happen frequently. If the emperor still insists on sending out armies to crush the rebellions, the troops will undoubtedly be wiped out. Even the emperor will have misfortunes. Furthermore, people are poor and the country's fortune has all been depleted. It takes more than 10 years to recover.

Xiang Chuan：It is dangerous for an emperor to lose himself and deviate from the moral path without knowing he is wrong. This is because he doesn't behave like a good emperor.

Suggestion：It is extremely dangerous to hold on obstinately to errors.

25. 無妄　Wuh-Whang

乾上 震下

天雷無妄

無妄：元、亨、利、貞。其匪正，有眚，不利有攸往。

象傳：天下雷行，物與無妄；先王以茂對時，育萬物。

Wuh-Whang：Not hypocritical. Never act recklessly or blindly. Never disregard laws and regulations.

Wuh-Whang insists that people respect four principles- comprehensiveness, propriety, harmony and ethics. If all the words and deeds comply with the ethics, it will bring good luck. If not, disasters will follow and it will be difficult to advance.

Xiang Chuan：The rumble of thunder travels the world. All the creatures are nourished by nature.

The emperors followed the natural rhythm to nourish all creatures.

Suggestion：Follow the natural laws. No imposing. No faking.

初九：無妄，往吉。

象傳：無妄之往，得志也。

In the first NINE : It is advantageous to be honest, sincere, selfless and to advance courageously.

Xiang Chuan：It is advantageous to be honest, sincere, selfless and to advance courageously. One can realize his goals.

Suggestion：It is fortunate to not act recklessly.

六二：不耕獲，不菑 *畬* ，則利有攸往。

象傳：不耕獲，未富也。

In the second SIX : It is unrealistic to wish to have achievements without making efforts or wish to harvest without ploughing the land. If one doesn't have such thought, it is positive.

Xiang Chuan：Wishing to get rich without making efforts is unrealistic.

Suggestion：It is unrealistic to have inordinate ambitions. To sit idle and enjoy the fruits of other's work.

六三：無妄之災，或繫之牛，行人之得，邑人之災。

＊註11：菑ㄗ，開墾荒地。

＊註12：畬ㄩˊ，已墾植三年的熟田。

象傳：行人得牛，邑人災也。

In the third SIX : It is an unimaginable disaster to have a cow that is tied up to the pole on the side of the road gets led along by a passerby. The passer-by is mistaken for a thief by the villagers.

Xiang Chuan：The passerby led the cattle away and was mistaken for a thief.

Suggestion： Sudden and unexpected disasters.

九四：可貞。無咎。

象傳：可貞無咎，固有之也。

In the fourth NINE : So long as you have self-control, are unselfish, do not behave recklessly and stick to a moral path, you can never be blamed.

Xiang Chuan：So long as you have self-control, are unselfish, do not behave recklessly and stick to the moral path, you can never be blamed. There are innate virtues of human beings.

Suggestion：Insistence on being ethical can prevent unexpected disasters. Refuse to be corrupted by evil influence.

九五：無妄之疾，勿藥，有喜。

象傳：無妄之藥，不可試也。

In the fifth NINE : Wishful thinking can be cured without medicine. It is positive.

Xiang Chuan：A healthy person shall not take any medicine.

Suggestion：It is miserable to be gullible. Moan about imaginary illness.

上九：無妄，行有眚，無攸利。

象傳：無妄之行，窮之災也。

In the topmost NINE : The event has come to an end. Avoid thinking yourself

smart, believing you can hassle people with a new system. It is impossible to have any benefits.

Xiang Chuan：Since you are in a dire situation, acting blindly and rashly will only lead to disasters.

Suggestion：When it is impossible to turn things around, you should stop in time and do not try to act tough.

26. 大畜 Da-shiu

 艮上 乾下
山天大畜

大畜：利貞。不家食，吉。利涉大川。

象傳：天在山中，大畜；君子以多識前言往行，以畜其德。

Da-shiu: Accumulation of virtues. It is favorable for people to be morally upright. Those of wisdom and virtues are supposed to contribute to the government instead of farming at homes. Their ambitions should be to make the world a better place. If so, it is fortunate. Their mission is sure to be a success just like taking risks to cross a big river.

Xiang Chuan：The sky is in the midst of the mountains. The man with noble character realizes that he should follow the good deeds of the ancestors to cultivate his virtues.

Suggestion：Cultivate virtues. One should not only improve himself but also make this world a better place.

初九：有厲，利已。

象傳：有厲利已，不犯災也。

In the first NINE：A new graduate is like a newborn calf. It is dangerous for him to act recklessly and have too much ambition. It is advantageous for him to cultivate virtues and accumulate wisdom before advancing his career.

Xiang Chuan：When one is in danger, it is advantageous to hold his horses to prevent disasters.

Suggestion：Get rich quick scheme is a one way ticket to failure.

九二：輿說輹。

象傳：輿說輹，中無尤也。

In the second NINE : The circumstances are not right, you should not advance. It means that when you are in danger, you should refrain yourself from hasty moves just as you remove the axle of a carriage to stop it from moving.

Xiang Chuan：Remove the axles to stop the carriage from going. This is a way to avoid falling into villains' traps.

Suggestion：To act according to circumstances.

九三：良馬逐，利艱貞，日閑輿衛，利有攸往。

象傳：利有攸往，上合志也。

In the third NINE : A man with noble character should be on high alert to accumulate energies that enable him to overcome difficulties as if a cavalryman works on his riding and defense skills every day to prepare for expeditions.

Xiang Chuan：Alertness and daily disciplines are favorable for a man to go on expeditions. This also meets the expectation of his superior.

Suggestion：Being active but not hasty to avoid failures.

六四：童牛之牿，元吉。

象傳：六四元吉，有喜也。

In the fourth SIX : The calf is kept in a closed space with bars to prevent it from

hurting people because it is not tamed. It is great fortune. Take preventative measure to keep the horns of a calf from hurting people.

Xiang Chuan：The calf is kept in a closed space with bars to prevent it from hurting people because it is not tamed. It is great fortune.

Suggestion：Take precautions to avoid disasters. To start well and end well.

六五：豶*豕之牙，吉。
象傳：六五之吉，有慶也。

In the fifth SIX ：The teeth of a pig are terrible and they hurt people easily. The surefire way is to castrate it so it becomes gentle. The farm is safe because it is gentle. Although it still has teeth, you can raise it safely.

Xiang Chuan：It is fortunate to castrate a pig so it becomes gentle.

Suggestion：To take away the firewood from under the caldron.

上九：何天之衢，亨。
象傳：何天之衢，道大行也。

In the topmost NINE ：The emperor undertakes a heavy responsibility to support the virtuous and the wise. The hiring opportunities for people with virtues and wisdom are wide open. It is a great omen.

Xiang Chuan：The emperor undertakes a heavy responsibility to support the virtuous and the wise.

The hiring opportunities for people with virtues and wisdom are wide open.

Suggestion：Consideration of every aspect leads to success.

---

*註13：豶ㄈㄣˊ，閹割過的豬。

27. 頤 Yi

 艮上 震下
山雷頤

頤：貞吉。觀頤，自求口實。

象傳：山下有雷，頤；君子以慎言語，節飲食。

Yi : Nourishment. People depend upon food and water to live. If one insists on the right way to maintain health, it is fortunate. Just look at how people feed themselves and how they cultivate their virtues, you will know if they follow the right way. Furthermore, just look at what people eat, you will understand how they make a living.

Xiang Chuan：Thunderclaps roam at the bottom of the hill. This phenomenon represents nourishment. The man with noble character realizes the importance of his words and deeds and the importance of moderate drinking and eating to maintain good health.

Suggestion：Eating and drinking are to nourish one's body. Mind one's words to cultivate one's virtues.

初九：舍爾靈龜，觀我朵頤，凶。

象傳：觀我朵頤，亦不足貴也。

In the first NINE : The mythical animal tortoise has the ability to nourish itself by breathing. If it abandons its ability and envies my pleasure of eating, it will bring bad luck. It means that gluttony is unhealthy.

Xiang Chuan：Instead of supporting himself, he envies being supported by others. This will be despised by the public.

Suggestion：He is better off creating opportunities on his own than envying other's wealth and positions. To look down upon oneself. To be insatiably avaricious.

六二：顛頤，拂經于丘頤，征凶。

象傳：六二征凶，行失類也。

In the second SIX : It is unreasonable for a superior to ask a subordinate to take care of him. It is greedy for a subordinate to ask the superior for more support.

Xiang Chuan : It is sensible for a subordinate to support the superior, but to ask for more either from the superior side or the subordinate side are both against the norms.

Suggestion : Blindly pursuing money and power is disgraceful.

六三：拂頤，貞凶，十年勿用，無攸利。

象傳：十年勿用，道大悖也。

In the third SIX : When one doesn't follow the right way to maintain his health, he gets in bad health. It is unfortunate. He spends a long period of time to restore his health but he is still very weak. Even if there are opportunities to let him utilize his talents, he dares not take them.

Xiang Chuan : Because of inappropriate diet, his body becomes weak. Even if he spends ten years trying to restore his health, he still has not recovered yet. Of course, he does not have a chance to be successful.

Suggestion : The proper way of taking care of oneself is through healthy diet and lifestyle. It is shameful to interfere with others' taking care of themselves.

六四：顛頤，吉。虎視眈眈，其欲逐逐，無咎。

象傳：顛頤之吉，上施光也。

In the fourth SIX : It is fortunate for the government to ask for contributions from people for the sake of serving people. In order to achieve this goal, one should be as fierce as a tiger staring at its preys. There will be no blames.

Xiang Chuan : Ask for contribution from the people. Then return the favor to the people. It is honest and above-board.

Suggestion：What is taken from the people is used for the interests of the people.

六五：拂經，居貞吉，不可涉大川。
象傳：居貞之吉，順以從上也。

In the fifth SIX : Although the emperor violates the norm of supporting people, it is still fortunate if his words and deeds are ethical. However, be careful not to have bad policies to make people suffer.

Xiang Chuan：It is favorable for the emperor to be ethical in his words and deeds. The fortune is due to the obedience to the will of his superior.

Suggestion：One who sticks to his folly and does nothing may not be necessarily incorrect, but it depends on the circumstance.

上九：由頤，厲吉。利涉大川。
象傳：由頤厲吉，大有慶也。

In the topmost NINE : Supporting the people is the responsibility of the emperor. The emperor should support people fairly. If the emperor is persistent to follow this principle, it is favorable for him to achieve great accomplishments in the future.

Xiang Chuan：If the emperor is persistent to follow these principles of supporting people, it is advantageous for him to achieve great accomplishments and will have things to celebrate in the future.

Suggestion：Supporting the people and cultivating their virtues, is the right thing to do.

28. 大過 Da-guo

 兌上 巽下

大過：棟撓，利有攸往，亨。

象傳：澤滅木，大過；君子以獨立不懼，遯世無悶。

Da-guo：Not sensible. It is as if the ridgepole of a house is bending, the house is unstable because of heavy weight on the center. It needs to be repaired to avoid danger. In the meantime, it is favorable to examine the problems and fix them. It means that a house is going to collapse, it needs a quick solution to be safe.

Xiang Chuan：Trees soak in the water of a lake. In theory, wood should float above the water, but a tree sinking in the water means the situation is against the norm. In the occasion, the man with noble character dares to face the world and not feel cynical at all. Even if he chooses to lead a life of seclusion, he will not feel depressed or agonized.

Suggestion：The man with noble character is able to take temporary setbacks and know when to give in and when not to.

初六：藉用白茅，無咎。

象傳：藉用白茅，柔在下也。

In the first SIX ：While worshiping to God, it is not wrong to use white couch grass as the bedding for the offerings to show respect. White couch grass is like a soft cushion and a symbol of purity, which is to harmonize the solemnity of praying.

Xiang Chuan：Although white couch grass is simple and cheap, it could be used in important religious situations.

Suggestion：Even a screw can play the leading role.

九二：枯楊生稊*，老夫得其女妻，無不利。

─────────────

＊註14：稊去一 ╱，新嫩葉。

象傳：老夫女妻，過以相與也。

In the second NINE : A withered poplar tree has a new branch just like an old man marries a young woman. It is not improper. There are no blames.

Xiang Chuan：Although the marriage between an old man and a young woman has a wide age gap, age, as long as they support each other, it is not unfavorable.

Suggestion：No need to adhere rigidly to formalities on unusual situation. Each takes what he needs.

九三：棟橈，凶。
象傳：棟橈之凶，不可以有輔也。

In the third NINE : The ridgepole of a house is bending. It is dangerous. It means that a condescending attitude when dealing with people results in relationship crisis because nobody will help you when you are in difficulty.

Xiang Chuan：The ridgepole of a house is bending. No other support can be of help to stabilize the structure. It signifies that condescending manners result in crisis.

Suggestion：It is difficult to make up for serious mistakes.

九四：棟隆，吉；有它，吝。
象傳：棟隆之吉，不橈乎下也。

In the fourth NINE : Use force to flatten the bulged ridgepole of a house. It looks safe from the outside. There should not be more issues, otherwise you will have regrets. It means that everything goes well in appearance, but in fact it is not like this.

Xiang Chuan：The bulged ridgepole of a house is pressed to flat and appears safe. It will not bend furthermore.

Suggestion：Be a pillar of the community.

九五：枯楊生華，老婦得其士夫，無咎無譽。

象傳：枯楊生華，何可久也？老婦士夫，亦可醜也。

In the fifth NINE : The withered poplar tree grows new flowers again as if an old woman marries a young husband. The marriage is neither blamed nor praised.

Xiang Chuan：The withered poplar tree grows new flowers again just like an old woman marries a young husband. Will this marriage last for a long time? This is indeed a scandal.

Suggestion：Blossoming but bearing no fruit is not worthy of being praised. The setting sun.

上六：過涉滅頂，凶。無咎。

象傳：過涉之凶，不可咎也。

In the topmost SIX : One feels the situation is beyond his capability but he does not know his limitations and insists on pushing it through. It is as if he doesn't know the depth of the river and is wading through the river. He will be drowned. It is a disaster, but it is too late to criticize him.

Xiang Chuan：One does not know his limitations and is wading through the river and drowns. He deserved to die. He can blame nobody.

Suggestion：There is no choice for one to sacrifice his life in an unusal situation.

29. 坎 Kaan

 坎上 坎下

坎為水

習坎：有孚，維心亨，行有尚。

象傳：水洊ｾ*至，習坎；君子以常德行，習教事。

Kaan: Multiple dangers and difficulties. One has to have confidence to turn peril into safety. It is fortunate. One's determination to be free from dangers and difficulties is lofty and worthy of encouragement.

Xiang Chuan：Water rolling continuously without stop is like dangers and difficulties keeping coming. The man with noble character realizes that he needs to constantly cultivate his own virtues to influence people.

Suggestion：Practice makes perfect.   To turn peril into safety.

初六：習坎，入於坎窞ｾ*，凶。

象傳：習坎入坎，失道凶也。

In the first SIX: One falls into multiple difficulties and dangers as if he is lost and falls into the deepest hole.

The situation is extremely dangerous.

Xiang Chuan：One encounters extreme difficulties and dangers. He is so lost that he couldn't pull himself out, because he doesn't follow the moral path. It is unfortunate.

Suggestion：There is no danger when there is preparedness.   One should not be affected by the present difficulties and become so discouraged to give up hope. On the contrary, one should be more positive, stand up bravely to face them and overcome them.

＊註15：洊ㄐㄧㄢˋ，一再地。

＊註16：窞ㄉㄢˋ，深坑。

九二：坎有險，求小得。

象傳：求小得，未出中也。

In the second NINE : Still in difficulty. The first priority is to improve from small areas and then think of ways to overcome present difficulties to be free from dangers.

Xiang Chuan : Presently he is not completely free of danger yet. He has to protect himself first as he is still in danger.

Suggestion : Unlimited potential. Do not be discouraged when in difficulty. Instead, one should be strong to face it.

六三：來之坎坎，險且枕，入於坎窞，勿用。

象傳：來之坎坎，終無功也。

In the third SIX : It is extremely dangerous to do anything because you are between a rock and a hard place. Do not act recklessly. Any efforts are futile.

Xiang Chuan : Stuck between a rock and a hard place. All efforts are futile.

Suggestion : Be patient under adversity. Smile at one's troubles. When in dangers and difficulties, do not act rashly. It takes patience and poise to come up with workable solutions.

六四：樽酒，簋*貳，用缶，納約自牖*，終無咎。

象傳：樽酒簋貳，剛柔際也。

In the fourth SIX : Deliver a bottle of wine and two bowls of rice held by the earthenware through the window. Although the food is simple, it is given with sincerity. There is no blame. It means that one is in danger and unnecessary formalities can be skipped.

Xiang Chuan : Though a bottle of wine and two bowls of rice are simple, it is given

---

*註17：簋ㄍㄨㄟ ˇ，古時的碗。

*註18：牖一ㄡ ˇ，窗戶。

with sincerity, which means the minds of the giver and the receiver are in sync.

Suggestion：Hope for the best. Do not give up any hope.   When in difficulties, unnecessary formalities can be skipped.

九五：坎不盈，祇*既平，無咎。

象傳：坎不盈，中未大也。

In the fifth NINE : Water has not filled up the cave, but the rock in the cave is nearly covered by water. It means that the situation is not hopeless yet. Be patient and it will all work out.

Xiang Chuan：Water has not filled up the cave, which means that one should be humble to follow the ethical path.

Suggestion：Not to stop until one reaches the goal. Do not give up easily.

上六： 係用徽纆*，寘*於叢棘，三歲不得，凶。

象傳：上六失道，凶三歲也。

In the topmost SIX : One is in extreme danger as if a criminal has been tied firmly in the prison of thorns for more than three years and has not been released yet. This is just like a person is in danger and has lost himself for quite a long time. It takes a long time to recover.

Xiang Chuan：One is lost and stops following the ethical path. Therefore, he has not been relieved from danger.

Suggestion：If you don't help yourself, it is the same as being fatalistic.

*註19：纆ㄇㄛˋ，繩索。

120

30. 離 Li

離上 離下

離：利貞。亨。畜牝ᵖⁱⁿ牛吉。

象傳：明兩作，離；大人以繼明照于四方。

Li：Interdependent. Be attached to. Li is fire. Fire relies on wood to burn and produces brightness.

All the creatures are interdependent. Therefore, all the attachments should comply with ethics to bring good luck. The virtuous assume heavy responsibilities for the country like obedient cows.

Xiang Chuan：The sun and the moon rise one after another in the sky. It is really splendid.

The great man apprehends virtues of brightness continuously distribute to the whole world impartially.

Suggestion：All creatures have something they'd like to depend on. It is no exception for men. Men have to follow the moral path.

初九：履錯然，敬之，無咎。

象傳：履錯之敬，以辟咎也。

In the first NINE：When you first start your career, you will inevitably make mistakes and be lost sometimes. If you are vigilant though, there won't be any faults. It means that to get close to a person, you must see his virtues clearly.

Xiang Chuan：Face life with caution, avoid making mistakes in a flurry.

Suggestion：Be devoted to one's career and treat it with seriousness.   To let things drift along. Do not make mistakes.

六二：黃離，元吉。

象傳：黃離元吉，得中道也。

In the second SIX : Get close to a great man with an open heart and selfless attitude. It is certainly auspicious.

Xiang Chuan：Get close to a great man with an open heart and selfless attitude. It is certainly auspicious because one follows moral path.

Suggestion：Neither overbearing nor servile.

九三：日昃*之離，不鼓缶而歌，則大耋之嗟，凶。
象傳：日昃之離，何可久也？

In the third NINE : One is old and weak just like the sun sets below the mountain. If he doesn't use the remaining days to enjoy himself by playing a pottery instrument and singing, he will regret and sigh for being old. It's unfortunate.

Xiang Chuan：One is old enough to retire, but he still hangs around. How long can sunset last?

Suggestion：When one is old, he should be happy with who he is. If one does not exert oneself in youth, one will regret it in old age.

九四：突如其來如，焚如，死如，棄如。
象傳：突如其來如，無所容也。

In the fourth NINE : He wants to get close to a great man, but he has bad intentions. His bad temper is like a sudden fire that burns violently to the point that everything turns to ashes. It means that one can not have bad intention when getting close to a great man, otherwise he will be despised by the public.

Xiang Chuan：His bad temper is just a sudden fire. There is no chance for him to be close to a great man.

Suggestion：Haste makes waste. When trying to get close to people, you should not take advantage of other's difficulties and loot a burning house.

＊註20：昃ㄗㄜˋ，太陽西下。

六五：出涕沱若，戚嗟若，吉。

象傳：六五之吉，離王公也。

<u>In the fifth SIX</u>: Because of the threats by sneaky villains, the newly enthroned emperor leads a life of tears and sorrow. He is constantly on alert in order to turn perils into safety. It is fortunate.

Xiang Chuan：It is fortunate because of the blessing from the ancestral temple and support from the dukes.

Suggestion：Arrogant. Commanding. There is no way out. Thick face. Black heart.

上九：王用出征，有嘉折首，獲匪其醜，無咎。

象傳：王用出征，以正邦也。

<u>In the topmost NINE</u>: The emperor sent the army out for the expedition. He rewarded those who killed the chief and won honor in the field as well as those who did not slaughter the innocent. There is no blame.

Xiang Chuan：The decision to send the army out for the expedition by the emperor is to unify and stabilize the nation.

Suggestion：Dispatch troops with just cause to crush the rebels.

31. 咸 Shian

  兌上 艮下

澤山咸

咸：亨，利貞，取女吉。

象傳：山上有澤，咸；君子以虛受人。

Shian：Mutual interactions. The interactions between a young girl and a young boy are derived from their true feelings. They love each other. Their feelings are the foundation of future marriage. It is fortunate.

Xiang Chuan：Water flows from the mountain. It means that water and mountains interact well with each other. The man with noble character should learn from it and be modest to accept criticism and get along with people.

Suggestion：Slow work yields fine products. With tolerance, morality is achieved.

初六：咸其拇。
象傳：咸其拇，志在外也。

In the first SIX ： Only the toe has feelings. It means that it is still too early to take action. It is like the love of a teenage girl, her feelings are not mature yet.

Xiang Chuan：Your toe already feels something, meaning that there are beginning signs of love.

Suggestion：Haste makes waste.

六二：咸其腓，凶；居吉。
象傳：雖凶居吉，順不害也。

In the second SIX ： You can feel it in the calves. It is extremely dangerous to take actions at the moment. There will be disaster. A young girl chasing a man without reservation is against the etiquette. Waiting for opportunities to come is fortunate.

Xiang Chuan：You can feel it in the calves. It means that it is extremely dangerous to act recklessly. If the young girl holds herself for a while, the young boy will certainly sweep her off her feet. It is not too late to agree to date him.

Suggestion：To wait at one's ease for an exhausted enemy. Forcing yourself on somebody will never end well.

九三：咸其股，執其隨，往吝。

象傳：咸其股，亦不處也；志在隨人，所執下也。

In the third NINE : Thighs are pulled by calves as if your marriage cannot be decided by yourself in ancient times. It is decided by matchmakers and your parents. If your marriage is decided by others, it won't end well because it is not based on your free will.

Xiang Chuan：Thighs are pulled by calves as if you have no say about your marriage. You only do what you're told to. It is pathetic.

Suggestion：Blindly following without your point of views will make you encounter difficulties. The less trouble, the better.

九四：貞吉，悔亡。憧憧往來，朋從爾思。
象傳：貞吉，悔亡，未感害也；憧憧往來，未光大也。

In the fourth NINE : Be loyal in love and there will be no regrets. On the contrary, if you fall in love with whoever comes along, you will regret.

Xiang Chuan：If the love of a couple is solid, there will be no regrets. However, if any of the two is unstable, changing mind easily, it is disgraceful.

Suggestion：Changing one's mind in love easily is irresponsible and shameful. To choose what is good and hold fast to it.

九五：咸其脢*，無悔。
象傳：咸其脢，志末也。

In the fifth NINE : Hold the lover's waist in his arm, there will be no regrets. It means that both parties love each other and enjoy each other being around, there is nothing wrong about it.

Xiang Chuan：Hold the lover's waist in his arm, there will be no regrets. Love is so solid that there is nothing more to ask for.

Suggestion：To make every effort.

＊註21：脢ㄇㄟˊ，背脊肉。

上六：咸其輔頰舌。

象傳：咸其輔頰舌，騰*口說也。

In the topmost SIX : You only feel it on the jaw, cheeks and the tongue. You can tell from the facial expressions. If the interaction is superficial, nobody will believe in his flattery and sucking up.

Xiang Chuan：You can only feel it on your jaw, cheeks and the tongue, meaning that his feelings are shallow, he is insincere.

Suggestion：It is useless to brag about one's eloquence.

32. 恆 Heng

雷風恆　　　震上 巽下

恆：亨，無咎，利貞，利有攸往。

象傳：雷風，恆；君子以立不易方。

Heng：Continuation and eternity. It is the way of eternity. So long as the family ethics are forever respected, it is a great omen.

Xiang Chuan：Thunderclaps and blowing winds represent eternity. The man with noble character realizes that he should always make the moral choice and should not change easily.

Suggestion：Perseverance brings success.

初六：浚恆，貞凶，無攸利。

象傳：浚恆之凶，始求深也。

In the first SIX : It is unfavorable to try to achieve eternity by being hasty, skipping

---

＊註22：騰ㄊㄥˊ，騰揚。

the necessary steps.

Xiang Chuan：To achieve eternity by cutting corners and acting hastily is flawed.

Suggestion：Proceed in an orderly way. Step by step. Eager for quick success and instant benefit.

九二：悔亡。

象傳：九二悔亡，能久中也。

In the second NINE : Make up one's mind to achieve eternity in the beginning, but regret afterwards. It means that he is not perseverant. A person without perseverance will never achieve anything.

Xiang Chuan：The laws of eternity are the laws of following the moral path and following the doctrine of the mean.

Suggestion：Follow rules and orders respectfully. The laws of eternity are the laws of following the moral path and following the doctrine of the mean.

九三：不恆其德，或承之羞，貞吝。

象傳：不恆其德，無所容也。

In the third NINE : If you cannot keep living your virtues, you will be humiliated because you cannot insist on making the moral choice.

Xiang Chuan：If you cannot keep living your virtues, you will have no room for survival.

Suggestion：Live without virtues or integrity.

九四：田無禽。

象傳：久非其位，安得禽也？

In the fourth NINE : No chickens are hunted because you keep hunting in the fields, not in the forests.

Xiang Chuan：He has been hunting in the wrong place. No wonder, he gets no chickens.

Suggestion：One who sticks to his folly and does nothing. What one is doing has nothing to do with one's training.

六五：恆其德，貞，婦人吉，夫子凶。
象傳：婦人貞吉，從一而終也；夫子制義，從婦凶也。

In the fifth SIX : It is fortunate for a woman to keep living female virtues and remain loyal to her man all her life, but it is inappropriate for a man to be inflexible to run his career.

Xiang Chuan：It is virtuous for a woman to keep her chastity, but a man should adapt according to the changing situations in business.

Suggestion：Sticking to one's virtues is important, but adapting to changing circumstances is also necessary.

上六：振恆，凶。
象傳：振恆在上，大無功也。

In the topmost SIX : It is unfortunate for a person to be impatient and reckless. A rolling stone gathers no moss.

Xiang Chuan：If the man of high position is impatient and reckless, he cannot achieve anything.

Suggestion：If a man is indecisive, capricious, impatient and reckless, it is tough for him to find a place to settle down.

33. 遯 Duen

乾上 艮下
天山遯

遯：亨。小利貞。

象傳：天下有山，遯；君子以遠小人，不惡而嚴。

Duen : Retreat. The villains are in power now. The man with noble character is unable to compete. The only way is to retreat and get far away from the villains to find a shelter. Although the retreat is a passive move, it brings safety. It is a small advantage.

Xiang Chuan：Even though the mountains are high, they are far away from the sky. It explains Duen- retreat. The man with noble character decides that he won't hate villains nor talk bad about them. He is strict with himself and prevents villains from approaching him.

Suggestion：Quit while you are ahead. A bird in the hand is worth two in the bush.

初六：遯尾，厲，勿用有攸往。

象傳：遯尾之厲，不往，何災也？

In the first SIX : Villains gain power, if you don't retreat fast enough and still follow others' tail like a cow, there will be danger. If you retreat too late, it can be useless.

Xiang Chuan：A wise man submits to fate.

Suggestion：One should not be swayed by feelings to act rashly. Make a firm decision to back away if the situation seems unfavorable, then there will be no danger. Do not leave any shortcomings to be exploited by others.

六二：執之用黃牛之革，莫之勝說。

象傳：執用黃牛，固志也。

In the second SIX : One shows his resolution not to retreat. His resolution is so strong that it seems that it is tied by leather strips of a yellow ox.

Xiang Chuan：One shows his resolution not to back away. His resolution is so strong that it seems that it is tied by strips of leather.

Suggestion：**You can't always do as you like, one has to compromise in this world.**

九三：係遯，有疾厲。畜臣妾，吉。

象傳：係遯之厲，有疾憊也；畜臣妾吉，不可大事也。

In the third NINE : If one is still sentimentally attached to his position and does not resign in time, it will lead to mental and physical fatigue. It would be better to resign and stay home to take care of his family than to deal with political affairs.

Xiang Chuan：If one is still sentimentally attached to his position and does not resign in time, it will lead to mental and physical fatigue. It would be better to resign and stay home to take care of his family than to deal with political affairs. Too much attachment to your position ruins your achievements.

Suggestion：**Decide in the nick of time.**

九四：好遯，君子吉，小人否。

象傳：君子好遯，小人否也。

In the fourth NINE : The man with noble character can give up everything and decide promptly to retire if the situation requires. It brings good fortune. On the contrary, the villains are sentimentally attached to their positions and hold on to their fame and fortune.

Xiang Chuan：The man with noble character will decide promptly to retire as the situation requires, but the villains are not because they are still sentimentally attached to the positions and fame.

Suggestion：**The biggest difference between a villain and a man with noble character is the level of attachment to fame and fortune. A loss may turn out**

to be a gain.

九五：嘉遯，貞吉。
象傳：嘉遯，貞吉，以正志也。

In the fifth NINE : Those who can grasp the opportunity and retire when the situation is bad is worthy of praise.

Xiang Chuan：Those who can seize the opportunity and withdraw when the situation is unfavorable are worthy of praise. However, if one cannot withdraw, he should be ethical and selfless, waiting for the right time to come.

Suggestion：A man of wisdom will definitely resign and wait for opportunities to come.

上九：肥遯，無不利。
象傳：肥遯無不利，無所疑也。

In the topmost NINE : To be able to give up emotional baggage and elegantly resign is very positive. When he is far from the bad impact of the villains, all of his worries will disappear.

Xiang Chuan：To be able to give up emotional baggage and elegantly resign is very positive because he will be free from all the worries and burden.

Suggestion：Don't worry about troubles of one's own imagination. Relaxed and graceful resignation causes no worries.

34. 大壯 Da-Juang

 震上 乾下

雷天大壯

大壯：利貞。

象傳：雷在天上，大壯；君子以非禮弗履。

Da-Juang：Powerful. Excessiveness eventually causes regret because too much power easily makes one conceited, condescending and arrogant, which can put one into danger. Therefore, this hexagram emphasizes righteousness, justice and temperance to avoid declining right after flourishing.

Xiang Chuan：The thunderclaps gain momentums in the sky. The man with noble character figures that his power doesn't come from surpassing others but from restraining himself so that his conduct complies with the rites.

Suggestion：To restrain oneself and observe the proprieties.

初九：壯於趾，征凶，有孚。

象傳：壯於趾，其孚窮也。

In the first NINE：He has strong intentions to advance, but his strength does not match his ambition. If he is still pushing forward, there will be disaster.

Xiang Chuan：He has strong intention to advance, but his strength does not match his ambition. If he is still pushing forward, there will be disaster as his sincerity will be exhausted.

Suggestion：A newborn calf. Anxiously manifesting one's ability in an immature situation will lead to regrets.

九二：貞吉。

象傳：九二貞吉，以中也。

In the second NINE : When one is in prosperity, it is easy for him to go beyond his ability. However, if he is composed, patient, righteous, restrained, it will be a great omen.

Xiang Chuan：When one is in propriety, it is easy for him to go beyond his ability. If he is righteous and restrained, it will bring good fortune as he follows the midway.

Suggestion："The modest receive benefit, while the conceited reap failure.

九三：小人用壯，君子用罔，貞厲。羝羊觸藩，羸其角。
象傳：小人用壯，君子罔也。

In the third NINE : The villains abuse their power and bully others, but the men with noble characters don't. The great men recruit the talents to assure people. Although they are decent and honest, their situation is rather dangerous as of a goat ramming into a fence and getting its horns entangled.

Xiang Chuan：The villains in power easily get carried away, they abuse their power and bully others but the great men don't. The great men recruit talents to assure people.

Suggestion：Advancing rashly without a plan will eventually burn you out.

九四：貞吉，悔亡；藩決不羸，壯於大輿之輹。
象傳：藩決不羸，尚往也。

In the fourth NINE : While in prosperity, one cannot do whatever he wants. This is fortunate as if a goat rams into the fence with his big horns to break open the fence. Because the horns are stronger than the carriage axle, it won't be entangled in the fence.

Xiang Chuan：The fence is dashed open by the goat. Its horns will not get entangled. The obstacles have been removed. Nothing will hinder the advancement.

Suggestion：The task goes smoothly like splitting bamboo. A little impatience spoils great plans.

六五：喪羊於易，無悔。

象傳：喪羊於易，位不當也。

In the fifth SIX : Things will develop in the opposite direction when they become extreme. In the time of prosperity, people will act like goats running in the field. It is easy for them to get lost. It is not surprising. Therefore, it won't cause regrets.

Xiang Chuan：The shepherd disregards the right place for the sheep so that the sheep get lost in the pasture. Wrong choice of place causes this loss. Remorse is useless.

Suggestion：To mend the sheepfold after a sheep is lost. To take precautions after suffering a loss.

上六：羝²羊觸藩，不能退，不能遂，無攸利，艱則吉。

象傳：不能退，不能遂，不詳也；艱則吉，咎不長也。

In the topmost SIX : A goat knocks on a fence and gets entangled. It can neither advance nor back off. Nothing is available. If you consider the difficulties in advance, it is fortunate.

Xiang Chuan：A goat knocks on a fence and gets entangled. It can neither advance nor back off. Nothing is available. If you consider the difficulties in advance, the suffering will be minimized.

Suggestion：Take precautions against a disaster. It is easy to fall into crisis if one bites off more than he can chew.

35. 晉 Jin

離上 坤下
火地晉

晉：康侯用錫馬藩庶，晝日三接。

象傳：明出地上，晉；君子以自昭明德。

Jin. Promotion. The dukes receive many horses and carriages awarded by the emperor due to their stellar performance. They receive three interviews from the emperor a day which represents extreme respect.

Xiang Chuan：The rising sun represents making progress. The man with noble character observes the phenomenon and wishes himself to be the sun to bless the world with his virtues.

Suggestion：Make achievements. To attain eminence step by step.

初六：晉如摧如，貞吉。罔孚，裕無咎。

象傳：晉如摧如，獨行正也；裕無咎，未受命也。

In the first SIX : Sometimes advancement will encounter setbacks. For a short while, he is not trusted by the people. However, he didn't complain, instead, he is strict with himself and flexible with people. Thus, his move won't cause any blame.

Xiang Chuan：Sometimes advancement will encounter setbacks. However, he is still sincere and morally upright. Although he hasn't been appointed any position yet, he won't have any regrets.

Suggestion：While there is life, there is hope. Act sincerely and ethically. Do not worry about gain or loss.

六二：晉如愁如，貞吉。 受茲介福，于其王母。

象傳：受茲介福，以中正也。

In the second SIX : Though one is promoted, he is still afraid of not being trusted. So long as he is sincere and morally upright, he will be blessed.

Xiang Chuan：He is blessed by big fortunes as he is ethical and fair.

Suggestion：Although the road to success is bumpy, if one follows the ethical path, success is not far away.

六三：眾允，悔亡。

象傳：眾允之志，上行也。

In the third SIX : In the meantime, one is promoted and enjoys immense support from people, there will be no regrets.

Xiang Chuan：Before achieving success, one's ambition should be fully recognized and supported by the public.

Suggestion：Public reliance and support is the path to success.

九四：晉如鼫 *鼠，貞厲。

象傳：鼫鼠貞厲，位不當也。

In the fourth NINE : A flying squirrel is talented. It can fly, swim, dig holes, run and climb, but it cannot do everything. The man with noble character would be prone to making mistakes if he is promoted to an important position without real capability.

Xiang Chuan：To promote a man without real ability like a flying squirrel is the same as blocking others' promotion.

Suggestion：To overestimate one's strength. Curses come home to roost. Keep up with the trends.

六五：悔亡，失得勿恤。往吉，無不利。

象傳：失得勿恤，往有慶也。

＊註23：鼫 ㄕˊ，螻鼠。

In the fifth SIX : Without anxiety or regrets, without concern of one's incompetence. If you don't care about personal gain or loss, just charging forward courageously is favorable.

Xiang Chuan：Do not worry about personal gain or loss, do the best you can. You will be blessed.

Suggestion：Do not worry about personal gain and loss, charge forward without fear. A loss may turn out to be a gain. To be indifferent to gains or losses.

上九：晉其角，維用伐邑，厲吉，無咎，貞吝。

象傳：維用伐邑，道未光也。

In the topmost NINE : Making progress to the point that there is no way up. Sending an army to squash rebellions in one's own territory is a shame because of improper management.

Xiang Chuan：Sending out an army to quash rebellions in one's territory is not just and honorable.

Suggestion：Making rebellions surrender peacefully is the best policy. Restraining oneself can prevent disasters.

36. 明夷 Ming-Yi

 坤上 離下

地火明夷

明夷：利艱貞。

象傳：明入地中，明夷；君子以蒞眾，用晦而明。

Ming-Yi. To perish. In a terrible situation, when one is facing difficulties, one has to follow the right and favorable direction, stand the test and never deviate from moral course.

Xiang Chuan：The sun is setting in the West, meaning that the light is blocked. The man with noble character realizes that seeing things in the dark brings more clarity. He leads the public to avoid the dangers and to move towards the bright future.

Suggestion：We see the light at the end of the tunnel.

初九：明夷于飛，垂其翼；君子于行，三日不食。有攸往，主人有言。

象傳：君子于行，義不食也。

In the first NINE : Because of the fatuous ruler, integrity is lacking. The man with noble character rushes to resign like a bird flying low to find a shelter. He would rather go hungry than give in to the reality. However, wherever he goes, there is gossip.

Xiang Chuan：The man with noble character rushes to resign and looks for a shelter. For the sake of justice, he would rather starve than succumbing.

Suggestion：Be worldly wise and play safe.

六二：明夷，夷于左股，用拯馬壯，吉。

象傳：六二之吉，順以則也。

In the second SIX : In a terrible situation, one is unable to utilize his talents as if his left leg was injured by the villains. He strives for turning things around. He makes uses of a strong horse to overcome the difficulties. It means that he has to cheer up and persevere to the end. Then it will bring fortune.

Xiang Chuan：It is fortunate if he always follows the moral path.

Suggestion：Do not give up any chance of survival.

九三：明夷於南狩，得其大首，不可疾貞。

象傳：南狩之志，乃大得也。

In the third NINE : In order to overturn the fatuous ruler, the assassination is secretly arranged during the royal hunting in the southern part. The movement should be confidential and cannot be executed prematurely.

Xiang Chuan : The mission to overturn the fatuous ruler during the Royal hunting in the southern part has achieved results.

Suggestion : It is easy for one to make mistakes while doing things too hastily.

六四：入于左腹，獲明夷之心，于出門庭。

象傳：入于左腹，獲心意也。

In the fourth SIX : As a confidant of the emperor, he can secretly gather information about the emperor's moves, understanding what's going on behind the scenes. Of course, he deeply understands what the emperor is thinking about. Because he is disappointed in the emperor, he plans to resign and run away since it is unlikely to turn things around.

Xiang Chuan : He infiltrates to gather information about the dark secrets of the emperor. Thus he knows the unspoken worries of the ruler.

Suggestion: Those who suit their actions to the time are wise.

六五：箕子之明夷，利貞。

象傳：箕子之貞，明不可息也。

In the fifth SIX : Chitz faked being crazy and acted like an idiot to conceal his wisdom to avoid danger. Actually he was not crazy. He took everyone's interests into consideration. His determination to leave was to reveal the wrongdoings of the emperor.

Xiang Chuan : The spirits of Chitz is decent. The light of his wisdom will never be extinguished.

Suggestion : Sacrifice oneself for the interests of the whole.

上六：不明晦，初登于天，後入于地。

象傳：初登于天，照四國也；後入于地，失則也。

In the topmost SIX : Extreme darkness. At the beginning the emperor is newly crowned and receives high praise, but then his stupidity leads the Court to disorder. Eventually he is despised by people.

Xiang Chuan : An emperor is newly crowned and receives high praise in the beginning, but his stupidity leads the Court to disorder. Eventually he is despised as he violates the moral principles.

Suggestion : A guilty conscience needs no accuser.

37. 家人 Jia-Ren

 巽上 離下

風火家人

家人：利女貞。

象傳：風自火出，家人；君子以言有物而行有恆。

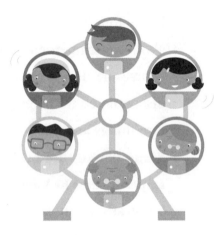

Jia-Ren : Families. The wife is in charge of the household chores and is thrifty in daily spending to help her husband. She plays a decisive role in the prosperity of the family. She is loyal with her husband from the beginning to the end. It is positive.

Xiang Chuan : Winds help fire burn fast. It represents that the foundation of morals and manners in a society come from every family. The man with noble character should be careful about his words and deeds. He should persevere in doing things.

Suggestion : The prosperity of a family largely depends on the harmony, tolerance, sincerity and the frugality of a wife.

初九：閑有家，悔亡。

象傳：閑有家，志未變也。

In the first NINE : If there are family rules and precautions in the beginning, there will not be regrets.

Xiang Chuan：If the family agree with the rules, nothing will change their hearts.

Suggestion：Family preaching in the beginning is more important than corrections after the events.

六二: 無攸遂，在中饋，貞吉。

象傳：六二之吉，順以巽也。

In the second SIX : A wife does not get involved in outside affairs, she focuses on household chores and cooking. She doesn't look like having special contributions to the family. She is obedient, virtuous and modest. She is also not involved in the husband's business as well.

Xiang Chuan：A wife is humble, gentle and agreeable. She manages the household chores so that her husband will be free of worries.

Suggestion：To stay at one's post and fulfill his best. If the family lives in harmony, all affairs will prosper.

九三: 家人嗃*嗃，悔厲，吉；婦子嘻嘻，終吝。

象傳：家人嗃嗃，未失也；婦子嘻嘻，失家節也。

In the third NINE : It would be much better for the family members to have severe family rules and even have complaints rather than to indulge family members freely. There will be regrets, but looking at it long term, it is auspicious. However, if you let the family members run wild, the family will eventually decline.

Xiang Chuan：Although the family members complain about severe family rules, the family is in order.

If the family members behave wildly, it is against the norms.

Suggestion: Lax family rules lead to the decline of a family.

＊註24：嗃ㄏㄜˋ，嚴酷。

六四：富家，大吉。
象傳：富家大吉，順在位也。

In the fourth SIX : Enable to prosper a family is fortunate.

Xiang Chuan : The prosperity of a family is mostly due to the contributions and the modesty of a wife.

Suggestion : To stick together through thick and thin. To share life's joys and sorrows for better or for worse.

九五：王假有家，勿恤，吉。
象傳：王假有家，交相愛也。

In the fifth NINE : The emperor uses his virtues to put his family in order and govern the nation. It is done without worries and efforts. It is fortunate.

Xiang Chuan : If an emperor is able to put his family in order, he is equally capable of governing the nation. It is fortunate because the royal family and the people get along and love each other like a big family.

Suggestion : Infinitely merciful and companionate.

上九：有孚，威如，終吉。
象傳：威如之吉，反身之謂也。

In the topmost NINE : If the head of the household is sincere and trustworthy, he will serve as an example for other family members. The family members will be trustworthy too.

Xiang Chuan : If the head of the household is sincere and trustworthy, he will serve as an example for other family members. This is because he examines himself on a regular basis.

Suggestion : Putting the family in order also needs firmness.

38. 睽 Kui

火澤睽　　離上 兌下

睽：小事吉。

象傳：上火下澤，睽；君子以同而異。

Kui：Opposition, deviation. It is a generation of deviation. Because each one has different characters and aspirations, things always turn out differently than they expected. Therefore, while dealing with people and things, one should be careful and discreet.

Xiang Chuan：Water and fire are naturally incompatible. It represents opposite forces. The man with noble character should be open-minded to tolerate differences so as to look for common grounds.

Suggestion：Give up subjective opinions to look for common ground.

初九：悔亡，喪馬勿逐，自復；見惡人，無咎。

象傳：見惡人，以辟咎也。

In the first NINE : In the times of deviation, if you can tolerate the differences of others, there will no regrets. It is just like when a horse goes astray, there is no need to chase after it because it is untamed, the more you chase, the farther it runs. However, if you go with the flow and let it do its own thing, the horse will come back eventually. By the same token, if a man holding opposite points of views wants to meet you, do not refuse. Just brush him off to avoid further misunderstanding. There will be no more conflict.

Xiang Chuan：If a man holding opposite points of views wants to meet with you, do not refuse. Just brush him off to avoid further misunderstanding. There will be no more conflict.

Suggestion：Magnanimity grants favors to whoever asks for it. Eliminate differences. Courteous treatment.

九二：遇主于巷，無咎。
象傳：遇主于巷，未失道也。

In the second NINE : One meets with his superior in the lane for business, though it doesn't fit the social norms. There is no blame. It means discouragement and destitution.

Xiang Chuan：As long as you don't meet a superior for personal interests in the lane, it is not against the social principles and ethics.

Suggestion：Adapt to the circumstances and make great concessions.

六三：見輿曳，其牛掣，其人天且劓，無初有終。
象傳：見輿曳，位不當也；無初有終，遇剛也。

In the third SIX : Personal relationships are seriously meddled just like a wagon is pulled backwards and the ox cannot move forward. Eventually the wagon got overturned and the driver is badly hurt as if a criminal is punished cruelly so his nose is cut off and his forehead tattooed. Although there are tortures initially, the wagon still arrives at the destination in the end. It means that forces coming from different directions create conflicts, you should stop being subjective and try to seek common ground among the differences.

Xiang Chuan：A wagon is pulled backwards. The ox cannot move forwards. The wagon is still stuck in the same place, but if the two forces find harmony, then the wagon can move forward.

Suggestion：Internal conflicts are equal to killing one another. Obstacles in life are unavoidable, but do not be discouraged because everyone has his time to shine.

九四：睽孤，遇元夫，交孚，厲無咎。
象傳：交孚無咎，志行也。

In the fourth NINE : In the times of uncertainty, two lonely men run across with

each other. They happen to be in a similar situation. Thus, they make friends with sincerity and they are finally free from disaster.

Xiang Chuan：They sincerely make friends. Their wishes to be free from loneliness can come true.

Suggestion：Friends in adversity.

六五：悔亡，厥宗噬膚，往何咎？

象傳：厥宗噬膚，往有慶也。

In the fifth SIX : If treating people and things with compassion and the principles of the middle-way can turn perils into good fortunes. Then the differences between people will disappear, which is replaced by harmony. Therefore, the regrets also disappear. The relatives all get along as easily as biting a piece of tender meat. Are there any inconveniences?

Xiang Chuan：The relatives all get along as easily as biting a piece of tender meat. This means that happy things are about to happen.

Suggestion：To be close as lips to teeth.

上九：睽孤，見豕負塗，載鬼一車，先張之弧，後說之弧。匪寇，婚媾。往，遇雨則吉。

象傳：遇雨之吉，群疑亡也。

In the topmost NINE : When differences between people get widened to the extreme, a man who lacks self-confidence and without trusted subordinates is prone to being suspicious of everything. He mistakenly took the followers to be the pigs covered with dirt in the wagon. When he was bending the arrow trying to shoot them, he realized that the coming people are not bandits. They are the people accompanying the marriage team. The shower cleaned their dirt, helping to clear up the misunderstanding.

Xiang Chuan：A shower cleans the dirt, helping to clear up the misunderstanding.

Suggestion：A man is even afraid of his own shadow. He should eliminate all

the grudges held in the past and cooperate with people.
Extremely suspicious.

39. 蹇 Jian

 坎上 艮下
水山蹇

蹇：利西南，不利東北。利見大人。貞吉。
象傳：山上有水，蹇；君子以反身修德。

Jian：Crippled. Difficult and hard. In such a difficult and hard situation, it is favorable to advance slowly toward the south west which leads to a flat road, but negative to advance toward the north east that leads to a steep slope. It is positive to meet with a great man to have good advice from him to overcome difficulties.

Xiang Chuan：Water runs from the summit of the mountains. If the water is washing off too much dirt, it is a sign of danger. The man with noble character should examine himself and cultivate his virtues when facing difficulties.

Suggestion：While encountering an obstacle or a setback, one should be calm to analyze the situation both subjectively and objectively and cross examine oneself. To clarify confusion and bring things back to order.

初六：往蹇，來譽。
象傳：往蹇，來譽，宜待也。

In the first SIX：If you run into a difficulty, it is advisable to retreat to a safe spot temporarily and come up with the measure to handle it. On the contrary, he will receive praises because he does not act blindly as he knows that it is not suitable to go ahead under present circumstances. He should instead wait for good timing.

Xiang Chuan：While encountering difficulties, one temporarily retreats to one's

shelter to come up with solutions. This way he will win praises because his action suits the timing. He would rather wait for good timing to take action.

Suggestion：Halting is not the same as stopping forever. It is like the rest required for one to go a long way.

六二：王臣蹇蹇，匪躬之故。

象傳：王臣蹇蹇，終無尤也。

In the second SIX : When the state is in trouble, the subjects are obliged to stand out and look for solutions for the emperor. Although they know it is not the right time to act, they will not turn away from the responsibilities.

Xiang Chuan：The subjects are loyal and devoted to the emperor without any complaints all the time.

Suggestion：Indifferent to the praise or blame and devoted to one's duty.

九三：往蹇，來反。

象傳：往蹇，來反，內喜之也。

In the third NINE : When encountering difficulties, one would rather retreat to a safe spot and examine oneself to look for solutions than advance blindly.

Xiang Chuan：One knows when to stop and when to move. His heart is full of happiness because he learns from valuable experience.

Suggestion：To retreat in order to advance. Rest well so that one has the energy to start again!

六四：往蹇，來連。

象傳：往蹇，來連，當位實也。

In the fourth SIX : When one is between a rock and a hard place, he has to examine himself and seek for support from comrades. It is pragmatic.

Xiang Chuan：One is between a rock and a hard place. He has to unite with the comrades to enhance their capabilities.

Suggestion：Working pragmatically wins confidence.

九五：大蹇，朋來。

象傳：大蹇，朋來，以中節也。

In the fifth NINE : When one is in great difficulties, there come many comrades to help and support him.

Xiang Chuan：When one is in great difficulties, there come many comrades to help and support him as he treated his friends nicely in the past and always made the moral choice.

Suggestion：Men of virtue will not feel lonely.

上六：往蹇，來碩，吉，利見大人。

象傳：往蹇，來碩，志在內也；利見大人，以從貴也。

In the topmost SIX : When moving forward, you never came across such an unprecedented difficulty. It is impossible for a single man to overcome it. In the occasion, he would rather cultivate his virtues than take action. It is fortunate to follow the good advice of the great men.

Xiang Chuan：When moving forward, you never came across such an unprecedented difficulty. You have to be determined. Listen to good advice from wise men. They are invaluable.

Suggestion： It would be better to seek support from comrades to reach the target rather than to work alone. There can be no rainbow without a cloud and a storm.

40. 解 Jie

震上 坎下
雷水解

解：利西南，無所往，其來復，吉；有攸往，夙吉。

象傳：雷雨作，解；君子以赦過宥罪。

Jie：Relieved from difficulties. Walking towards the south west, which is a flat road, means to free from dangers and land in a safe place. Obstacles have already been removed, people and the troops are eager to rest and build up strength. However, when facing an emergency, the rescue better be quick and without delay.

Xiang Chuan：Thunder and rain clear the smog, all creatures become active. The man with noble character realizes that kind policy will enable the criminals to be reborn. Therefore, we should lighten the sentence of a criminal.

Suggestion：Moral education is more important than criminal sentencing.

初六：無咎。

象傳：剛柔之際，義無咎也。

In the first SIX: Any difficulty is settled or error is corrected immediately in the beginning. There will be no blame because the moral path is followed.

Xiang Chuan：Behaving according to ethics is not wrong.

Suggestion：Working together with one heart in times of difficulty.

九二：田獲三狐，得黃矢，貞吉。

象傳：九二貞吉，得中道也。

In the second NINE: Capturing three foxes while hunting, you found copper arrowheads in the foxes. Three foxes represent hidden dangers are relieved. The copper arrowheads stand for a morally upright man. The lesson here is that it takes amorally upright man to get you out of danger.

Xiang Chuan：To get help from amorally upright man is without fail.

Suggestion：In order to fix a problem, you need to eliminate hidden worries in advance.

六三：負且乘，致寇至，貞吝。

象傳：負且乘，亦可醜也；自我致戎，又誰咎也?

In the third SIX : While riding on a wagon, one normally leaves the heavy bag on the ground. Instead, he is still carrying it on his back. No wonder it invites gangsters to eye on his pack. He asked for it.

Xiang Chuan：While taking a wagon, one normally leaves the heavy bag on the ground. Instead, he is still carrying it on his back. His behavior is ugly and suspicious. It invites bandits to eye it. He deserves it. Who can he blame but himself?

Suggestion：Never trouble trouble until trouble troubles you.

九四：解而拇，朋至斯孚。

象傳：解而拇，未當位也。

In the fourth NINE : Getting rid of the corns on the thumb is just like breaking away from the villains to win confidence from men of noble character. The man with noble character takes precautions in time to avoid the disasters. Thus, all his comrades come to follow him.

Xiang Chuan：He is easily targeted by the villains because of his improper behaviors.

Suggestion：One who mixes with vermilion will turn red. One who touches pitch shall be defiled therewith.

六五：君子維有解，吉，有孚于小人。

象傳：君子有解，小人退也。

In the fifth SIX : If the man with noble character categorically turns down the

villains, it is a great omen.

His sincerity and decisiveness to reject the villains makes them give up evil and return to good. It naturally makes the villains afraid and retreat.

Xiang Chuan：The man with noble character firmly declines the villains. It naturally makes the villains scared and retreat.

Suggestion：Far away from villains, the difficulties disappear.

上六：公用射隼于高墉之上，獲之，無不利。

象傳：公用射隼，以解悖也。

In the topmost SIX：The duke bends his arrows to shoot down the fierce falcons that stand on the high walls.

It means that to expel villains or to eradicate obstacles in such a favorable situation needs fast and firm decisions.

Xiang Chuan：The duke bends his arrows to shoot down the falcons that stand on the high walls to relieve the dangers. It means that the duke gets rid of the bad guys.

Suggestion：To cut weeds and eliminate the roots.

41. 損　Suen

山澤損　艮上 兌下

損：有孚，元吉，無咎。可貞，利有攸往。曷之用？二簋可用享。

象傳：山下有澤，損，君子以懲忿窒欲。

Suen：Frugality. Depletion. Frugality is widely accepted by the public and complies with the ethics. Frugality is a good principle. It is not wrong to stick with it. Applying frugality into worship in the ancient times means reducing the offerings to two small bowls of food plus a sincere heart and respect. These are enough.

Although the offerings are less, the sincerity is not discounted.

Xiang Chuan：There is a lake beneath a mountain which decreases earth of the mountain as if heavy taxation on people is an excess decrease on the people; the superior man apprehends restraints on personal angers, desires and greediness.

Suggestion：The gift is insignificant but it is the thought that counts!

初九：已事遄*往，無咎。酌損之。

象傳：已事遄往，尚合志也。

In the first NINE：In essence, there will be no blame to help others immediately after one finishes his work, but benefiting others one needs to consider one's capability.

Xiang Chuan：Good deeds should be done according to one's capability. It should meet the expectation of the benefits people can receive and the value you can provide. In a word, you need to take your ability into consideration when helping people.

Suggestion：Everything should be done according to one's capability.

九二：利貞。征凶，弗損，益之。

象傳：九二利貞，中以為志也。

In the second NINE：All the behaviors must follow the moral path. It is right to give up one's own interests for the sake of others, but if there is a win-win situation, it couldn't be better.

Xiang Chuan：One should insist on being ethical, but before helping others, one should always evaluate one's capability.

Suggestion: Balancing between yours and other people's benefits flexibly. Do not be stuck with formality. A rash decision will be more of a hindrance than a help.

---

*註25：遄ㄔㄨㄢˊ，迅速地。

六三：三人行，則損一人，一人行，則得其友。

象傳：一人行，三則疑也。

In the third SIX : Balance is created by constant adjusting. Two is just right, but three is a crowd. When there are three people, two are close. While the third person is isolated, the balance is destroyed. The third person will then look for his own balance.

Xiang Chuan：One person goes alone on a trip. He will find another one to join him, but when there are three people, the third one will easily get suspicious and starts to find his balance.

Suggestion：Compromise and find its balance.

六四：損其疾，使遄有喜，無咎。

象傳：損其疾，亦可喜也。

In the fourth SIX : To heal one's disease and to recover from an illness soon is a pleasant thing. It is nothing wrong.

Xiang Chuan：Heal one's diseases. Cut bad habits. Change bad temper. Quit smoking. These may be regarded as improving oneself. It's a happy and pleasant thing.

Suggestion：Heaven helps those who help themselves.

六五：或益之，十朋之龜，弗克違，元吉。

象傳：六五元吉，自上祐也。

In the fifth SIX : Sacrificing yourself to help others makes you receive a precious tortoise as a return. One should not decline as this is a warm feedback. It is very fortunate.

Xiang Chuan：One receives blessing from Heaven as he is humble to sacrifice his interests to benefit others.

Suggestion：Sacrificing oneself to benefit others is a sure way to win people's hearts.

上九：弗損益之，無咎，貞吉，利有攸往，得臣無家。

象傳：弗損益之，大得志也。

In the topmost NINE : Do not take away from people but instead give back to the people. Basically there is no blame as it is ethical. If the emperor's policies follow this principle, the subjects will wholeheartedly contribute to the nation to the point that they even forget their homes.

Xiang Chuan : Do not take away from people, but instead give back to the people. This is the emperor's ambition to give favors and love to the people.

Suggestion : People will be convinced when you benefit people within your capability. Giving up ones' interests to benefit others is also an act of kindness to the people.

42. 益 Yih

 巽上 震下

風雷益

益：利有攸往。利涉大川。

象傳：風雷，益；君子以見善則遷，有過則改。

Yih : Increase benefits. Use the surplus of the superior to give back to the inferior as if the superior shows sympathy for the people, reduces their material comfort to benefit the people. Thus, even when facing difficulties, they will all strive hard to overcome them.

Xiang Chuan : Winds and thunders occurring simultaneously represents that they enhance each other.

The man with noble character realizes that he should follow the good examples of others without hesitation like the winds and correct his faults immediately like the firmness of thunderclaps.

Suggestion : The man with noble character should pay more attention to his own moral cultivation and the correction of his faults. Helping people without

asking anything in return.

初九：利用為大作，元吉，無咎。

象傳：元吉，無咎，下不厚事也。

In the first NINE : If one is fully supported and authorized by the superior, he is able to make use of his talents and abilities to do something worthwhile. It will be a great omen and there will be no blame.

Xiang Chuan：Because of his lower rank, he is unable to complete any big project unless he is fully supported and authorized. Without being delegated by the superior, even if you expect highly of him, he cannot achieve much.

Suggestion：The gratitude for trusting an important position.

六二：或益之，十朋之龜，弗克違，永貞吉。王用享於帝，吉。

象傳：或益之，自外來也。

In the second SIX : When somebody brings valuable gifts, there is no need to decline. The beneficiary should be grateful and remain ethical forever to have good fortunes. It will bring a great omen if the emperor uses the presents as the offerings to worship the God.

Xiang Chuan：Somebody gives you valuable gifts, it is merely worldly possessions. The beneficiary should be ethical forever.

Suggestion：Icing on the cake means making the good better. As you sow, so shall you reap.

六三：益之用凶事，無咎。有孚中行。告公用圭。

象傳：益用凶事，固有之也。

In the third SIX : During the years of famine, it is not wrong to relieve the people in disaster provided that you're sincere and fair. What is taken from the people is used in the interests of the people. In principle, there is no blame, but it is necessary that he report the facts about the famine faithfully and ask immediate permission for disaster relief.

Xiang Chuan：The help to relieve the famine is originally from the people. All he does is to give it back to the people and fulfills his obligation.

Suggestion：What is taken from the people is used for the interests of the people.

六四：中行告公從，利用為依遷國。
象傳：告公從，以益志也。

In the fourth SIX：In the years of famine, people are suffering from starvation. The biggest fortune to the people is nothing more than moving the Capital to a rich and populous land. Now that the change of Capital is beneficial to the people, the Dukes agree to follow up, which shows their decency. There will be no disadvantages.

Xiang Chuan：The Dukes agree to move the capital to a richer area, which is beneficial to the people and the biggest present they could have given to the people. It is also their wish.

Suggestion：For the wellbeing of the whole, all the measures must comply with the benefits of the people.

九五：有孚惠心，勿問元吉。有孚惠我德。
象傳：有孚惠心，勿問之矣；惠我德，大得志也。

In the fifth NINE：It is a great fortune to benefit people with complete sincerity. People will undoubtedly return gratitude to the emperor.

Xiang Chuan：There is no need to do a poll about people's satisfaction on the benefits they receive. Apparently, the feed- back from people will prove if your goal has been fulfilled.

Suggestion：It's better to give than to take.

上九：莫益之，或擊之。立心勿恆，凶。

象傳：莫益之，偏辭也。或擊之，自外來也。

In the topmost NINE : To increase benefits of the people is essentially his duty, but he is unable to persist. He is even accused of exploiting people.

No wonder, he is suffering attacks from people as his behaviors are against the norms. It brings misfortune.

Xiang Chuan : Nobody supports him. It is his biased view. Suffering attacks from people is just like an unexpected disaster to him.

Suggestion : High ranking officials are greedy and do things only for personal benefit. This will trigger public anger.

43. 夬 （ㄍㄨㄞˋ） Guai

兌上 乾下

澤天夬

夬：揚于王庭，孚號有厲，告自邑。不利即戎，利有攸往。

象傳：澤上於天，夬；君子以施祿及下，居德則忌。

Guai : Crack-down. To expose the crimes of the villains, which will stop the wrongdoers and also warn the inhabitants not to commit any crimes. You should be well prepared to crack down on the gangsters. Launch a fatal attack instead of alerting them.

Xiang Chuan : The air is very humid. It looks like it's going to rain. The man with noble character realizes that it is a taboo not to give favors to people and only focus on personal interests.

Suggestion : To be overly lenient is to breed evil.

初九：壯于前趾，往不勝為咎。

象傳：不勝而往，咎也。

In the first NINE : Challenging boldly and rashly just because you have a strong toe will make you encounter difficulties. It signifies that a newborn calf that is reckless to act will easily suffer losses.

Xiang Chuan：Without certainty to win, but one still boldly takes action. One will suffer losses.

Suggestion：Be more brave than wise.

九二：惕號，莫夜有戎，勿恤。
象傳：有戎勿恤，得中道也。

In the second NINE : When facing the villains, you should always remain alert to prevent possible attacks. If you are fully prepared, there are no worries about any night attacks. It means that be prepared at any time to face the challenges.

Xiang Chuan：If fully prepared, there are no worries about sudden attacks from the villains.

Suggestion：Forewarned is forearmed.

九三：壯于頄⃨*，有凶。君子夬⃨夬，獨行遇雨，若濡有慍，無咎。
象傳：君子夬夬，終無咎也。

In the third NINE : If a man with noble character shows discontent, his resolution to drive out villains will attract disaster because he shows his hostility on the face. If a man with noble character is determined to kick out villains, he should be like a pedestrian walking alone in the rain. Even if his clothes are all wet, he has to conceal his unpleasant mood and shows calmness in the appearance. If he can keep his cool, the villains will be cracked down without mistakes.

Xiang Chuan：The resolution of a man with noble character to break off the villains will not be blamed.

*註26：頄ㄑㄧㄡˊ，臉。

Suggestion：To endure all the disgrace and insults in order to accomplish difficult tasks.

九四：臀無膚，其行次且。牽羊悔亡，聞言不信。

象傳：其行次且，位不當也；聞言不信，聰不明也。

In the fourth NINE：To eradicate the villains, the action should be decisive. Hesitation is useless to get things done. A shepherd never pulls the sheep. Instead, he always goes behind the sheep. If one follows the advice of the virtuous, he will never have regrets. However, if you just listen to the advice but never take action, you will mess things up.

Xiang Chuan：To eradicate the villains, the action should be decisive. If one is hesitant and doesn't follow the advice of the virtuous, or he just hears, but doesn't listen, he is not clever.

Suggestion：One doesn't know what course to take. A clever person may become the victim of his own ingenuity.

九五：莧陸夬夬，中行無咎。

象傳：中行無咎，中未光也。

In the fifth NINE：Expelling out the villains is like eradicating the purslane, it should be fast and without hesitation. If the process is reasonable and follows the principle of middle way, there will be no disasters.

Xiang Chuan：The best way to make villains give up evil and return to good is to reform them. If not, the eradication is sure to fail due to the lack of the final push.

Suggestion：To eradicate villains one must be decisive without any hesitation even if there are personal considerations involved.

上六：無號，終有凶。

象傳：無號之凶，終不可長也。

In the topmost SIX : The villains are lawless. They will have to face punishment. Their cries and regrets cannot reverse the situation. All their wrongdoings will lead to misfortune in the end.

Xiang Chuan：The villains and their wicked behaviors are destined to fail. Their arrogance will not last long after all.

Suggestion：Money from injustice and ridiculous self-flattery cannot last forever.

44. 姤 Guo

天風姤　　乾上 巽下

姤：女壯，勿用取女。

象傳：天下有風，姤；后以施命誥四方。

Guo：Come across unexpectedly. The young girl is so horny that she dates five young men at the same time, which is extremely immoral. Do not marry such a promiscuous girl.

Xiang Chuan：The winds blow to the world, helping all the creatures to meet by chance. The emperor declares the regulations to the nation.

Suggestion：Falling in love at first sight is not wrong. The good or bad cannot be judged immediately. It depends on the "relationship status" (married or single) and motives (good or evil) of a person.

初六：繫于金柅*，貞吉。有攸往，見凶，羸豕孚蹢躅*。

象傳：繫於金柅，柔道牽也。以靜制動。

---

*註27：柅ㄋㄧ∨，古時剎車之木條。

*註28：蹢ㄉㄧˊ躅ㄓㄨˊ，來回走。

[In the first SIX]: Seriously monitor the villains to avoid the chaos just like stepping on the brakes of a carriage to avoid danger. It is fortunate. It means that persistence of moral choice creates good fortunes. On the contrary, to be overly lenient is to breed evil. The man with noble character will be sabotaged by the villains as a thin and weak pig moves restlessly because of worries. At this very moment, if you follow the rule of "calmness over hastiness", it will not have misfortune.

Xiang Chuan：The villains are restless and anxious, they should be restrained just like a car needs brakes.

Suggestion：To take every precaution at the beginning. Calmness over hastiness.

[九二]: 包有魚，無咎，不利賓。
象傳：包有魚，義不及賓也。

[In the second NINE]: You accidentally find some raw fish in the kitchen. There is nothing wrong. However, you cannot serve the fish to the guests because it does not belong to you. It means that one should resist the temptation to take things without permission.

Xiang Chuan：Some raw fish is found in the kitchen which should not be cooked to serve the guests without the owner's permission. From the view of ethics, taking the fish to treat the guests without permission is not right.

Suggestion：Do not make undeserved money.

[九三]: 臀無膚，其行次且，厲，無大咎。
象傳：其行次且，行未牽也。

[In the third NINE]: Due to the injured thigh, he is feeling uneasy when sitting and standing. He cannot move freely as if his hands are tied by the villains.

Apparently, the situation is not favorable for him but if he still insists to take action, it is sure to bring him misfortune. On the contrary, if he can judge the timing and size up the situation, there will be no disaster.

Xiang Chuan：Because of injuries on the thigh, he is unable to move freely. His movements are limited as if he is restrained by the villains.

Suggestion：Only when you are not involved with the villains can you be safe.

九四：包無魚，起凶。

象傳：無魚之凶，遠民也。

In the fourth NINE：You cannot find fish in the kitchen. If there is any dispute, it is unfortunate.

Xiang Chuan：You cannot find fish in the kitchen. If there is any dispute, it is unfortunate.

It represents that an emperor is unable to limit the villains and his decisions are away from public opinions. He cannot win trust and confidence from people. It is unfortunate.

Suggestion：Without preparation, all the efforts are futile.

九五：以杞包瓜，含章，有隕自天。

象傳：九五含章，中正也；有隕自天，志不舍命也。

In the fifth NINE：The shadow of the willow protects sweet melons beneath as if a virtuous sovereign recruits the virtuous and talented people for the country. The emperor shows his open-mindedness to recruit talented people and protect the people. The villains will fail just like the falling meteoric rocks.

Xiang Chuan：The emperor has the virtue of respecting the middle-way. He never goes against the will of heaven.

Suggestion：To desire greatly to win the support of the wise.

上九：姤其角，吝，無咎。

象傳：姤其角，上窮吝也。

In the topmost NINE : One is so arrogant that he is reluctant to lower himself to initiate communication with others. He is isolated as if he is pushed to the corner. However, since he is only conceited and aloof, he won't cause any harm.

Xiang Chuan : One is so arrogant that he is reluctant to communicate with others. He is isolated as if he is compelled to the corner. In fact, he has nowhere to go.

Suggestion : To transcend the worldly affairs. To hold oneself aloof from the world.

45. 萃 Tsui

澤地萃　　　兌上 坤下

萃：亨，王假有廟。利見大人，亨，利貞。用大牲，吉。利有攸往。

象傳：澤上於地，萃；君子以除戎器，戒不虞。

Tsui : Gathering together. The emperor comes to the ancestral temple to worship and makes use of the occasion to meet with those of great virtue. The purpose is to consult those of wisdom and virtue. What matters is that the motive of the gathering is pure, otherwise it becomes a potential turmoil. It is fortunate to treat the virtuous with the livestock used in worshipping the God.

Xiang Chuan : Water flowing to the lakes, it is convergence. The water flowing to the lake consists of different mix of sand and stones. The man with noble character realizes that it is necessary to have good maintenance of weapons in case of emergency.

Suggestion : The rise and fall of a country is nothing more than the gathering and separation of people.

初六 : 有孚不終，乃亂乃萃，若號，一握為笑，勿恤，往，無咎。

象傳：乃亂乃萃，其志亂也。

[In the first SIX] : If one cannot be sincere from the beginning to the end, the gathering will turn into chaos. If one recruits comrades in the name of justice, they will come and shake hands with one other without worries. Such a gathering is sure to accomplish something worthwhile. There is no blame.

Xiang Chuan：The gathering is sometimes in order, sometimes in chaos because everyone has different agendas.

Suggestion：Where there is sincerity, there is opportunity.

六二 : 引吉，無咎。孚乃利用禴。

象傳：引吉無咎，中未變也。

[In the second SIX] : One is led to gather with others, it is fortunate. There is no blame. Treating people with sincerity instead of giving sumptuous gifts is just like giving a small offering in the religious ceremony. Even if it is not ceremonious, it is acceptable.

Xiang Chuan：One is led to gather with others. There is no blame. Treating people with sincerity instead of giving sumptuous gifts is just like giving small offerings in the religious ceremony. Although it is not ceremonious, it is still acceptable because one's heart hasn't changed.

Suggestion： Let's hope for the best.

六三 : 萃如嗟如，無攸利，往，無咎，小吝。

象傳：往無咎，上巽也。

[In the third SIX] : Although everybody joins together to discuss, there are still unresolved matters, which makes people sigh because they have a sense of loss. However, sincerity can reconcile them without regrets. At most, there are inconveniences, but there won't be disaster.

Xiang Chuan：Though the gathering will not reach a conclusion, following the advice of the elderly will not be blamed since you demonstrate the virtue of piety.

Suggestion：To compromise out of consideration for the general interest.

九四：大吉，無咎。

象傳：大吉無咎，位不當也。

In the fourth NINE : The wish to gather the masses together is fulfilled. It is a great fortune. There is no blame because the gathering helps to form public opinion.

Xiang Chuan：The gathering that helps to form public opinion brings great fortune, but watches your words and deeds so that you do not do things outside the authority of your position.

Suggestion：Do not appoint oneself as the leader when gathering together with the mass. So great is one's achievements as to make one's boss feel uneasy.

九五：萃有位，無咎。匪孚，元永貞，悔亡。

象傳：萃有位，志未光也。

In the fifth NINE : In the gathering, one is recommended to be the leader because of his virtues. It is not inappropriate. If his virtues are not extensively recognized by the people, he should examine himself and be always morally upright. When doing so, regrets will disappear.

Xiang Chuan：In the gathering, one is recommended to be the leader, but his virtues have not been extensively recognized by the people because his virtues have not been well seen yet.

Suggestion： To convince people by means of one's virtues.

上六：齎⁺咨ᵖ*涕洟，無咎。

象傳：齎咨涕洟，未安上也。

In the topmost SIX : One is isolated from the public and feels disturbed. He weeps and sighs as he is aware of his loneliness and helplessness. If he reflects on himself and corrects things he has done wrong, it will be helpful to his future.

Xiang Chuan：One is isolated from the public and feels disturbed. He weeps and

＊註29：齎ㄐㄧ 咨ㄗ，嗟嘆。

sighs as he is aware of his loneliness and helplessness.

Suggestion： Failure is the mother of success. One has to examine himself on why he cannot win people's hearts.

46. 升 Shen

 坤上 巽下
地風升

升：元亨，用見大人，勿恤，南征，吉。

象傳：地中生木，升；君子以順德，積小以高大。

Shen：Rising, to make progress. It is required to advance step by step and through the assistance of a great man. There will be no worries. It is advantageous to move towards the target on the south to look for opportunities.

Xiang Chuan：Tree growing gradually from earth represents the hexagram of Shen. The man with noble character should cultivate his virtues like the growth of trees. Many a little makes a nickel.

Suggestion：All creatures make their progress gradually. A man should not constantly seek fame and wealth but should concentrate on cultivating his virtues.

初六：允升，大吉。

象傳：允升大吉，上合志也。

In the first SIX： When one tries to get close to a great man, if he is sincere, talented and fits the expectations of the great man, it is in his favor to be promoted. It is a great luck.

Xiang Chuan：It is a great fortune to be promoted because of one's sincerity and talents.

Suggestion：To help somebody to fulfill his wishes. Promotion happens

because of reliability and confidence. Man proposes, God disposes.

九二：孚乃利用禴，無咎。
象傳：九二之孚，有喜也。

In the second NINE : Sincerity will help you to get promotion. Even though you only have simple offerings while praying, if your attitude is sincere, you will win support from people. Sincerity is the ladder to promotion. There is no blame.

Xiang Chuan：Sincerity will help you to get promotion. Even though you only have simple offerings while praying, if your attitude is sincere, you will win support from people. Sincerity is the ladder to promotion. It will bring joy.

Suggestion：As you sow, so will you reap.

九三：升虛邑。
象傳：升虛邑，無所疑也。

In the third NINE : One is promoted so smoothly as if he enters into an empty city.

Xiang Chuan：No worries ahead of him. The future is bright.

Suggestion：Do more, talk less. The future will be bright and the road to success will easy as if walking through an empty space.

六四：王用亨於岐山，吉，無咎。
象傳：王用亨於岐山，順事也。

In the fourth SIX : The emperor worships and prays for prosperity and safety for his country and the people in Mt. Chi annually. It is fortunate. There is no blame.

Xiang Chuan：The emperor and the people pray for the same things because they have the same wishes. He will practice justice and respect public opinions.

Suggestion：Obedience to the superior, closeness to the inferior.

六五：貞吉，升階。

象傳：貞吉升階，大得志也。

In the fifth SIX : Moral deeds and words allow one to rise higher. Lofty ambitions achieved.

Xiang Chuan：Moral deeds and words allow one to rise higher. Because one is positive and ambitious he has opportunities to achieve many future successes.

Suggestion：To know subordinates well enough to assign them jobs commensurate with their abilities.

上六：冥升，立於不息之貞。

象傳：冥升在上，消不富也。

In the topmost SIX : Satisfy your material and career desires moderately. Don't get lazy. Always make the moral choice.

Xiang Chuan：Blindly pursuing material and career desires are the same as digging their own grave.

Suggestion：Merits and achievements are transient, but virtues last forever.

47. 困 Kuen

 兌上 坎下
澤水困

困：亨。貞，大人吉，無咎。有言不信。

象傳：澤無水，困；君子以致命遂志。

Kuen：Poverty, predicament. Overcoming difficulties brings fortune. If one is ethical, he can turn poverty into prosperity. At a minimum, he won't have any disasters. When one is poor, if he is still content with his lot, he can get along with

people and deal with things sensibly. Poor people are not convincing because their words and deeds are not recognized. Therefore, a poor man would rather shut his mouth.

Xiang Chuan：There is no water in the lake. This represents poverty. The man with noble character would rather sacrifice his life to realize his purpose than to live in disgrace.

Suggestion：Words from a man of lowly position carry little weight.

初六：臀困于株木，入於幽谷，三歲不覿。
象傳：入于幽谷，幽不明也。

In the first SIX ：One is poor and helpless. He is forced to retreat to a secluded valley. He is so pathetic as if his naked buttocks were sitting on a hard tree. He has been trapped by his own worries for three years.

Xiang Chuan：Because he is secluded for a long time, he became a nobody.

Suggestion：Poverty chills ambition. When one is poor, if he opens his mind, all the difficulties will soon be resolved.

九二：困于酒食，朱紱方來。利用享祀。征凶，無咎。
象傳：困於酒食，中有慶也。

In the second NINE ：One has been trapped by his own worries and distressed due to the lack of food and drinks, but somehow luck found him and he is awarded a position by the emperor. On this occasion, he has to be grateful for the blessings and avoid slipping into poverty again.

Xiang Chuan：Being penniless and distressed, if one keeps on making the moral choice, luck will arrive soon.

Suggestion：Contented in poverty and devoted to spirituality.

六三：困于石，據于蒺蔾 *，入于其宮，不見其妻，凶。

象傳：據于蒺蔾，乘剛也；入于其宮，不見其妻，不祥也。

In the third SIX : One is extremely distressed as if he were pressed against a big rock. He is suffering from pain as if he sits on thorny vines. He is between the hammer and the anvil. To make things worse, when going home, his wife is gone. It is a misfortune.

Xiang Chuan：He is suffering from pains as if he is sitting on thorny vines. He is now between the hammer and the anvil. To make things worse, when going home, his wife is gone. It is a misfortune.

Suggestion：Only wisdom and stamina can free him from pressure. Because of one's extramarital relationship, he is suffering. It is of his own making.

九四：來徐徐，困于金車，吝，有終。

象傳：來徐徐，志在下也；雖不當位，有與也。

In the fourth NINE : One's luxurious wagon arrives late because of an accident. It means that even a big shot person may sometimes have accidents. However, the difficulty is only a temporary obstacle, he will eventually get out of trouble.

Xiang Chuan：The wagon comes late, things will not turn around. It means that it is difficult for one's wish to come true. If one is patient, he will have the help he needs.

Suggestion：When in need of assistance, help always comes late.

九五：劓刖，困于赤紱，乃徐有說，利用祭祀。

象傳：劓刖，志未得也；乃徐有說，以中直也；利用祭祀，受福也。

In the fifth NINE : One is sabotaged by the rich and the powerful as if he were sentenced to a penalty of cutting off his nose and feet. He falls into the extreme difficulty. However, eventually he gets out of it and is acquitted. He prays to console his ancestors.

---

*註30：蒺ㄐㄧˊ 蔾ㄌㄧˊ，海邊沙地之草有刺。

Xiang Chuan：One is sabotaged by the rich and powerful and suffers the punishment of nose cutting and feet cutting, he hits rock bottom. However, eventually he gets out of the trouble by being upright. He prays to console the ancestors and is blessed by gods.

Suggestion：Punishing severely is not as good as influencing with virtues.

上六：困于葛藟，于臲卼*；曰動悔，有悔，征吉。

象傳：困于葛藟，未當也，動悔，有悔，吉行也。

In the topmost SIX：One slips into extreme difficulties as if he was entangled by vines and cannot move. If he acts rashly and blindly, things will get worse, but if he can correct his past mistakes, it is auspicious.

Xiang Chuan：One slips into extreme difficulties as if he was entangled by vines and cannot move. If he can repent and correct his past mistakes, it is auspicious.

Suggestion：Accounts differ and opinions vary. If you are moral, there won't be chaos.

48. 井 Jing

坎上 巽下

水風井

井：改邑不改井，無喪無得。往來井井。汔至，亦未繘*井，羸其瓶，凶。

象傳：木上有水，井；君子以勞民勸相。

Jing：The well. Inexhaustible. The town can be changed, but the well cannot. The water in a well stays constant. It neither dries out nor increases. The inhabitants frequently draw buckets of water to drink from the well, the water still remains

---

＊註31：臲ㄋㄧㄝˋ卼ㄨˋ，動搖不安。

＊註32：繘ㄐㄩˋ，取井水之繩。

clean and pure. While drawing a bucket of water from the well, the bucket nearly reaches the mouth of the well. Suddenly the bucket crashes and breaks due to the broken rope. The water from the bucket drops right back into the well, which is unfortunate.

Xiang Chuan：A tree sucks water from the earth to deliver to the leaves. It means that people draw buckets of water from a well. The water is inexhaustible and always available for use.

A man with noble character learns from the virtues of a well to serve people without regret and to encourage people to work hard to improve their lives.

Suggestion：To avoid failing due to the lack of a final effort.

初六：井泥不食。舊井無禽。
象傳：井泥不食，下也；舊井無禽，時舍也。

In the first SIX ：The well has not been used for a long time, the water is contaminated by mud and is undrinkable. Even birds won't drink from it. The old well should be discarded.

Xiang Chuan：The well has not been used for a long time. The water is contaminated by mud and is undrinkable. Even birds won't drink from it. The well is abandoned.

Suggestion：Those who lost touch with the times are destined to be eliminated by selection.

九二：井谷射鮒*，甕敝漏。
象傳：井谷射鮒，無與也。

In the second NINE ：There is only a little water left in the bottom of the well, only enough for small fish to live. People should stop using the well. This well is like a broken bucket and is no longer suitable to draw water.

Xiang Chuan：There is only a little water running in the bottom of the well. It means that the virtuous cannot find faithful friends.

---

*註33：鮒 ㄈㄨˋ，小鯽魚。

Suggestion：He who has talent but cannot find opportunities to use it. It is unlucky to be born at such a time when he can't put all his knowledge into use.

九三：井渫ㄒㄧㄝˋ*不食，為我心惻。可用汲，王明並受其福。

象傳：井渫不食，行惻也。求王明，受福也。

In the third NINE：The well has been cleaned, but nobody drinks from it, which makes me feel sad. Under such circumstances, the talents should be recommended to the emperor. This will benefit people.

Xiang Chuan：The water of the well has been cleaned, but nobody drinks from it. If the emperor is wise, he will recruit the virtuous to work for him so that their talents benefit people.

Suggestion：It is unlucky to be born in the wrong era. Time will not wait for me.

六四：井甃ㄓㄡˋ*，無咎。

象傳：井甃無咎，修井也。

In the fourth SIX：The well is now under construction and repair to make the water drinkable again.

Xiang Chuan：The well is now under construction and repair to make the water drinkable again. The superior man cultivates his virtues as if the well is kept in good condition.

Suggestion：To do charity happily. The talents should cultivate virtues to enrich themselves and get prepared for opportunities.

九五：井洌ㄌㄧㄝˋ*，寒泉食。

＊註34：渫ㄒㄧㄝˋ，掏出污泥。

＊註35：甃ㄓㄡˋ，以磚修井壁。

＊註36：洌ㄌㄧㄝˋ，清澈的。

象傳：寒泉之食，中正也。

In the fifth NINE : The well provides fresh, clean and cool water for drinking. Everybody likes it.

Xiang Chuan：The well provides cool, fresh and clean water to share with everybody as if a virtuous emperor grants his favors to people selflessly and fairly.

Suggestion：It doesn't matter if a hero has humble roots.

上六：井收，勿幕；有孚，元吉。
象傳：元吉在上，大成也。

In the topmost SIX : The construction and repair of a well are completed. It needs not a cover when it's fixed because everyone is sincere. It brings great fortune.

Xiang Chuan：The well gives water selflessly to people just like a virtuous person uses his talents to benefit people, which is a huge achievement.

Suggestion：The ruler should learn from the generosity of the well to give to the people and make great achievements. It will satisfy everyone.

49. 革　Ger

兌上 離下

澤火革

革：巳日乃孚。元、亨、利、貞，悔亡。
象傳：澤中有火，革；君子以治曆明時。

Ger：Reform. After a period of reform, people gradually get used to and convinced of the new laws. People believe the success of reform needs to consist of four virtues which are creativeness, prosperity, harmony and righteousness. The initial stage of the reformation is painful because people are suspicious and hold a wait-

and-see attitude. After the results of the reform are gradually shown, people will turn to support it. The concerns naturally disappear.

Xiang Chuan：Fire in the lake produces conflicts. The man with noble character is inspired by natural phenomenon and makes a new calendar to serve as a guide for planting crops.

Suggestion：A good reform takes all things on a new aspect.

初九：鞏用黃牛之革。

象傳：鞏用黃牛，不可以有為也。

In the first NINE : The thinking of the elderly is as stubborn as a piece of hard cattle leather. If the reform does not get their approval, the implementation at the beginning will be very difficult.

Xiang Chuan：At the beginning of the reform, one should be flexible to consolidate people's ideas without attempting to do something big.

Suggestion：Timing is not mature yet. Do not take action.

六二：巳日乃革之，征吉，無咎。

象傳：巳日革之，行有嘉也。

In the second SIX : The timing to reform is mature. Thus, the measures taken for the reform will not be blamed.

Xiang Chuan：The timing for the reform is mature. The implementation of the reform will win praise from people.

Suggestion：Strike while the iron is hot. Grasp good timing to proceed with the reform.

九三：征凶。貞厲。革言三就，有孚。

象傳：革言三就，又何之矣？

In the third NINE : Rushed reform will bring bad luck. Therefore, we should discuss it all over again and should welcome opinions from all sides. Wait to reach a conclusion before taking any action.

Xiang Chuan：Hearing opinions from all sides and repeated discussions can prevent failures. If it is repeatedly debated again and again, when will the conclusion be reached?

Suggestion：Reform cannot be done in one step.

九四：悔亡，有孚，改命，吉。
象傳：改命之吉，信志也。

In the fourth NINE : In the process of reform, there are no regrets because the stakeholders are sincere and understanding so they win people's trust and confidence. A successful reform is established on the foundation of public opinion, which is fortunate.

Xiang Chuan：The reform is launched based on people's understanding and trust. There are no concerns as we have strong ambitions about the reform.

Suggestion：To remove the old and to constitute the new. To sift the wheat from the chaff.

九五：大人虎變，未占有孚。
象傳：大人虎變，其文炳也。

In the fifth NINE : Supported by the people, the leader of the reform tries his best to implement the reform. The reform gives people a fresh outlook just like a tiger sheds its old fur to reveal his new striped fur. People respond well to it. There is no need to predict the future. People know the reform is going to work.

Xiang Chuan：The leader tries his best to implement the reform. The reform gives people a fresh outlook just like a tiger sheds its old furs to reveal his new striped furs Things are going well because the leader is fair and ethical.

Suggestion：Reform should give people a fresh outlook and win trust and

support from people.

上六：君子豹變，小人革面，征凶，居貞，吉。
象傳：君子豹變，其文蔚也；小人革面，順以從君也。

In the topmost SIX : The man with noble character is dedicated to implementing the reform like a panther sheds his fur to reveal his dazzling new look. However, the villains always focus on the superficial. At this time, the reform is nearly completed. If the reform still continues, it is unfortunate because people need to rest and rehabilitate.

Xiang Chuan：The man with noble character is dedicated to implementing the reform like a panther sheds his fur to reveal his dazzling new look. However, the villains always focus on the superficial. They only pretend to follow the reform of the leader.

Suggestion：The successful leader of the reform gives people time to recuperate and rest.

50. 鼎 Ding

火風鼎　　離上 巽下

鼎：元吉，亨。
象傳：木上有火，鼎；君子以正位凝命。

Ding：A kind of pot. A cooking utensil or utensil for religious ceremony. The meaning of the word ding is also extended to "providing food and care for the virtuous in the ancient." Ding symbolizes new era, monarchical power and luck. Ding also signifies great achievements and prosperity.

Xiang Chuan：Wood is burned to cook food. The man with noble character

understands that his mission is to consolidate the new government and not to disappoint people.

Suggestion：To support the virtuous and people is the mission of a nation.

初六：鼎顛趾，利出否。得妾以其子，無咎。

象傳：鼎顛趾，未悖也。利出否，以從貴也。

In the first SIX ：Flip over the Ding to make it convenient to pour out dirty stuff in the Ding and refill fresh food. This is a positive change as if a concubine has a son to carry on the family name.

Xiang Chuan：Cleaning the bottom of the Ding means to remove the old and to introduce the new. It is not against the norms. There is no blame.

Suggestion：Judge a thing by looking at all the aspects, not just one aspect.

九二：鼎有實，我仇有疾，不我能即，吉。

象傳：鼎有實，慎所之也。我仇有疾，終無尤也。

In the second NINE ：A Ding that is full of food is just like a virtuous and talented man. He will not be afraid of any jealousy from the enemies. So long as he behaves cautiously, they cannot do anything against him. It is appropriate.

Xiang Chuan：A Ding that is full of food is just like a virtuous and talented man. He will not be afraid of any jealousy from the enemy. So long as he behaves cautiously, they cannot do anything against him.

Suggestion：A talented man is not afraid of any challenge. Just, honest and unselfish.

九三：鼎耳革，其行塞，雉膏不食。方雨虧悔，終吉。

象傳：鼎耳革，失其義也。

In the third NINE ：The handles of the Ding are broken. They need to be repaired.

Without the handles, it is difficult to move it to serve the delicious pheasant meat unless the rain comes in time to cool down the temperature of the Ding so that we don't need to move it to let people enjoy delicious food.

Xiang Chuan：A Ding without handles has lost the function of serving food.

Suggestion：Virtues and talents are both indispensable.

九四：鼎折足，覆公餗*，其形渥，凶。

象傳：覆公餗，信如何也！

In the fourth NINE : A leg of the Ding is broken because of the heavy content. The delicious food held by the Ding for the Dukes is knocked over. The spilled food wet the Duke's clothes and made him feel embarrassed. It is unfortunate. It means that if one doesn't have enough capability and wisdom to shoulder heavy responsibilities, he is bound to suffer.

Xiang Chuan：The food in the Ding is knocked over, meaning one's capability may be not enough to bear heavy responsibilities.

Suggestion：An excellent supervisor assigns the right persons to the right positions.

六五：鼎黃耳金鉉，利貞。

象傳：鼎黃耳，中以為實也。

In the fifth SIX : The reform is completed. New systems are working perfectly as if the Ding is equipped with copper handles and bronze rings. It means that the reform has achieved satisfactory results.

Xiang Chuan：The Ding has solid copper handles, bronze rings for people to carry. It can hold food to serve people. Ding represents a person with both perseverance and virtues.

Suggestion：Actual strength and images.

---

*註37：餗ㄙㄨˋ，鼎中食物。

上九：鼎玉鉉，大吉，無不利。
象傳：玉鉉在上，剛柔節也。

In the topmost NINE : The Ding is decorated with jade on the rings. It looks graceful and auspicious. It brings great fortune. The Ding is now perfectly accessorized, which stands for the monarchial power. So long as the emperor rules the country with both carrot and stick, it is fortunate.

Xiang Chuan：The Ding is decorated with jade on the rings. It looks graceful but the jade attached on the rings should be well placed, with a style that is neither too masculine nor too feminine.

Suggestion：A combination of hardness and softness.

51. 震　Soong

　震上 震下
震為雷

震：亨。震來虩虩*，笑言啞啞，震驚百里，不喪匕鬯*。
象傳：洊雷，震；君子以恐懼修省。

Jehn：Thunderclaps. Spring thunder wakes up all the creatures. Although thunderclaps scare people, the man with noble character is at ease and composed. He goes on talking and laughing as if nothing had happened. He is so composed that he looks like a priest holding a religious utensil in the middle of the ceremony unimpacted by anything, even the roaring thunder.

Xiang Chuan：Thunderclaps keep striking and the man with noble character realizes that he should examine himself and cultivate his virtues.

Suggestion：Sense of urgency.

＊註38：虩ㄒㄧˋ，驚恐的樣子。
＊註39：鬯ㄔㄤˋ，古代祭祀用之香酒。

初九：震來虩虩，後笑言啞啞，吉。

象傳：震來虩虩，恐致福也；笑言啞啞，後有則也。

In the first NINE : When thunderclaps roar, people are frightened and don't know what to do at first. However, the second time around, they are used to it and stay calm. They go on talking and laughing as if nothing had happened. It brings fortune.

Xiang Chuan：People are frightened by thunderclaps. They learn from the experience and know if they remain cautious, they can turn peril into safety.

Suggestion：You can't gain knowledge without experience.

六二：震來厲，億喪貝，躋于九陵，勿逐，七日得。

象傳：震來厲，乘剛也。

In the second SIX : The shocks come brutally and suddenly. Nobody can predict the loss.

You would rather lose your money and run to the mountains than lose your life. At the critical moment, one should be composed and not care about money. After the shock, the situation has changed. Soon you will get your money back.

Xiang Chuan：When bad things happen and you cannot resist it, you should bear with it and come up with a plan to bring the situation under control.

Suggestion：While there's life, there's hope.

六三：震蘇蘇，震行無眚。

象傳：震蘇蘇，位不當也。

In the third SIX : The thunder and lightning frighten people and make people slip on the muddy road. It represents that you should handle people and things cautiously to avoid making mistakes.

Xiang Chuan：The thunder and lightning frighten people because they stay at the wrong place.

Suggestion：Adapt according to circumstances.

九四：震遂泥。

象傳：震遂泥，未光也。

In the fourth NINE : One is frightened by the thunderclaps and doesn't know what to do. He slips into the mud.

Xiang Chuan : One is frightened and slips into the mud because he indulges himself and his words and deeds are not frank and ethical.

Suggestion : Once bitten, twice shy.

六五：震往來，厲，意無喪，有事。

象傳：震往來厲，危行也；其事在中，大無喪也。

In the fifth SIX : Thunderclaps and lightening keep on striking. Accidents could happen any time. Although one tends to believe that nothing will happen, things always come unexpectedly.

Xiang Chuan : Thunderclaps and lightening keep on striking. Accidents could happen any time.

At this time, one should be more attentive. As long as one handles things morally, he will certainly succeed.

Suggestion : Beyond one's expectations. Excessive confidence in oneself.

上六：震索索，視矍矍*矍，征凶。震不于其躬，于其鄰，無咎。婚媾有言。

象傳：震索索，中未得也；雖凶無咎，畏鄰戒也。

In the topmost SIX : Thunderclaps and lightning keep on striking. Everyone is panicking. Suddenly his neighbor was struck by lightning. Although this accident had nothing to do with him, he was blamed by his friends. At this time, any discussion of marriage will invite gossip.

Xiang Chuan : Thunderclaps and lightning keep on striking. Everyone is panicking. If the lightning happens again, facing it in time is positive.

＊註40：矍ㄐㄩㄝˊ，驚恐四方觀望的樣子。

Suggestion：To harm others to benefit oneself. To make gains at others' expense.

52. 艮 Gen

艮為山　　艮上 艮下

艮：艮其背，不獲其身；行其庭，不見其人，無咎。

象傳：兼山，艮；君子以思不出其位。

Gen：Restrain. Hold. One can neither see his own back nor his own silhouette. When two people are walking in a courtyard back to back, neither one can see the face of the other. It means that one should grasp the best opportunity when it comes and hold himself from evil desires. This way, he will not have any disasters. Passively speaking, one doesn't worry about what the eyes don't see.

Xiang Chuan：Two mountains overlap each other but each stands independently. The man with noble character realizes the meaning of independence and noninterference, he will not do things against his duties and will restrain from having evil desires.

Suggestion：To stop before going too far. Well water does not intrude into river water. To hold no rank without making inquiry about it.   The man with noble character should know to stop indulging in desires.

初六：艮其趾，無咎，利永貞。

象傳：艮其趾，未失正也。

In the first SIX：Finding something wrong before action and immediately stop it. It is not wrong. However, it is advantageous to always follow the moral path.

Xiang Chuan：Finding something wrong before action and immediately stop it. It does not violate the moral principles.

Suggestion：Last-minute efforts are useless if no preparatory work has been done beforehand.

六二：艮其腓，不拯其隨，其心不快。

象傳：不拯其隨，未退聽也。

In the second SIX ：One's calves are constrained so that they are unable to move. It means one is restrained and cannot follow the great man as an apprentice. Thus he feels unhappy.

Xiang Chuan：It is difficult for one to make up his mind. He is in a dilemma and feels unhappy.

Suggestion：One's strength does not match one's ambitions. Refusing to receive good advice is sure to cause regrets.

九三：艮其限，列其夤，厲熏心。

象傳：艮其限，危熏心也。

In the third NINE ：Too many restrictions in handling people and things are just like one's loins are torn and is unable to move. This restraint negatively impacted his interpersonal relationship. The pain is as if his heart suffers from pain-causing smoke.

Xiang Chuan：Too much restraint in handling people and things negatively impacts his interpersonal relationship as if his heart suffers from pain-causing smoke. It makes him fall into danger.

Suggestion：Appropriate restrictions can sometimes buffer uneasy situations to avoid having a loss. To get the opposite of what one wants.

六四：艮其身，無咎。

象傳：艮其身，止諸躬也。

In the fourth SIX : To restrain one's upper body from moving around, which means that holding one's behaviors to avoid acting rashly. If one can give up everything, having faith to regain the peace of mind, he will not have blame.

Xiang Chuan：One can exercise self-control and not do anything that is outside of his position.

Suggestion：Whether grasping an opportunity or not sometimes decides one's fate. To fulfill one's obligation, but not haggle over trifling matters.

六五：艮其輔，言有序，悔亡。

象傳：艮其輔，以中正也。

In the fifth SIX : Holding one's mouth from talking rashly. His speeches will be well-founded and well organized. The regrets disappear.

Xiang Chuan：Only talk when it is appropriate. Your speech should follow the middle way.

Suggestion：Disaster emanates from careless talk. To speak on the grounds without nonsense.

上九：敦艮ㄎ，吉。

象傳：敦艮之吉，以厚終也。

In the topmost NINE : To restrain evil desires by means of honesty, sincerity and caution. It is a great omen.

Xiang Chuan：Insisting on being sincere, honest and discreet to the end is noble.

Suggestion：Good to begin well, better to end well. Honesty and sincerity can keep one from having distracting thoughts.

53. 漸 Jiang

巽上 艮下

風山漸

漸：女歸吉，利貞。

象傳：山上有木，漸；君子以居賢德善俗。

Jiang：Slowing evolving. Everything is developed gradually, just like the wedding of a young girl. If it follows traditional etiquette, people will give blessings and accept it.

After the wedding, a young girl becomes a member of a new family. She should follow "the three obedience's and four virtues". It is fortunate.

Xiang Chuan：Trees grow gradually and flourish in the mountains, which represents gradual development.

The man with noble character realizes that it is necessary to cultivate virtue in order to set an example for social customs.

Suggestion：Virtue cultivation and setting an example for social customs are achieved one step at a time. To change and influence unobtrusively and imperceptibly.

初六：鴻漸于干。小子厲，有言，無咎。

象傳：小子之厲，義無咎也。

In the first SIX：The big wild geese are approaching the river shore slowly. Some geese are lost and can't keep up with the rest of the team. They are nervous and uneasy as if kids encounter difficulties and get scolded.

So long as these geese fly orderly, they will not be blamed. It means that when young people just start their career, if they handle people and things properly, there is no blame.

Xiang Chuan：When young people encounter difficulties, fairly speaking, they shouldn't be blamed.

Suggestion：So long as you are realistic, progress gradually and don't act rashly, there will be no blame.

六二：鴻漸于磐ㄆㄢˊ，飲食衎ㄎㄢˋ*衎，吉。
象傳：飲食衎衎，不素飽也。

In the second SIX：The geese are approaching the rocks of the shore slowly. They find food and water on their own and have happy lives. It brings good fortune. It means that the first priority for young people is to work hard to make ends meet and look for prosperity later.

Xiang Chuan：The geese find food and water on their own and have happy lives. They are not those who have free lunch.

Suggestion：Work pragmatically to have a solid foundation in one's career, then aim at higher positions. Not to be a good-for-nothing.

九三：鴻漸于陸。夫征不復，婦孕不育，凶。利禦寇。
象傳：夫征不復，離群醜也；婦孕不育，失其道也；利用禦寇，順相保也。

In the third NINE：The geese are lost and can't help but approach the land gradually as if one's husband has been sent to the battlefield for years and never comes home. His wife has an affair and is pregnant, but bringing up the baby will be a big problem to the family. It is a misfortune. It is good for the husband to sacrifice for the nation, but it is bad for his family.

Xiang Chuan：The husband has been sent to the battlefield for years and never returns home. He neglects his family and now his wife is pregnant with another's baby. It is against the feudal ethics. It is positive for people to unite to defend against foreign aggressors and to protect the homeland.

Suggestion：To make use of one's qualities and overlook the defects. To repent in time.

＊註41：衎ㄎㄢ ˋ，快樂。

六四：鴻漸于木，或得其桷*，無咎。

象傳：或得其桷，順以巽也。

In the fourth SIX : The big wild geese approach the low and flat branches of a tree lowly to perch on so that they can rest safely. No blame.

Xiang Chuan：Perhaps the reason that the geese can find low and flat branches of a big tree to perch on is because of their virtue of patience.

Suggestion： **Even under an unstable situation, if you respond to it humbly and one step at a time, there will be no disaster. Step back and you'll see boundless sea and sky.**

九五：鴻漸于陵，婦三歲不孕，終莫之勝，吉。

象傳：終莫之勝，吉，得所願也。

In the fifth NINE : The wife can't get pregnant as the couple have not been together for three years. Eventually they overcome difficulties to get back together as if the geese quit their habits and land on the foothills. It means that difficulties are inevitable before having successes. If you make efforts continuously, the goals will be fulfilled in the end.

Xiang Chuan：The husband and wife have not been together for three years. They overcome difficulties to have a reunion. Finally, they have their wishes come true.

Suggestion： **Where there is a will, there is a way. Return to the moral course after being lost.**

上九：鴻漸于陸，其羽可用為儀，吉。

象傳：其羽可用為儀，吉，不可亂也。

In the topmost NINE : The big wild geese gradually fly away as they grow up. They fly freely around the world. Their spotless feathers can be used as religious ornaments. Even the geese appear proud and aloof, they still serve as a good

---

*註42：桷ㄐㄩㄝˊ，承屋瓦的方木。

example for future generations. It is fortunate.

Xiang Chuan：The spotless feather can be used for dancing ornamentals in the worship. It is good fortune.

It images not because of his achievements but neglects the sense of integrity.

Suggestion：Not to claim personal credit for achievement.

54. 歸妹 Gui- Mei

 震上 兌下
雷澤歸妹

歸妹：征凶，無攸利。
象傳：澤上有雷，歸妹；君子以永終知敝。

Gui- Mei：Marriage. The young girl is willing to marry a much older man, which violates social norms. Marriage is one of the most important things in life. If the marriage doesn't respect etiquette, it will not be blessed by the relatives. It means more haste, less speed.

Xiang Chuan：Thunder strikes the lake. The water is shaken by thunderclaps.

The man with noble character realizes how to enjoy a long-lasting and harmonious marriage and how to prevent mistakes to avoid regret.

Suggestion： Both sides are willing to do the thing. Respect the seniority.

初九：歸妹以娣。跛能履，征吉。
象傳：歸妹以娣，以恆也；跛能履吉，相承也。

In the first NINE ：The younger sister marrying with her elder sister to the same man as a concubine is like a crippled man is contented with his fate and keeps trying to walk. Although she cannot decide her own fate, she knows the etiquette and sticks to the principles, which brings good fortune.

Xiang Chuan：Even if she has low status, she is content with her lot as a concubine and obedient to both the first wife and the husband.

Suggestion：To be contented with one's lot.

九二：眇能視，利幽人之貞。

象傳：利幽人之貞，未變常也。

In the second NINE : For the sake of harmony at home, a wife or a husband should not be stubborn, otherwise they will fight even for the small stuff. Each should be tolerant of the other as if one of his or her eyes is closed. She never complains and never wants to get divorced even if she lives like a nun.

Xiang Chuan：The young girl is suffering from a bad marriage. She lives like a nun but still remains loyal to her husband.

Suggestion：Harmony in the family is the foundation for every success.

六三：歸妹以須，反歸以娣。

象傳：歸妹以須，未當也。

In the third SIX : Theoretically, a younger girl followed her elder sister to marry, but she pretends to be the elder sister because she prefers to be the first wife. Eventually, she still has to go back to her original status to marry as a concubine. Her attempt violates ethics.

Xiang Chuan：A young girl has inappropriate ambition to become the first wife and not a concubine. She doesn't respect the social norms that only the eldest sister becomes the first wife. She really does not know her position.

Suggestion：A slow fire makes sweet malt.

九四：歸妹愆*期，遲歸有時。

象傳：愆期之志，有待而行也。

＊註43：愆ㄑㄧㄢ，延誤。

In the fourth NINE : The young girl turns down marriage offers many times. She is expecting a Prince Charming. Although she postponed marrying herself off, she is patient to have love at first sight.

Xiang Chuan：The young girl would rather wait for an ideal husband than settle down with the first man that comes along. It is her own wish.

Suggestion：A slow fire makes sweet malt.　The road to happiness is strewn with setbacks.　He would rather go without than have something shoddy.

六五：帝乙歸妹，其君之袂，不如其娣之袂良；月幾望，吉。
象傳：帝乙歸妹，不如其娣之袂良也；其位在中，以貴行也。

In the fifth SIX : The royal family is marrying their eldest daughter off with the younger sister as the concubine. The dresses of the bride are not as glamorous as those of the younger sister. Although the groom is poor, the bride is contented with the marriage as if the moon is going full. It is very fortunate.

Xiang Chuan：The dresses of the bride are not as glamorous as those of the concubines but the bride is elegant and noble.

Suggestion：Neither money nor status can make one give up his own values. To set an example to practice female virtues.

上六：女承筐，無實，士刲*羊，無血，無攸利。
象傳：上六無實，承虛筐也。

In the topmost SIX : A wedding ceremony is held in the temple. The bride carries a bamboo basket without offerings inside to worship. The bridegroom kills a goat, but no blood is found for religious ceremony. Apparently, the wedding doesn't fit the etiquette. All guests left the wedding in disappointment. It means that the marriage exists in name only without substance.

Xiang Chuan：Carry a basket without any offerings in the wedding. It means that the marriage will not have a good result.

*註44：刲 ㄎㄨㄟ，宰殺。

Suggestion : A marriage without substance is difficult to find its happiness. Though it is tasteless, it is a pity to throw it away.

55. 豐 Feng

 震上 離下
雷火豐

豐：亨，王假之，勿憂，宜日中。
象傳：雷電皆至，豐；君子以折獄致刑。

Feng : Abundant harvest; prosperity. The country is prosperous and the people are living in safety. The emperor should make his nation prosperous just like the sun in the middle of the day, shining bright light to all sides.

Xiang Chuan : Thunder and lightning come together. This represents abundance and prosperity. The man with noble character realizes that the trials should be just and fair and is able to differentiate the smallest details. No one is suffering injustice, but the criminals receive punishment.

Suggestion : To maintain good luck by restraint. One's tolerance and open-mindedness lead to one's greatness.   To support the weak and keep the powerful under control.

初九：遇其配主，雖旬無咎，往有尚。
象傳：雖旬無咎，過旬災也。

In the first NINE : One fortunately meets a superior who appreciates and recognizes his worth. Do not overlook the ethics or bypass the superior. After a period of working together and adjusting himself, he will be highly respected.

Xiang Chuan : One fortunately meets a superior who appreciates and recognizes his worth. Do not overlook the ethics or bypass the superior. After a period of working

together and adjusting himself, he will be highly respected. So long as he does not transgress what is right, there will be no disaster.

Suggestion：Hold on to and secure present advantages.

六二：豐其蔀＊，日中見斗。往得疑疾；有孚發若，吉。

象傳：有孚發若，信以發志也。

In the second SIX ：The man with noble character at the peak of his career is just like the midday sun. Unfortunately, he is persecuted and hit as if the sunlight is completely covered by immense clouds. Even the Big Dipper can be seen in the daytime. If he tries to clarify things, it will make the misunderstanding even worse. Only sincerity can give him the strong will to overcome this challenge. It is fortunate.

Xiang Chuan：Firmly hold one's sincerity and conviction to clarify the misunderstanding. It is driven by his strong wish.

Suggestion：The rights and wrongs can eventually be identified.

九三：豐其沛，日中見沫，折其右肱，無咎。

象傳：豐其沛，不可大事也；折其右肱，終不可用也。

In the third NINE ：The villains are in power now. The sky is completely covered by the clouds. Little stars twinkle in the daytime as if the right arm of a talent is broken and he can achieve nothing. Now that he is in such a situation, he is seeking only to avoid blame and play safe.

Xiang Chuan：The villains are in power now, the sunshine is completely covered as if the right arm of the talent is broken and unable to utilize his talent to do anything worthwhile. His arm is broken, he is unable to fully use his talent in the long run.

Suggestion： While there's life, there's hope. To compromise out of consideration for the general interest. To be worldly wise and play safe to avoid blame.

＊註45：蔀ㄅㄨˋ(bu)，遮蔽。

九四：豐其蔀，日中見斗；遇其夷主，吉。

象傳：豐其蔀，位不當也；日中見斗，幽不明也；遇其夷主，吉行也。

In the fourth NINE : While he is looking to enrich his life, he always comes across obstacles as if the sunshine is completely covered by the clouds, only the Dipper can be seen in the daytime. If he is appreciated by a virtuous emperor, he will not go astray.

Xiang Chuan：While he is looking to enrich his life, he always comes across obstacles as if the sunshine is completely covered by the clouds, only the Dipper can be seen in the daytime. If he is appreciated by a virtuous sovereign, he is lucky enough to fulfill his ambition.

Suggestion：Never lose oneself because of setbacks. A muddle-head regime would rather adopt the democratic system of Cohabitation.

六五：來章，有慶譽，吉。

象傳：六五之吉，有慶也。

In the fifth SIX : An emperor should be farsighted and have the sense to make uses of talents to make the country prosperous. It deserves blessings.

Xiang Chuan：It is fortunate as he brings in the talent.

Suggestion：Diligence makes up for deficiency. A ruler will not desert the virtuous. It brings good fortune to the nation.

上六：豐其屋，蔀其家，闚其戶，闃*其無人，三歲不覿，凶。

象傳：豐其屋，天際翔也；窺其戶，闃其無人，自藏也。

In the topmost SIX : By living in a large and impressive mansion to glorify his family, he selfishly alienates his family from people. Nobody can visit the house easily. As a result, the house has been vacant for years.

The situation continues without changes for three years. The house owner closed

---

*註46：闃ㄑㄩˋ，靜寂的。

himself from the outside world and alienates himself from others. It is unfortunate.

Xiang Chuan：By living in a large and impressive mansion to glorify his family, he alienates himself from the outside world. He is like a bird soaring alone in the sky and contented with himself. He selfishly secludes himself and the family from the world.

Suggestion：Arrogance causes isolation and misfortune.

56. 旅 Lu

 火山旅   離上 艮下

旅：小亨，旅貞吉。

象傳：山上有火，旅；君子以明慎用刑，而不留獄。

Lu: Traveling. People who travel for business ask only for convenience, not for luxury. The travelers are forced to leave home and wander about from place to place. They only ask for safety, which is their basic requirement. It is too early to talk about good fortune.

Xiang Chuan：The fire in the mountain keeps burning. This means travelling. The man with noble character realizes that all trials should be examined carefully without delay and avoid mistrials.

Suggestion：When in Rome, do as the Romans do.

初六：旅瑣瑣，斯其所取災。

象傳：旅瑣瑣，志窮災也。

In the first SIX：Haggling over details in travelling is due to his lowly character. All the troubles are derived from improper deeds and of one's own making.

Xiang Chuan：Haggling over details in travelling is due to his lowly character and

poor upbringing. Poverty chills his ambition, all the troubles are derived from improper deeds and of one's own making.

Suggestion：Haggling over every penny hurts one's reputation.

六二：旅即次，懷其資，得童僕，貞。

象傳：得童僕，貞，終無尤也。

In the second SIX：During travelling, meals and accommodations are well arranged. With sufficient money and a faithful young boy servant in company, one can follow the right path.

Xiang Chuan：During the travelling, having a loyal young boy servant in company makes it easy to run your errands, he will not have any complaints finally.

Suggestion：While travelling, money is everything but your behavior should be modest and low-profile.

九三：旅焚其次，喪其童僕，貞厲。

象傳：旅焚其次，亦以傷矣；以旅與下，其義喪也。

In the third NINE：The hotel caught fire during the trip. Unfortunately, his young boy servant left him because he generally mistreats him. He lost his help, so he has to handle everything by himself. At this moment, he has to keep following the ethical route to avoid disaster.

Xiang Chuan：The hotel caught fire during the trip. It is surely a misfortune. The master is arrogant to his servant. In a sense, he deserves to lose his help. It is of his own making.

Suggestion：A guilty conscience needs no accuser.

九四：旅于處，得其資斧，我心不快。

象傳：旅于處，未得位也；得其資斧，心未快也。

In the fourth NINE : A temporary accommodation is found while travelling. He found a hatchet to cut down thistles and thorns to build a temporary lodge but he feels unhappy. It represents "east or west, home is best" or it might also imply that one has not been recognized and supported by his superior. He still encounters many difficulties.

Xiang Chuan : While travelling, he found a temporary lodge. Although he got a hatchet to cut down thistles and thorns to build a temporary place for the night, he feels depressed and frustrated as his lofty ambition has not been fulfilled yet.

Suggestion : A hero has no chance of using his might.

六五 : 射雉，一矢亡，終以譽命。
象傳 : 終以譽命，上逮也。

In the fifth SIX : He shoots a pheasant but loses an arrow. Even if there is the loss of an arrow, he gains some and loses some. He still receives praise and promotion. It means that travelling inevitably encounters inconvenience and loss. If the traveler is humble and modest to follow local customs, he will have a smooth trip and unexpected gains.

Xiang Chuan : He shoots a pheasant but loses an arrow. Even if there is the loss of an arrow, he gains some and loses some. He still receives praise and promotion. Because of his good relationship with others, he eventually has the blessings to get promotion as he pleased the emperor.

Suggestion : Do not worry about personal gains and losses. Do not lose big things because you try to haggle over small things.

上九 : 鳥焚其巢，旅人先笑後號咷；喪牛于易，凶.。
象傳 : 以旅在上，其義焚也；喪牛于易，終莫之聞也。

In the topmost NINE : The bird nest in the tree caught fire. The traveler who saw it didn't feel sad as if his house were burned down. Worse of all, he laughed at it. Never did he expect to see his place get burned down as well afterwards. He couldn't help but cry out. The traveler lost the calmness as if a tamed cow goes wild. His future trip will be even more difficult.

Xiang Chuan：Normally, a traveler shouldn't be arrogant and hard to deal with. If he is like this, nobody will care about how tough his trip gets.

Suggestion：Extreme pleasure is followed by sorrow.

57. 巽 Xun

巽為風　　巽上 巽下

巽：小亨，利有攸往，利見大人。

象傳：隨風，巽；君子以申命行事。

Xun：Unassuming, submissive. To deal with people with an unassuming attitude enables you to change people's adversity and give you a favorable situation. Therefore, things go smoothly for him everywhere and fortune always finds him. He is so modest that great men appreciate him so much that they give him an important position which benefits his future career.

Xiang Chuan：The wind blows into every little crack of any surface as if the laws are put into effect thoroughly. The man with noble character realizes that it takes repeated reminding to effectively put the law into practice just like the wind has to keep blowing to cover all the surface.

Suggestion： Where the wind passes, the grass bends.

初六：進退，利武人之貞。

象傳：進退，志疑也; 利武人之貞，志治也。

In the first SIX：When one doesn't know whether he should step out or retreat, he is sometimes too humble and hesitates to make a fast decision. If he can learn the

virtues from a soldier to make up his flaws of being indecisive, it is fortunate.

Xiang Chuan：Indecisiveness and irresolution make one confused and inefficient. The virtues of a soldier can encourage and strengthen his will.

Suggestion： Humbleness can help you to progress. The reason that you miss opportunities for success is because of indecisive character.

九二：巽在床下，用史巫紛若，吉，無咎。

象傳：紛若之吉，得中也。

In the second NINE ： The subject kneels down under the bed of the emperor to report to him. There is no blame as he just shows his deference and loyalty to win the trust from the emperor. The devotion is like that of witchcraft or a missionary. In principle, there is no blame.

Xiang Chuan：The subject frequently shows his sincerity and deference to the emperor. This corresponds to the spirits of the "golden mean".

Suggestion：Neither overbearing nor servile. To be the same outside and inside.

九三：頻巽，吝。

象傳：頻巽之吝，志窮也。

In the third NINE ： One is totally unwilling to follow, but the situation forces him to pretend to be obedient. The humiliation is completely caused by himself.

Xiang Chuan：One is not willing to become a cow that follows others, but he still does due to the lack of ambition.

Suggestion：A shaky and unsteady mind will not achieve anything.

六四：悔亡，田獲三品。

象傳：田獲三品，有功也。

In the fourth SIX : If you take the chance firmly and make use of it, you will not have regrets. The subject is instructed by the emperor to promote the useful and abandon the harmful, eventually he enjoys both success and fame as if he got many kills in the hunting to provide rich offerings to God, treating guests or personal meals.

Xiang Chuan：Immediately he got three hunting kills, he did establish merits and achievements and win promotion.

Suggestion：Do not think opportunity will knock at your door twice.

九五：貞吉，悔亡，無不利。無初有終，先庚三日，後庚三日，吉。
象傳：九五之吉，位正中也。

In the fifth NINE : There will not be disadvantages if you follow the ethical way. Nobody can be sure of the outcome of the new laws. In order to be certain of the feasibility of the new laws and see if they are accepted by the people, the notice is issued three days before they are put into practice. The cautious attitude will bring good fortune.

Xiang Chuan：In order to be certain of the feasibility of the new laws and see if they are accepted by the people, the reminder is sent to the public again and again before the announcement. Then the government will review and improve some time after the announcement of the new laws to check the pros and cons. The cautious attitude will bring fortunes as it is doing the right thing.

Suggestion：World belongs to everybody.

上九：巽在床下，喪其資斧，貞凶。
象傳：巽在床下，上窮也；喪其資斧，正乎凶也。

In the topmost NINE : One is so humble that he kneels down beside the bed and disregards his dignity. He ignores the moral path and even lost his travel money and his hatchet. He has to persist on the moral path to avoid disaster.

Xiang Chuan：One is so humble that he kneels down beside the bed and disregards

his dignity. He is really at the end of his rope. He even lost his travel money and the drive (hatchet). It is totally unfortunate.

Suggestion：To bow and scrape. Worry about gains and losses. Over-correcting a mistake is not the right way to be successful.

58. 兌 Duei

 兌為澤 兌上 兌下

兌：亨，利貞。

象傳：麗澤，兌；君子以朋友講習。

Duei：Joyful. While meeting people, no one wouldn't want to hear pleasant words and deal with sincere people. However, pleasing others needs to be based on principles too.

Xiang Chuan：Two lakes connect together. This represents enjoyable communication. The man with the noble character realizes that gathering with friends to discuss principles and truths benefits one another.

Suggestion：To learn from each other by exchanging views to avoid being ignorant and ill-informed.

初九：和兌，吉。

象傳：和兌之吉，行未疑也。

In the first NINE：Treat people with joy and sincerity. You will get along with them and you'll not have any worries. It is a good omen.

Xiang Chuan：Treat people with joy and sincerity. You won't be blamed or suspected.

Suggestion：Do not play favorite and do not be selfish. Then you won't be suspected.

九二：孚兌，吉，悔亡。
象傳：孚兌之吉，信志也。

In the second NINE : It is auspicious if you treat people with sincerity and a joyful mind. Then the remorse disappears.

Xiang Chuan：If you treat people with sincerity and a joyful mind, it will bring fortune because of your trustworthiness.

Suggestion：Long term friendship depends on mutual sincerity.

六三：來兌，凶。
象傳：來兌之凶，位不當也。

In the third SIX : To please others hypocritically in order to have gains will attract bad luck.

Xiang Chuan：Trying to benefit from hypocritical flattery will bring bad luck.

Suggestion：To flatter to gain favor is shameful.

九四：商兌未寧，介疾有喜。
象傳：九四之喜，有慶也。

In the fourth NINE : Trying to use flattery to please others only makes one lose his peace of mind. He should rather give up the evil thought so that the positive things can happen.

Xiang Chuan：Getting rid of evil thoughts is worthy of celebration.

Suggestion：To refuse the evil so as to avoid trouble and attract good luck.

九五：孚于剝，有厲。
象傳：孚于剝，位正當也。

In the fifth NINE : When one has power and status, there easily come many

flatteries and support from all sides. He will easily be tempted. It is unfortunate.

Xiang Chuan：If you occupy a critical position, the villains will possibly suck up to you. Thus, the sincerity is compromised. The serious outcome is not difficult to imagine.

Suggestion：He who gives fair words feeds you with an empty spoon.

上六：引兌。

象傳：上六引兌，未光也。

In the topmost SIX : Using every possible way to flatter is shameful.

Xiang Chuan：Tempting or flattering people to have personal gain is not honorable.

Suggestion：To do things offensive to God and reason.

59. 渙 Huan

巽上 坎下

風水渙

渙：亨。王假有廟，利涉大川，利貞。

象傳：風行水上，渙；先王以享于帝立廟。

Huan. Slacking. Breaking up. It is fortunate to unite people's hearts. Because people are of different minds, the emperor should invite clan relatives and subjects to gather together at the ancestral temple to worship to unite people. The gathering can help to cope with the adventures and adversities. It also enables one to stick to the moral choice.

Xiang Chuan：The winds blow on the surface of the water and create ripples. Ripples represent that people are of different minds. The emperor realized that to unite people, he needs to build ancestral temples for people to pray to God together.

Suggestion：Make herculean efforts to turn the situation.

初六：用拯馬壯，吉。

象傳：初六之吉，順也。

In the first SIX : Take advantages of powerful and effective measures to reunite and motivate people in the beginning. It will turn the adverse situation into a good one.

Xiang Chuan：It is fortunate for an emperor to listen to constructive advice and take timely measures to prevent people from having different minds.

Suggestion：In case of emergency, handling it timely is always the key to success. As urgent as sparks that may start conflagration, it is not allowed to incur loss through delay.

九二：渙奔其机，悔亡。

象傳：渙奔其机，得願也。

In the second NINE : When people are facing dangers because of breaking apart, they are always finding shelters first for survival.

They flee to find a low stool to take a refuge when there is natural disaster such as an earthquake. There will be no regrets.

Xiang Chuan：When people are facing dangers because of breaking apart, they will react immediately by instinct to seek for shelter.

Suggestion：To look for a better job while holding on to the present one.

六三：渙其躬，無悔。

象傳：渙其躬，志在外也。

In the third SIX : While people are of different minds, the man with noble character should restrain his personal desires and take the priority to consider public interests. There will be no regret.

Xiang Chuan：The ambition of a man with noble character is to relieve the public and bring justice to the whole world.

Suggestion：Disregard oneself and consider the public interest as the first priority.

六四：渙其群，元吉。渙有丘，匪夷所思。

象傳：渙其群，元吉，光大也。

In the fourth SIX ：When private political parties are breaking apart, it is a great omen. Because diverse small groups can form a big group to unite the whole country. It is beyond imagination and will bring good fortune.

Xiang Chuan：Uniting people through small groups for the wellbeing of the whole nation is honorable.

Suggestion：Unity of will is an impregnable stronghold.

九五：渙汗其大號，渙王居，無咎。

象傳：王居無咎，正位也。

In the fifth NINE ：When there are centrifugal forces dividing people, the emperor still enforced the laws without compromise, as if the sweat never goes back to your body. The emperor should be composed when giving command to avoid chaos. This is his duty. There is no blame.

Xiang Chuan：When there are centrifugal forces dividing people, the emperor should be composed when giving command in order to stabilize the people to avoid chaos. It is his obligation.

Suggestion：Military orders cannot be challenged or revoked. Suit the actions to the words.

上九：渙其血去逖出，無咎。

象傳：渙其血，遠害也。

In the topmost NINE ：Things will go in the opposite direction when they become extreme. When people are divided by centrifugal forces to the extreme, eventually some opposite forces will pull them back and they will be reunited together. The worries and terrors will be gone. There is no blame.

Xiang Chuan：When people are divided by centrifugal forces to the extreme, the situation looks too serious to reverse but if the emperor is not too worried or scared about it, there will be disaster.

Suggestion：After a long period of division, the country tends to unite. After a long period of union, the country tends to divide.

60. 節 Jier

 坎上 兌下
水澤節

節：亨。苦節，不可貞。

象傳：澤上有水，節；君子以制數度，議德行。

Jier：Temperance. Temperance is a virtue. When there is neither too much nor too little, the balance is reached. In short, if temperance suits the actual condition, it is fortunate. If there is too much temperance, it is to impose a difficult task on the people. Too much restraint on the public will make people feel painful. This is not right.

Xiang Chuan：Water flows into the lake. If water is overflowing, it will be wasteful or cause flooding. The man with noble character realizes the criteria for etiquette on food, clothing, housing and transportation and makes relevant laws and principles so that people have standards to follow.

Suggestion：Too much is as bad as too little. The most difficult is set a standard. Taking measures according to the time and the place.

初九：不出戶庭，無咎。

象傳：不出戶庭，知通塞也。

In the first NINE : One is aware that the timing is inappropriate. He restrained himself to stay at home to wait for good opportunities. He will act when the time is right. Before that, he will be cautious about his words and deeds. He carefully judges and decides if it is suitable to step out of the courtyard. Because he is so prudent, there will be no blame.

Xiang Chuan：One knows the value of temperance. He knows whether the time is right to step out of the house. If the timing is not mature yet, he never leaves his house. He is prepared for the opportune moment to take action.

Suggestion：Waiting it out to make the right move. He that talks much errs much.

九二：不出門庭，凶。

象傳：不出門庭，凶，失時極也。

In the second NINE : Too much self-constraint makes him never leave home for a long time. The isolation will bring misfortune as the opportunity only comes once.

Xiang Chuan：One is extremely restrained and never steps out of the courtyard. He missed a good opportunity.

Suggestion：Hesitate to move forward. Miss the boat.

六三：不節若，則嗟若，無咎。

象傳：不節之嗟，又誰咎也。

In the third SIX : He got out of control and depleted all the resources and ended up sighing with regrets. However, if he can correct in time, there will be no blame.

Xiang Chuan：One lost control, he reaps the fruit of his own making. He can blame nobody but himself.

Suggestion：One regrets that things haven't been done the other way.

六四：安節，亨。

象傳：安節之亨，承上道也。

In the fourth SIX : People are content to exercise self-control. The nation is in prosperity and people live in safety. It is a great omen.

Xiang Chuan：People are content to exercise self-control. Their behavior shows that they surrender to the will of the emperor.

Suggestion：Let nature take its course and have an easy conscience in mind, which leads to prosperity.

九五：甘節，吉，往有尚。

象傳：甘節之吉，居位中也。

In the fifth NINE : Moderate control makes people totally willing to cooperate. Reasonable policies make people develop habits to follow them. The administration is efficient and highly praised.

Xiang Chuan：Moderate control brings good fortune as it is followed in accordance with the doctrine of the means.

Suggestion：Moderate control takes both reason and people's feelings into consideration.

上六：苦節，貞凶，悔亡。

象傳：苦節貞凶，其道窮也。

In the topmost SIX : Impose too much control on people, then, they will think it is an oppression because it has deviated from its good will. Therefore, control has to be appropriate to avoid regret.

Xiang Chuan：Too much control on people will not work out. It will cause more pain than results.

Suggestion：Food is next to the God to the people.

61. 中孚 Zhong Fu

 巽上 兌下
風澤中孚

中孚：豚魚，吉。利涉大川，利貞。

象傳：澤上有風，中孚; 君子以議獄緩死。

Zhong Fu：Sincerity. If you are sincere, even offering pigs and fish while praying is not shabby. It makes good fortune. Sincerity is applicable everywhere in the world so long as one always does the right things. With this conviction, any challenge will be overcome.

Xiang Chuan：The winds blow over the lake, which represents virtues widely spread over the nation.

The man with noble character realizes that you need to be fair and sincere to judge criminal cases and he also recommends that criminals with death penalty be treated humanely.

Suggestion：God values the lives of all creatures. It is our innate virtue to cherish the lives of all creatures.

初九：虞吉，有它不燕。

象傳：初九虞吉，志未變也。

In the first NINE：Never trust somebody in the beginning too fast, but evaluate his sincerity first before believing him. This is fortunate. As soon as you stop being doubtful, your belief in him will be unswerving. Otherwise, you will feel uneasy.

Xiang Chuan：As soon as you stop being doubtful, your belief in him will be unswerving. If the sincerity remains unchanged from the start to the end, it is fortunate.

Suggestion：If there is doubt in his mind, he will not be free from worries.

九二：鳴鶴在陰，其子和之；我有好爵，吾與爾靡*之。
象傳：其子和之，中心願也。

In the second NINE : Although they are far apart from each other, their sincerity echoes with each other just like the crane is singing under the trees, while baby cranes naturally respond nearby. The joy from the warm interaction is just like when I have delicious wine, I share with you happily.

Xiang Chuan：The sincere response from the baby cranes comes truly from their hearts.

Suggestion：Misfortune tests the sincerity of friends. Sincerity makes hearts echo perfectly with one another.

六三：得敵，或鼓或罷，或泣或歌。
象傳：或鼓或罷，位不當也。

In the third SIX : A man without sincerity is a man without achievement. After all, he will not be trusted. When the war happens, you can see changing emotions from the following scenes: enemies were beating drums to advance bravely, they stopped, they lost their morale, they were crying due to a defeat or they were singing because of a triumph. If the soldiers do not have firm conviction, they will be lost.

Xiang Chuan：One minute the soldiers are beating drums to advance, the next minute they start to retreat. It means that the soldiers are not under good command.

Suggestion：It is dangerous for you to have half-assed sincerity.

六四：月幾望，馬匹亡，無咎。
象傳：馬匹亡，絕類上也。

In the fourth SIX : Having reliance and full support from people is just like the

---

*註47：靡ㄇㄧˇ，共同。

lunar full moon has the unmatched brightness. On the contrary, losing people's trust is like a weak horse unable to compete in the race, falling into a pathetic situation. However, from the standpoint of pure competition, that's life. No one should be blamed.

Xiang Chuan：For survival, horses compete in racing. The weaker ones have pitiful fates and the strong ones dominate the world.

Suggestion：The law of the jungle. Survival of the fittest. Leaving temporarily doesn't mean you lost everything. It just means you adapted to the circumstances.

九五：有孚攣如，無咎。
象傳：有孚攣如，位正當也。

In the fifth NINE : Winning people's confidence and support with sincerity is just like twin brothers support each other from the bottom of their hearts. There will be no blame. It means that sincerity can win positive response from people.

Xiang Chuan：Being able to grasp opportunities and meet the expectation of the public reflects the virtue of the doctrine of the mean.

Suggestion: Winning the public is a solid foundation for a government. To show utter devotion.

上九：翰音登於天，貞凶。
象傳：翰音登於天，何可長也？

In the topmost NINE : A rooster sings so loudly that its voice travels across the sky but it doesn't sound solid. It means that one feels so cocky that he thinks he is the king of the world. He better start practicing modesty. Otherwise, his arrogance will bring misfortune.

Xiang Chuan：A rooster sings so loudly that its voice travels across the sky but it doesn't sound solid. It represents that while lacking sincerity, how can his words and deeds last long?

Suggestion：Unrealistic speech and empty fame will not have favorable responses from the public.

62. 小過　Xiao Guo

 震上 艮下
雷山小過

小過：亨，利貞。可小事，不可大事；飛鳥遺之音，不宜上，宜下，大吉。
象傳：山上有雷，小過；君子以行過乎恭，喪過乎哀，用過乎儉。

Xiao Guo：A small mistake. Small mistakes are inevitable. As long as you learn from your mistakes, correct them and guide yourself back to the ethical path, it will bring luck. You should start by handling small things. Do not promise things that are beyond your ability. Do not let small problems worsen into big troubles that are difficult to fix. You should stay low profile to give people a good impression. Even when a bird flies very high, its loud singing can still be heard by people. It is much more auspicious for a bird to quietly fly low such as a person should stay low profile.

Xiang Chuan：The thunderclaps are a little louder at the peak of a mountain. The man with noble character realized that he should be humble, frugal, stay low profile and show true sorrow during a funeral to set good example and enlighten people.

Suggestion：Neither too much nor not enough is good.

初六：飛鳥以凶。
象傳：飛鳥以凶，不可如何也。

In the first SIX：A bird flaunts its ability to fly high without knowing that it would be easily shot.

Xiang Chuan：A bird flaunts its ability to fly high without knowing that it is easily

shot. It means that a person overdoes things without listening to others. He is hopeless.

Suggestion：To reach for what is beyond one's grasp. To get into the blind alley. A trouble of one's own making.

六二：過其祖，遇其妣²，不及其君，遇其臣，無咎。

象傳：不及其君，臣不可過也。

In the second SIX : Ancient people value ethics very much. One wants to meet with his grandfather but happens to meet his grandmother. It's a coincidence. One wants to be summoned by the emperor but instead he happens to see his subordinate. It is also a coincidence. In both cases, there is nothing to be blamed.

Xiang Chuan：Although it is a pity not to be summoned by the emperor but one cannot force his chance. There are certain principles to be followed.

Suggestion：Keep one's duty and having a sense of priority. Know how far to go and when to stop.

九三：弗過防之，從或戕之，凶。

象傳：從或戕之，凶如何也。

In the third NINE : Even if there are no mistakes, one should still take precautions. Not taking any precaution will invite disasters.

Xiang Chuan：If you let things be or indulge yourself, it is easy for you to be set up by villains. How terrible it is!

Suggestion：To take precautions against a disaster.

九四：無咎。弗過遇之，往厲必戒，勿用永貞。

象傳：弗過遇之，位不當也；往厲必戒，終不可長也。

In the fourth NINE : Because of low rank, one dare not act beyond his position. There is no blame. If the circumstance forces him to act outside of his responsibilities, he surely has to bear the risk. Everything should be done according to different requirements of individual cases instead being done inflexibly.

Xiang Chuan：Even when you're only dealing with a small mistake, you can still prevent it. Don't wait until a mistake is made to act upon it. Prior precaution prevents poor performance.

Suggestion：Adapt according to different circumstances.

六五：密雲不雨，自我西郊；公弋-取彼在穴。
象傳：密雲不雨，已上也。

In the fifth SIX : Dark and dense clouds are floating from the western suburbs, but no rain is brought. The Duke ties a rope to an arrow to shoot birds, but he still catches nothing. The duke can only find prey in the cave. It means that the subordinates cannot come up with any tactic to give to the emperor. The will is strong but the body is weak. Even when there is a coming opportunity, he is still incompetent for the task.

Xiang Chuan：Dark clouds are taking over the sky, but they bring no rain as if the evil stands at a favorable spot.

Suggestion：The will is strong but the body is weak.

上六：弗遇過之，飛鳥離之，凶，是謂災眚。
象傳：弗遇過之，已亢也。

In the topmost SIX : To act arrogantly just like a bird flaunts its superiority of flying very high but ends up getting caught by the net. The tragedy is completely of its own making. It means that one cannot face his mistakes honestly.

Xiang Chuan：Suffering from pain as a result of his arrogance.

Suggestion：Stop before going too far. Turn bad luck into good fortune. To think highly of oneself.

63. 既濟 Jih-Jih

 坎上 離下

水火既濟

既濟：亨小，利貞，初吉終亂。

象傳：水在火上，既濟；君子以思患而豫防之。

Jih-Jih：Completeness. One has completed one's business goals. It is fortunate. To rise or fall in life is uncertain. One has to do good deeds and restrain himself from doing bad things. Be careful that extreme joy is always followed by extreme sorrow as things will develop in the opposite direction when they become extreme.

Xiang Chuan：Water can flow above fire, which represents cooking is complete. However, water and fire are not compatible. The man of noble character learned that if he doesn't plan for the long-term future, he will have worries in the near term.

Suggestion：Be prepared for danger in times of peace.

初九：曳-其輪，濡其尾，無咎。

象傳：曳其輪，義無咎也。

In the first NINE：The wheels of a wagon are pulled backwards to reach a balance to avoid fast driving. A fox wets its tail to slow its speed to cross the river. Such caution will prevent tragedies.

Xiang Chuan：To pull the wheels of a wagon backwards so the wagon can go in balance and move steadily. In a sense, it is prepared for danger in times of peace.

Suggestion：Precaution against any tragedy. To maintain the achievements of our predecessors is not easy.

六二：婦喪其茀*，勿逐，七日得。

象傳：七日得，以中道也。

---

*註48：茀ㄈㄨˊ，飾物。

In the second SIX : When you are successful and well off, never sweat over trivial things just like a woman lost her jewelry. Pay attention to the big picture. Be patient and the lost items would be returned in a week. After all, money is not an inherent part of the human being. It means to never look back but welcome the future with caution. Avoid suffering a big loss for a little gain.

Xiang Chuan：The jewelry will be returned in seven days. Trust that people tend to do the right thing.

Suggestion：Have confidence and take the world as it is. Don't look back, but care for the future.

九三：高宗伐鬼方，三年克之，小人勿用。
象傳：三年克之，憊也。

In the third NINE : During the Shang dynasty, the monarch Kao-Zong launched a war against the rebellion in Gui Feng without a justified cause. It took three years before the rebellion was crushed. Afterwards, it is unwise to assign important positions to people without virtue. On the contrary, you should give them rewards to calm them down.

Xiang Chuan：It took three years to squash the rebellion. The nation is exhausted and the people are poor.

Suggestion：Militarism exhausts public funds and manpower.

六四：繻＊有衣袽＊，終日戒。
象傳：終日戒，有所疑也。

In the fourth SIX : For safety reasons while sailing the boat, the sailors always have ragged clothes ready to serve as stuffing in case of leaking. The sailors are attentive and cautious on the lookout for possible leakages.

Xiang Chuan：The sailors are always attentive and on the lookout for possible

---

＊註49：繻ㄒㄩ，彩帛。

＊註50：袽ㄖㄨˊ，破舊衣物。

leakages. They do their best to guard the safety of the boat.

Suggestion：Be industrious and frugal. There is no danger if you're well prepared. No danger of anything going wrong.

九五：東鄰殺牛，不如西鄰之禴祭，實受其福。

象傳：東鄰殺牛，不如西鄰之時也；實受其福，吉大來也。

In the fifth NINE : The neighbor country from the east provides a cow to worship the God while some other country from the west only provides simple offerings. However, the former country's blessing is not as big as the latter. It represents that the neighbor country from the east doesn't respect the principles of frugality.

Xiang Chuan：The country in the east provides a handsome sacrifice. However, its blessing is not as big as the other country that only prepares simple offering. This is because the country from the west worships regularly and sincerely so it receives more blessing from the gods.

Suggestion：Hold on your faith and things will go your way.

上六：濡其首，厲。

象傳：濡其首厲，何可久也？

In the topmost SIX : While the fox almost crossed a river, it got so excited that it was drowning. It was dangerous. It means that if a successful man cannot control his desires and act cautiously, his success won't last long.

Xiang Chuan：While the fox almost crossed a river, it got so excited that it was drowning. It is dangerous. If there were no solid rescue plans, how can it last long?

Suggestion：To be faced with imminent disaster. Pride leads to loss while modesty brings benefits.

64. 未濟　Weih-Jih

 離上 坎下
火水未濟

未濟：亨，小狐汔ˋ*濟，濡其尾，無攸利。

象傳：火在水上，未濟; 君子以慎辨物居方。

Weih-Jih：Incomplete. The target has not been reached yet, one has to continue to the end. It brings fortune. It is just like a fox intending to cross a river, but it carelessly soaks its tail. It turns all the previous labor to nothing.

Xiang Chuan：Fire is on water, which can't cook the food. It means that things cannot be done. The man with noble character carefully identifies and categorizes things to make everything fall into the right place.

Suggestion：To fall short of success for lack of a final effort. It reminds and encourages people to carry out an undertaking from start to end.

初六：濡其尾，吝。

象傳：濡其尾，亦不知極也。

In the first SIX：The fox really goes out of its depth to cross the river alone only to find that it soaks the tail and still doesn't know it is time to stop. What a shame!

Xiang Chuan：The fox really goes out of its depth to cross the river alone only to find that it soaks the tail. His wish of crossing the river was crushed. The fox doesn't even know how deep the river is now.

Suggestion：Be conservative. Do not act rashly. Wait it out.

九二：曳其輪，貞吉。

象傳：九二貞吉，中以行正也。

---

*註51：汔ㄑ一ˋ，接近，幾乎。

In the second NINE : A man with noble character should watch his words and deeds as if a wagon has brakes to control the wheels to avoid disasters. If one insists on doing the right things, it is fortunate.

Xiang Chuan : The man with noble character handles people carefully just like a wagon has brakes to avoid driving out of control. If he is ethical, his words and deeds will be appropriate and unprejudiced.

Suggestion : Haste makes waste.

六三 : 未濟，征凶。利涉大川。
象傳：未濟，征凶，位不當也。

In the third SIX : The ambition has not been achieved yet. If you rush it, it is dangerous. On the contrary, if you are fully prepared beforehand and advance fearlessly, it will be fortunate.

Xiang Chuan : The ambition has not been fulfilled yet. If you advance hastily, it is dangerous. The failure is always due to inadequate preparations.

Suggestion : Nothing ventured, nothing gained.

九四 : 貞吉，悔亡，震用伐鬼方，三年有賞于大國。
象傳：貞吉，悔亡，志行也。

In the fourth NINE : One should always do the right things. It is auspicious. Naturally, you won't have any regrets.

In the name of justice, it takes three years to crush the tribe Guei Feng. The commander receives heavy rewards and praises from the emperor.

Xiang Chuan : It is fortunate for you to insist on doing the right things. Naturally, you won't have any regrets. The wish of squashing the foreign tribes is fulfilled.

Suggestion : To persevere continuously.

六五 : 貞吉，無悔。君子之光，有孚，吉。

象傳：君子之光，其暉吉也。

In the fifth SIX : Do the right things consistently and naturally you won't have regrets. The virtues of a man with noble character are just like sunshine, bringing good wishes and luck to people.

Xiang Chuan：The virtues of a man with noble character are just like sunshine illuminating the world. It not only brightens himself but also benefits the people.

Suggestion：The virtues of an emperor are like the sunshine. People enjoy the kindness happily.

上九 ：有孚於飲酒，無咎；濡其首，有孚失是。
象傳：飲酒濡首，亦不知節也。

In the topmost NINE : One is confident to succeed. Sharing delicious wine with friends happily is not wrong, but if you drink so much as to pour wine over your heads, you have overdone it.

Xiang Chuan：One is confident to succeed. Share delicious wine with friends happily is not wrong, but if you drink so much as to pour wine over your head, you have overdone it. It turns all the previous efforts to nothing.

Suggestion：If you cannot control yourself, it is very likely for you to be reminded by this saying later-"Extreme pleasure is followed by sorrow."

第二篇 **Part Two**

現代風水
Modern
Feng Shui

北

西　　　　　　　東

南

Chapter 1 Feng Shui consultation examples 風水勘查實例

1. Electric pole 電線桿

There was a residence in Tu Cheng City, which was located on the SE side and faced the NW side. An electric pole with transformers stood right on the Si (NW) -front right of the house. The house owner, always drunk, rambled on all day and often slept in front of neighbors' houses, causing lots of inconvenience to the community. The owner was born in 1941(Xin Si zodiac sign is snake). I immediately took out a convex mirror and attached it to the wall of his house reflecting right back to that problem electric pole.

Two months later, I called his wife to ask if her husband situation has improved. She happily replied that her husband was no longer drunk all day and was now working in his son's printing shop.

2. Birdcage and money problems 鳥籠與寅吃卯糧

A husband bought a birdcage with several lovely birds from some night market. Strange to say, afterwards the family always ran into money problems. After the feng shui survey, the key issue was that the birdcage was inappropriately placed at the rear balcony.

👍 Solution : The birdcage should be replaced at the front balcony.

3. Sewing machine leads to marriage problems 縫紉機/夫妻失和

Many years ago, a popular American sewing machine was promoted with installment plans and the payment was collected by the salesman monthly at home. Therefore, the convenience was much appreciated by the housewives. Like her neighbors, Mrs. Huang bought one as well. Half a year later, the husband and wife were growing apart because of small problems. I was invited to do a Feng Shui inspection of the house and found the location of the sewing machine in the bedroom was causing their marriage problems.

👍 Solution : Remove the sewing machine from the bedroom.

4. Climbing the separation ladders　樓梯/太太回娘家

I was once brought by a woman to her younger brother's house to inspect the Feng Shui. Her brother had a fight with his wife due to small issues but the wife was so angry that she left and went back to her parents' home for over two weeks. After the inspection, I found the problem was caused by a ladder misplaced at the position of Zi which was in conflict with the zodiac sign of his wife. (The wife was born in 1948 – zodiac sign: rat.) In fact, the ladder, used to climb up to the attic, was only taken out when someone needed to access the attic. However, because of the inconvenience, people started to leave the ladder there.

👍 Solution : Always remember to remove the ladder after use.

5. Fireplace/ fire accident　火爐/火災

I was invited to Denver, USA to do a Feng Shui consultation for a Chinese businessman - Mr. Wang. He was very sociable and knew a lot of people. Among the guests that day, a journalist said to me, "I'm sorry to say that many westerners don't believe in Feng Shui. To convince them, could you tell us what has happened in this house?" For a few seconds, like a switch, the room became dead silent. I immediately took out a Chinese Compass (Luo-Pan) and checked the house. A few minutes later, I smiled to the journalist and said the house had a fire accident. It might have happened in 1993. All of a sudden, the room burst into applause.

The reason is : The house is on the Yin (NE) side and the fireplace was located on the Si (SE). No wonder a fire accident happened. The accident occurred in 1993 when the goblin star entered into the SE where the fireplace was.

👍 Solution : The location of the fireplace should be moved forward about two feet at Bing (丙). Accidents like this will never happen again.

6. The importance of changing the location of an Altar　神明桌之更動

A woman invited me to conduct a Feng Shui inspection of her house in 2011. She complained that her husband, who used to be easy going, has had a bad temper for the past two years. She also mentioned that the location of the altar had been moved to a more spacious space.

After the inspection, I found that the house was situated on the Zi (north) side and the malevolent side is on the east of the house. The altar was set on the Mao, Yi (east), directly conflicting her husband's zodiac sign that is rabbit (Mao) as well. The bad temper of her husband was then clearly understood.

👍 Solution：2011 was Xin Mao year so the altar should not be set on the west facing east. The altar should not be located on the malevolent side-east. I suggested that the altar be moved around 3 feet backwards, to the north east side of the house.

Chapter 2 Basic Concepts of Feng Shui 風水基本概念

1. Origins 風水緣由

Feng Shui was developed by Chinese about three thousand years ago. It is a philosophy of harmonizing people with the surrounding environment–

天，乾卦，代表西北方；

澤，兌卦，代表西方；

火，離卦，代表南方；

雷，震卦，代表東方；

風，巽卦，代表東南方;

水，坎卦，代表北方;

山，艮卦，代表東北方;

地，坤卦，代表西南方。

heaven (hexagram Chian- NW),

lake (hexagram Duei-W), a large area of water that is surrounded by land,

fire (hexagram Li- South),

thunder (hexagram Jehn- E),

wind (hexagram Xun- SE),

water (hexagram Kaan- N),

mountain (hexagram Gen- NE)

and land - surface of the earth (hexagram Kun- SW).

Modern Feng Shui is a guide to orient a house and working environments (interior and exterior) in an auspicious manner to bring luck, fortunes, longevity, happiness and wealth to people.

2. A house that optimizes all the Feng Shui principles in ancient China 中國古代 風水之樣板屋

The ancient Chinese paid a lot of attention to their health and the harmony of their living environment because Chinese believe that physical health is a reflection of the harmony of environment.

A good Feng Shui house follows some basic guidelines: it sits on the North side and faces on the South side. The left side of a Feng Shui house should have a stream called "Blue Dragon", serving as the water source that is crucial for day-to-day living. The "Blue Dragon" symbolizes the career development of the family members. The right side is called the "White Tiger", symbolizing the property and wealth of the family. The South side should have a pond called "Red Bird", signifying the potential and the prospect of the family. If the house is overlooking a spacious land, its residents are sure to enjoy plenty room to grow and free from worry. The rear end or the North side of the house is called the "Xuan Wu", or "Black Tortoise", which symbolizes strong backing. The residents tend to feel comfortable as if they were sitting on armchairs.

北 N
後玄武(靠山)
"Xuanwu"(tortoise) signifies strong backing.

西 W
右白虎(長廊)

Right side of a house is a long lane called "White Tiger".

東 E
左青龍(溪流)

Left side of a house Should have a stream that is called "Blue Dragon".

南 S
前朱雀(池塘)
The pond in front of a house is called "Red Bird".

鑫富樂文教編輯部繪製

樣板屋 The typical Feng Shui house

座北朝南 A Feng Shui house should sit on the North and face on the South. A typical Feng Shui house is sitting on the North and facing the South. Most houses in ancient were constructed like this. The main reason was that people living in this type of houses could stay warm in winter and cool in summer. If the main door is located on the left side or dragon side (southeast) of the house, the people would not suffer chilly winds from the Northwest. This was their principle.

Currently, every piece of land is worth a lot of money in the city. It is almost impossible to own a house completely satisfying the criteria of a Feng Shui house. Because "Blue Dragon" is afraid of foul smell, putting the toilets on the dragon side is a no-no. Thus people will at least require dragon side to be taller than white tiger side. Moreover, since the "Dragon" side doesn't fear bustling, in fact, the more people coming in and out, the more money it helps to generate, the front door of a house should open on the "Dragon" side. On the contrary, the "White Tiger" (right side) is afraid of bustling. Consequently, people should not insist on Feng Shui directions inflexibly, we shall use Ba-Gua as a tool to analyze the Feng Shui energy to bring positive change.

Q&A

Q1: If a house neither has a stream on the left nor a corridor on the right. Is there any way it can still attract good energy?

A1:

Busy streets in the city center can be seen as streams (but it is a taboo for a shop to face the cut of a road curve), the arcade of the shops on the right is also suitable for business purpose.

Q2: If you sit in the living room and face the front door, your left side of the house is the dragon side and your right side of the house is the white tiger side?

A2:Yes.

Q3: It is said the tiger side of the house shouldn't be taller than the dragon side. Please explain.

A3:

The dragon side of the house represents "men" in the family. In Chinese culture, men have higher position in the family because he has to earn money for the whole family. However; "women" in the family have to take care of the house and raise children. Therefore, the main door on the dragon side of the house is equal to an air hole that people get in and out frequently. It will make the family prosperous and wealthy. On the contrary, if the white tiger side is taller than the dragon side, it is equal to a tiger opening its mouth to hurt people, which leads to family disputes and financial problems.

Q4: The dragon is afraid of foul smells and the tiger is afraid of noises. Is it true? Please explain.

A4:

The Feng Shui model house is sitting on the north and facing the south. If the toilets are located on the dragon side, the wind from southeast in the summer will generate bad smell and make the whole house unsanitary. In addition, it easily attracts ill-fated loves. The tiger side of the house favors quietness. If the two sides switch, the women in the family tend to gain a lot of power and cause the family live in disagreement.

3. 現代風水原理：Modern Feng Shui can also be defined as a philosophy to balance the energies of any given space to assure mental and physical health and good fortunes for people inhabiting it.

For example, people's blood contains iron, so our blood circulation as well as our overall health are influenced by magnetic fields of the earth. In addition, the year you were born and the gender difference-male (Yang) or female (Yin) also have an impact on your birth karma.

4. 基本瞭解 Basic Knowledge

天干地支 The Decimal Cycle											
天干 The Decimal Cycle	甲 Jia	乙 Yi	丙 Bing	丁 Ding	戊 Wu	己 Ji	庚 Geng	辛 Xin	壬 Ren	癸 Gui	
地支 Earthly branch	子 Zi	丑 Chou	寅 Yin	卯 Mao	辰 Chen	巳 Si	午 Wuu	未 Wei	申 Shen	酉 You	戌 Xu	亥 Hai

生肖與地支 Zodiac symbols and Earthly branch											
生肖 Zodiac symbols	鼠 Rat	牛 Ox	虎 Tiger	兔 Rabbit	龍 Dragon	蛇 Snake	馬 Horse	羊 Goat	猴 Monkey	雞 Rooster	狗 Dog	豬 Pig
地支 Earthly branch	子 Zi	丑 Chou	寅 Yin	卯 Mao	辰 Chen	巳 Si	午 Wuu	未 Wei	申 Shen	酉 You	戌 Xu	亥 Hai

天干地支與生肖五行方位關係

Relationships among heavenly stems, earthly branches, zodiac signs, five elements & directions:

五行 Element	天干 Decimal	地支 Zodiac	生肖 Symbol	方位 Direction
木 Wood	甲乙 Jia, Yi	寅卯 Yin, Mao	虎兔 Tiger, Rabbit	東 East
火 Fire	丙丁 Bing, Ding	巳午 Si, Wuu	馬蛇 Horse, Snake	南 South
土 Earth	戊己 Wu, Ji	辰戌丑未 Chen, Xu, Chou, Wei	龍狗牛羊 Dagon, Dog, Ox, Goat	中央 Central
金 Metal	庚辛 Geng, Xin	申酉 Shen, You	猴雞 Monkey, Rooster	西 West
水 Water	壬癸 Ren, Gui	亥子 Hai, Zi	豬鼠 Rat, Pig	北 North

六十年甲子(干支表) Table of sexagenarian cycles

1 甲 Jia	2 乙 Yi	3 丙 Bing	4 丁 Ding	5 戊 Wu	6 己 Ji	7 庚 Geng	8 辛 Xin	9 壬 Ren	10 癸 Gui
甲子 Jia Zi 1804 1864 1924 1984	乙丑 Yi Chou 1805 1865 1925 1985	丙寅 Bing Yin 1806 1866 1926 1986	丁卯 Ding Mao 1807 1867 1927 1987	戊辰 Wu Chen 1808 1868 1928 1988	己巳 Ji Si 1809 1869 1929 1989	庚午 Geng Wuu 1810 1870 1930 1990	辛未 Xin Wei 1811 1871 1931 1991	壬申 Ren Shen 1812 1872 1932 1992	癸酉 Gui You 1813 1873 1933 1993
甲戌 Jia Xu 1814 1874 1934 1994	乙亥 Yi Hai 1815 1875 1935 1995	丙子 Bing Zi 1816 1876 1936 1996	丁丑 Ding Chou 1817 1877 1937 1997	戊寅 Wu Yin 1818 1878 1938 1998	己卯 Ji Mao 1819 1879 1939 1999	庚辰 Geng Chen 1820 1880 1940 2000	辛巳 Xin Si 1821 1881 1941 2001	壬午 Ren Wuu 1822 1882 1942 2002	癸未 Gui Wei 1823 1883 1943 2003
甲申 Jia Shen 1824 1884 1944 2004	乙酉 Yi You 1825 1885 1945 2005	丙戌 Bing Xu 1826 1886 1946 2006	丁亥 Ding Hai 1827 1887 1947 2007	戊子 Wu Zi 1828 1888 1948 2008	己丑 Ji Chou 1829 1889 1949 2009	庚寅 Geng Yin 1830 1890 1950 2010	辛卯 Xin Mao 1831 1891 1951 2011	壬辰 Ren Chen 1832 1892 1952 2012	癸巳 Gui Si 1833 1893 1953 2013
甲午 Jia Wuu 1834 1894 1954 2014	乙未 Yi Wei 1835 1895 1955 2015	丙申 Bing Shen 1836 1896 1956 2016	丁酉 Ding You 1837 1897 1957 2017	戊戌 Wu Xu 1838 1898 1958 2018	己亥 Ji Hai 1839 1899 1959 2019	庚子 Geng Zi 1840 1900 1960 2020	辛丑 Xin Chou 1841 1901 1961 2021	壬寅 Ren Yin 1842 1902 1962 2022	癸卯 Gui Mao 1843 1903 1963 2023
甲辰 Jia Chen 1844 1904 1964 2024	乙巳 Yi Si 1845 1905 1965 2025	丙午 Bing Wuu 1846 1906 1966 2026	丁未 Ding Wei 1847 1907 1967 2027	戊申 Wu Shen 1848 1908 1968 2028	己酉 Ji You 1849 1909 1969 2029	庚戌 Geng Xu 1850 1910 1970 2030	辛亥 Xin Hai 1851 1911 1971 2031	壬子 Ren Zi 1852 1912 1972 2032	癸丑 Gui Chou 1853 1913 1973 2033
甲寅 Jia Yin 1854 1914 1974 2034	乙卯 Yi Mao 1855 1915 1975 2035	丙辰 Bing Chen 1856 1916 1976 2036	丁巳 Ding Si 1857 1917 1977 2037	戊午 Wu Wuu 1858 1918 1978 2038	己未 Ji Wei 1859 1919 1979 2039	庚申 Geng Shen 1860 1920 1980 2040	辛酉 Xin You 1861 1921 1981 2041	壬戌 Ren Xu 1862 1922 1982 2042	癸亥 Gui Hai 1863 1923 1983 2043

5. Feng Shui Compass (Luo-Pan) 風水指南針(羅盤)

A Chinese feng shui compass, also called (Luo-Pan), is used to access deeper information on a site. It has Ba-Gua（*eight basic trigrams or eight directions), each trigram contains 3 mountains. Eight directions therefore have 24 mountains. The compass is a basic instrument to determine the precise direction of a structure. With the use of the compass, a Feng Shui consultant can decide whether a dwelling is auspicious to the habitants or not.

6. 8 basic Gua (trigrams) 八個基本卦 / 八個方位：

	基本卦 8 Basic Gua	方位 Direction
一 1	乾卦 Chian	西北 NW
二 2	兌卦 Duei	西 W
三 3	離卦 Li	南 S
四 4	震卦 Jehn	東 E
五 5	巽卦 Xun	東南 SE
六 6	坎卦 Kaan	北 N
七 7	艮卦 Gen	東北 NE
八 8	坤卦 Kun	西南 SW

鑫富樂文教編輯部繪製

7. "8 Feng Shui Fate" produced 八個風水命

東四命：1 坎、3 震、4 巽、9 離

4 East Fate:1 Kaan, 3 Jehn, 4 Xun, 9 Li

西四命：2 / 5 坤、6 乾、7 兌、8 艮

4 West Fate:2/5 Kun, 6 Chian, 7 Duei, 8 Gen

Each birth year corresponds to a different "Feng Shui Fate". The followings are the references of the Feng Shui Fate.

項目 Item	風水命 Feng Shui Fate	命卦 Fate divined by trigrams	五行屬 Five Elements	男性 Male	女性 Female
\multicolumn{6}{	c	}{八個風水命出生西元年份 The conversion of Eight Feng Shui fates from Lunar years into Western years.}
1	東四命 4 East Fates	坎 Kaan	水 Water	1918, 1927, 1936, 1945, 1954, 1963, 1972, 1981, 1990, 1999, 2008, 2017	1914, 1923, 1932, 1941, 1950, 1959, 1968, 1977, 1986, 1995, 2004, 2013
2	西四命 4 West Fates	坤 Kun (同5) (Same as 5)	土 Earth	1917, 1926, 1935, 1944, 1953, 1962, 1971, 1980, 1989, 1998, 2007, 2016	1915, 1924, 1933, 1942, 1951, 1960, 1969, 1978, 1987, 1996, 2005, 2014
3	東四命 4 East Fates	震 Jehn	木 Wood	1916, 1925, 1934, 1943, 1952, 1961, 1970, 1979, 1988, 1997, 2006, 2015	1916, 1925, 1934, 1943, 1952, 1961, 1970, 1979, 1988, 1997, 2006, 2015
4	東四命 4 East Fates	巽 Xun	木 Wood	1915, 1924, 1933, 1942, 1951, 1960, 1969, 1978, 1987, 1996, 2005, 2014	1917, 1926, 1935, 1944, 1953, 1962, 1971, 1980, 1989, 1998, 2007, 2016
5	西四命 4 West Fates	坤 Kun (同2) (Same as 2)	土 Earth	1914, 1923, 1932, 1941, 1950, 1959, 1968, 1977, 1986, 1995, 2004, 2013	1918, 1927, 1936, 1945, 1954, 1963, 1972, 1981, 1990, 1999, 2008, 2017
6	西四命 4 West Fates	乾 Chian	金 Metal	1913, 1922, 1931, 1940, 1949, 1958, 1967, 1976, 1985, 1994, 2003, 2012	1919, 1928, 1937, 1946, 1955, 1964, 1973, 1982, 1991, 2000, 2009, 2018
7	西四命 4 West Fates	兌 Duei	金 Metal	1912, 1921, 1930, 1939, 1948, 1957, 1966, 1975, 1984, 1993, 2002, 2011	1920, 1929, 1938, 1947, 1956, 1965, 1974, 1983, 1992, 2001, 2010, 2019
8	西四命 4 West Fates	艮 Gen	土 Earth	1920, 1929, 1938, 1947, 1956, 1965, 1974, 1983, 1992, 2001, 2010, 2019	1912, 1921, 1930, 1939, 1948, 1957, 1966, 1975, 1984, 1993, 2002, 2011

項目 Item	風水命 Feng Shui Fate	命卦 Fate divined by trigrams	五行屬 Five Elements	男性 Male	女性 Female
9	東四命 4 West Fates	離 Li	火 Fire	1919, 1928, 1937, 1946, 1955, 1964, 1973, 1982, 1991, 2000, 2009, 2018	1913, 1922, 1931, 1940, 1949, 1958, 1967, 1976, 1985, 1994, 2003, 2012

8. 五行相生相剋 Five elements are the basic elements of the universe and everything in our world is a compound of the five elements, which are either "mutual generating" or "mutual overcoming".

相生 Mutual Generating	
木 Wood	火 Fire
火 Fire	土 Earth
土 Earth	金 Metal
金 Metal	水 Water
水 Water	木 Wood

相剋 Mutual Overcoming	
木 Wood	土 Earth
土 Earth	水 Water
水 Water	火 Fire
火 Fire	金 Metal
金 Metal	木 Wood

235

9. To decide the central point of a house 房子中心點量測

The magnetic needle of the Compass（Luo-pan）always points to the central point of Zi, which is exactly at the central point of the north. The central point of a house is located at the cross area of two diagonal lines. If the center isn't on an auspicious location for a house, the family will have trouble bonding. If the central point is located in the restrooms, on the toilet bowls, elevators or escalators, the family members will not be able to live in harmony and will also encounter financial difficulties.

There are eight directions and twenty-four mountains. Each direction has three mountains, which amounts to 24 mountains. 八個方位二十四山：每個方位有三個山，八個方位共二十四山。

	方位 Directions	二十四山　24 Mountains		
(1)	（北 N） （坎 Kaan）	壬 Ren (337.5-352.5)	子 Zi (352.5-7.5)	癸 Gui (7.5-22.5)
(2)	（東北 NE） （艮 Gen）	丑 Chou (22.5-37.5)	艮 Gen (37.5-52.5)	寅 Yin (52.5-67.5)
(3)	（東 E） （震 Jehn）	甲 Jia (67.5-82.5)	卯 Mao (82.5-97.5)	乙 Yi (97.5-112.5)
(4)	（東南 SE） （巽 Xun）	辰 Chen (112.5-127.5)	巽 Xun (127.5-142.5)	巳 Si (142.5-157.5)
(5)	（南 S） （離 Li）	丙 Bing (157.5-172.5)	午 Wuu (172.5-187.5)	丁 Ding (187.5-202.5)
(6)	（西南 SW） （坤 Kun）	未 Wei (202.5-217.5)	坤 Kun 217.5-232.5)	申 Shen (232.5-247.5)
(7)	（西 W） （兌 Duei）	庚 Geng (247.5-262.5)	酉 You (262.5-277.5)	辛 Xin (277.5-292.5)
(8)	（西北 NW） （乾 Chian）	戌 Wu (292.5-307.5)	乾 Chian (307.5-322.5)	亥 Hai (322.5-337.5)

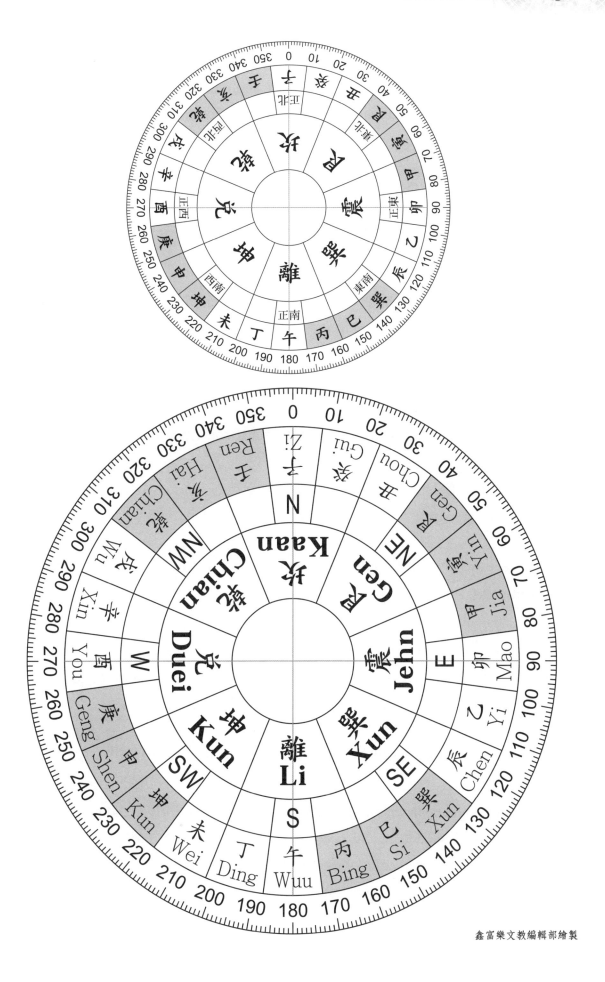

鑫富樂文教編輯部繪製

10. The Sitting and Facing Direction of a House 房屋座向

1st floor：Stand in the center of the house and face the direction of the door plate. The house is usually located on the same direction of the front door. Use the Compass to determine the sitting and facing direction.

Condos or apartments on the 2nd floor or higher: Stand in the center of the apartment and face the front balcony. Use the Compass to decide the sitting and facing direction.

Sites in a building on the 2nd floor or higher : Stand in the center of the house and face the direction of the front of the building, then find your direction.

☯ Feng Shui Q&A

Q1: How to find out the central point of a three-floor house?

A1:

Each floor has different central point. For a three-floor house, we have to measure each floor separately.

Q2: It is said the tiger side of the house shouldn't be taller than the dragon side. Please explain.

A2:

Front and rear balconies of a house should be ignored from the study of landscape as they do not have foundations. However, if the balcony has foundations laid under, it should be taken into considerations of the study of landscape.

Q3: How to locate the central point of a building (1-3 fl) with arcade?

A3:

The arcade should be taken out from the study of landscape. Even though the landlord owns the arcade legally, people have the right to pass through. Therefore, when locating the central point of the 1st, 2nd and the 3rd floor, arcades need not be considered.

Q4: Some buildings have terraces that are similar to balconies with foundations under. Shall we include the terraces when we do the study of landscape?

A4:

As long as the terraces have foundations beneath, they should be included.

Q5: Some buildings use the 1st and the 2nd floor as corridor or walkway. The 3rd floor above serves as offices and apartments. How to decide central points of this type of buildings?

A5:

If the 1st and the 2nd floors are used as the walkway of the building and there are no walls defining inside from outside, the apartments/offices above have no central points. Of course, it is not good from Feng Shui perspective. Unless the business units are in busy districts, they tend to have big sales pressure. For example, the stations of MRT have open entrances and exits on the 1st floor. Above the station are offices or apartments, which have no foundations. When locating the central point of an apartment, the study of landscape should exclude the areas without foundations.

Q6: If the basements (B1, B2 and B3) serve as parking lots of the building, the central points of the residents above should ignore the parking lot to find central points? Many buildings are mostly like this.

A6:

If B1, B2 and B3 of the building are parking lots, the residents above need not consider the foundations to find the central points as the parking lots are owned by everyone living in the building. Therefore, central points can be easily found.

Q7: If the basements are rented out to be a shopping mall, the residents above should exclude the shopping mall to find their central points?

A7:

If the basements of the building are rented out to be a shopping mall, the residents above can find their central points normally because the basements are owned by the community of this building.

Q8: While finding the central points, is there any level of differences in spaces opening to the outside without any compartments?

A8:

Yes, there is.

Q9: If the 1st floor serves as business space and the 2nd floor above are apartments, when doing the study of landscape, should we ignore the foundations?

A9:

If the 1st floor serves as business space and the 2nd floor above are apartments, you can easily locate the central points since the business unit does not belong to the public area.

Chapter 3 Easy guide to pick a house with good Feng Shui
住屋之基本選擇

1. 風水命：The first step is to align the "Feng Shui Fate" of the house owner with the sitting and facing direction of the house.

	戶長的風水命 Feng shui fates of the house owner			避免的住屋座向 Avoids to live the house sites	
(1)	1 坎命 Kaan			辰 Chen 戌 Xu	丑 Chou 未 Wei
(2)	2 坤命 Kun	5 坤命 Kun	8 艮命 Gen	乾 Chian	兌 Duei
(3)	4 巽命 Xun	3 震命 Jehn		乾 Chian	兌 Duei
(4)	6 乾命 Chian	7 兌命 Duei		離 Li	
(5)	9 離命 Li			坎 Kaan	

2. To decide which floor to live in for an apartment or a condo, the Chinese element of the house owner needs to be at least compatible or preferably "mutual generating" with the element of the number of the floors. The Five Elements are Wood, Fire, Earth, Metal and Water. Each element is strongly related to one another.

屋座向 House directions	1 樓 1F	2 樓 2F	3樓 3F	4樓 4F	5樓 5F
東 E	木 Wood	火 Fire	土 Earth	金 Metal	水 Water
東南 SE	木 Wood	火 Fire	土 Earth	金 Metal	水 Water
南 S	火 Fire	土 Earth	金 Metal	水 Water	木 Wood
西南 SW	土 Earth	金 Metal	水 Water	木 Wood	火 Fire
東北 NE	土 Earth	金 Metal	水 Water	木 Wood	火 Fire
西 W	金 Metal	水 Water	木 Wood	火 Fire	土 Earth
西北 NW	金 Metal	水 Water	木 Wood	火 Fire	土 Earth
北 N	水 Water	木 Wood	火 Fire	土 Earth	金 Metal

Example：

Feng Shui fate of "8 Gen" has the Element of Earth. The sitting direction of the apartment is on the South (Fire). Which floor is suitable for the Feng Shui fate of 8 Gen to live in?

Answer： Sitting direction on the south (Fire)：1st FL (Fire) & 2nd FL (Earth) are both suitable for fate 8 Gen (Earth) to live in as 1st FL(Fire) is mutually generating to 8 Gen (Earth), 2nd FL (Earth) is compatible with the 8 Gen (Earth) .

Chapter 4 Feng Shui and the front door 門

A door is the entrance to a house, like the face of a man.

通常下列不應在屋前或屋門前：**Thus you should avoid having or facing the following objects or constructions in front of a house or the house door.**

1. A Temple, Church or a "cross" of a church with the exception of the cross of a hospital.

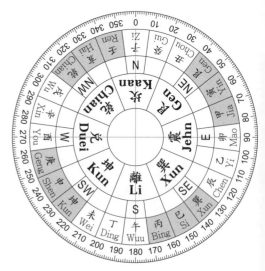

2. An electric pole, a power plant, or an electric tower.

3. Public restrooms, a garbage dump, an incinerator.

4. A crematorium, a cemetery, a withered tree, a vine covered wall.

5. A gas station or a chemical plant.

6. A court house, a garage entrance or a pedestrian bridge.

7. A tunnel, a small alley, a crooked road, the gap between two buildings.

8. A chimney, a police station and a fire department.

9. The ridge of a roof, the corner of a house and a triangle-shaped building.

10. A cliff and a river bank.

11. An archway or an archway taller than the front door could spoil the Feng Shui and might attract fire accidents.

12. Frequent use of the side doors instead of the main door might cause the husband of the house to become lazy.

13. A good feng shui front door should not face the elevator. It might cause the male master to lose money.

14. Avoid the direct alignment of the front door with the back door as good energy coming from the front door would escape easily through the back door.

15. Avoid a front door that opens in to a cramped space and directly connected to a road. This might attract danger.

16. A crooked tree in front of the house.

17. A well in front of the house is not good.

18. The front door should not directly face a warehouse entrance.

19. The front door should avoid facing the road with either of the following direction - Zi, Wuu, Mao or You thus it might cause the inhabitants to have extramarital relationships.

20. The front door that is next to a restroom might bring bad luck.

21. Too many doors in a business space, especially in a shop, might cause quarrels among customers and the employees, with the exception of a department store or a mall.

22. If a front door with another door very close to it, the male master of the house might be prone to have mistresses.

23. The front door faces a corner of another house.

24. The front door is located at the hollow corner on the NW.

25. The front door is located at the hollow or protruding corner on the SW.

26. The front door of a corner house faces the intersection of two crossing roads.

27. The front door of a corner house opens to a cramped space and directly faces a road.

28. The front door should not face any corner or sharp object.

29. The front door should not face a fence entrance.

30. The front door should not be at the protruding part of a house.

31. Avoid wiring on the front door.

32. Any house or door(s) should not face a Y-shaped road.

33. Any house or door(s) should not face a dead end.

34. For in-home businesses, avoid the front door located on the SW or on the NE.

35. A small house with more than two doors might cause the family members to disagree with one another.

1. **住家大門設點建議 The good Feng Shui locations of the front doors are suggested**

as follows:

It is recommended that the front door be located facing the following directions:

North: Ren, Gui;   **East**: Jia, Yi;   **South**: Bing, Ding;

West: Geng, Xin.

Other mountains (directions) are good as well but it depends on the Chinese zodiac signs of the family members since some directions may conflict the family's animal signs.

House door location suggested as followings:

住家大門 Main Door	設點建議 Suggested Locations	
北方 North	壬 Ren（337.5-352.5）	癸 Gui（7.5-22.5）
東方 East	甲 Jia（67.5-82.5）	乙 Yi（97.5-112.5）
南方 South	丙 Bing（157.5-172.5）	丁 Ding（187.5-202.5）
西方 West	庚 Geng（247.5-262.5）	辛 Xin（277.5-292.5）

2. 營業場所之大門 The Main Door of a Business

Many people believe that for a business to make money easily, the main door should have the following locations:

屋座向 House directions	店門設點 Preferred door location	忌諱門 Taboo door location
壬 Ren	艮、丙 Gen, Bing	巽、午 Xun, Wuu
子 Zi	兌、丑、丁、巳 Duei, Chou, Ding, Si	坤、亥 Kun, Hai
癸 Gui	兌、丁、巳、丑 Duei, Ding, Si, Chou	坤、乙、辰 Kun, Yi, Chen
丑 Chou	子、癸、申、辰 Zi, Gui, Shen, Chen	坤、申 Kun, Shen
艮 Gen	午 Wuu	庚、丁、丑 Geng, Ding, Chou

屋座向 House directions	店門設點 Preferred door location	忌諱門 Taboo door location
寅 Yin	丙、艮 Bing, Gen	坤、丁、未 Kun, Ding, Wei
甲 Jia	辛、巽 Xin, Xun	坤、申 Kun, Shen
卯 Mao	坤、乙 Kun, Yi	乾、乙、辰 Chian, Yi, Chen
乙 Yi	庚、卯、亥、未 Geng, Mao, Hai, Wei	巽、丑 Xun, Chou
辰 Chen	兌、丁、巳、丑 Duei, Ding, Si, Chou	巽、丁、未 Xun, Ding, Weih
巽 Xun	乾、甲 Chian, Jia	乙、丙、子 Yi, Bing, Zi
巳 Si	子、癸、申、辰 Zi, Gui, Shen, Chen	巽、乙、辰 Xun, Yi, Chen
丙 Bing	巽、午、壬、寅 Xun, Wuu, Ren, Yin	乾、亥 Chian, Hai
午 Wuu	艮、丙 Gen, Bing	乾、艮、丁、未 Chian, Gen, Ding, Wei
丁 Ding	子、癸、申、辰 Zi, Gui, Shen, Chen	艮、丁、未 Gen, Ding, Wei
未 Wei	坤、乙 Kun, Yi	艮、乙、辰 Gen, Yi, Chen
坤 Kun	庚、卯、亥、未 Geng, Mao, Hai, Wei	甲、癸、午 Jia, Gui, Wuu
申 Shen	巳、丑、丁、兌 Si, Chou, Ding, Duei	艮、亥 Gen, Hai
庚 Geng	坤、乙 Kun, Yi	艮、丁、未 Gen, Ding, Wei
酉 You	子、癸、申、辰 Zi, Gui, Shen, Chen	艮、巽、申 Gen, Xun, Shen
辛 Xin	乾、甲 Chian, Jia	丑、巽 Chou, Xun
戌 Xu	艮、丙 Gen, Bing	巽、丁、未 Xun, Ding, Wei
乾 Chian	巽 Xun	乙、酉、子 Yi, You, Zi
亥 Hai	乙 Yi	巽、乙、辰 Xun, Yi, Chen

Chapter 5 Bedroom臥室

Your bedroom is a place to rest and sleep. There is no need of bright lighting. Curtains can be installed if necessary. 一般臥室的禁忌 The taboos in your bedroom.

1. Avoid hanging swords in your bedroom.

2. A dressing table located in the east of a sleeping room is not good. Avoid a dressing table facing to the beds as well.

3. Mirrors should not face your bed. The same rule applies to a mirror facing another mirror.

4. The television set shouldn't face the bed.

5. Needles, knifes, scissors are not allowed to put into the dressers of a bed, especially a bed of a pregnant woman.

6. Sewing machine should not be put in the bedroom, because it will make couples to have fights.

7. No need to put potted plants in your bedroom.

8. A home aquarium in your bedroom is not recommended, but a small fish bowel is permitted.

9. Avoid installing a bed under the beams of a house.

10. The headboard of a bed usually is set against the wall. Avoid having a bed which three sides are against the walls, at most two sides.

11. The room of a domestic helper should not be on the NW, N, W and the SW of a house.

12. Avoid having an open skylight in your bedroom.

13. Having too many art lamps in a bedroom is not good.

14. The door of a bedroom should not face the staircase, kitchen, rest rooms and especially the toilet bowel.

15. The doors of two bedrooms should not face each other as it would cause the inhabitants to have fights easily.

246

16. Facing the door of a bedroom, the doorknob should not be on the right side of the door. A good feng shui doorknob should be on the left side.

17. The bed facing the door of another room is not good.

18. It is not allowed to have hanging objects such as cabinets, shelves or paintings in a bedroom.

19. Don't hang anything above the headboard of a bed in case of falling objects.

20. Beds are not allowed to be located under the toilets of an upper apartment as it would attract misfortunes to the person sleeping under.

21. Too many round objects in a bedroom is not good.

22. A tea or a coffee maker beside the bed is not allowed.

23. Beds are usually 70 cm（not over 85 cm）above the ground.

24. The headboard of a bed should be kept closely against the wall.

25. The bed of a pregnant woman should not be moved at all even for cleaning.

26. The pictures of ancestors should not be hung in your bedroom.

27. Lighting installed right on top of the headboard is not good.

28. A bedroom should not have round windows.

29. A bedroom should not have a big clock as the noise will have adverse impact on sleeping.

The positions of your pillows are very important to the health of the sleepers. A school of Feng Shui indicates that people with "4 East Feng Shui fates" should have their pillows placed on the east, southeast and the south north but those with "4 West Feng Shui fates" should have their pillows placed on the northwest, southwest, west and the northeast. This shows that if pillows are not properly placed, the sleepers' health will have problems.

不同生肖有其不宜之枕頭的位置，除外其餘皆安全，就會有好的睡眠與健康。

Here are the detailed "forbidden positions" for each of the animal signs in Chinese astrology. Except for the forbidden positions, the rest is safe for placing the pillows. Properly placed pillows will enable you to enjoy a sound sleeping and good health.

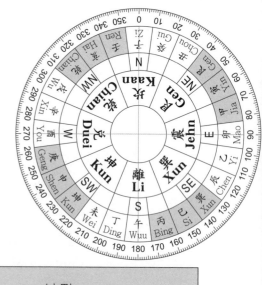

	生肖 Chinese Signs		枕頭位置 pillows location (差 wrong)	缺點 shortage
(1)	鼠 Rat	馬 Horse	子 Zi	神經衰弱、記性變差及肝臟的毛病。 Neurasthenia, memory loss and liver problems.
(2)	牛 Ox	羊 Goat	丑 Chou	肝臟、胃及神經衰弱的問題。 liver, stomach and nervous systems problems.
(3)	虎 Tiger	猴 Monkey	寅 Yin	肝臟疾病的問題。 Lung problems.
(4)	兔 Rabbit	雞 Rooster	卯 Mao	下肢，大腸，便秘，血壓的問題。 the trouble on lower legs, large intestines, blood pressure problems that are linked to constipation
(5)	龍 Dragon	狗 Dog	辰 Chen	胃的疾病。 Stomach problems.
(6)	蛇 Serpent	豬 Pig	巳 Si	脾臟、血癌的問題。 Troubles on spleen and leukemia.
(7)	馬 Horse	鼠 Rat	午 Wuu	心臟病的問題。 Heart attack
(8)	羊 Goat	牛 Ox	未 Wei	小腸、不孕症的問題。 Small intestines and infertility issues.
(9)	猴 Monkey	虎 Tiger	申 Shen	子宮、膀胱的問題。 Uterus and bladder issues
(10)	雞 Chicken	兔 Rabbit	酉 You	口腔、腎臟的問題。 Oral and kidney problems

	生肖 Chinese Signs		枕頭位置 pillows location (差 wrong)	缺點 shortage
(11)	狗 Dog	龍 Dragon	戌 Xu	心臟病的問題。 heart problems
(12)	豬 Pig	蛇 Serpent	亥 Hai	膽、淋巴腺、白血球數量的問題。 Troubles on gall, lymph and white blood (cell) counts.

Chapter 6 Kitchen &Dining Room
廚房與餐廳

1. 廚房與餐廳禁忌 *18* feng shui taboos in your kitchen and dining room

　(1) A kitchen should not be located on the SW of a house.

　(2) The stove should not be placed above the drain even if it is covered.

　(3) The stove should not face the west.

　(4) Avoid installing a stove next to the toilets.

　(5) A Stove should be not placed behind a toilet bowel or a bed even if there is a wall in between.

　(6) The kitchen is recommended not to be situated next to the dining room.

　(7) A dining table should not face the door of a house.

　(8) A dining table should not be situated under a beam, a skylight or beneath the restrooms.

　(9) Avoid having a skylight in your kitchen.

　(10)Do not put a well in the kitchen.

　(11)A Feng Shui kitchen is recommended not to have an opening on the roof.

　(12)Don't put a stove right in front of a window.

　(13)Don't install a stove or kitchen utensils in the center of a house.

　(14)The stove should not be placed under a beam.

　(15)Do not install a stove in front of a water pump or a well.

　(16)Keep faucets away from your stove.

　(17)Stoves should be kept closely against the wall and should not have a space in the back.

　(18)Don't put a fish bowel in the kitchen.

2. According to the Feng Shui principles, the reasons that fire accidents occur are often due the improper locations of your stoves, ranges, especially high power appliances such as ovens, stoves, ranges, microwave ovens, conventional ovens, water heaters, bottle gas, gas ranges, rice cookers, induction cookers, slow cookers etc.

屋座朝向 House Direction	爐具放置不當地點 Improper Stoves location 👎
子 Zi	亥 Hai 👎
丑 Chou	申 Shen 👎
寅 Yin	巳 Si 👎
卯 Mao	寅 Yin 👎
辰 Chen	亥 Hai 👎
巳 Si	申 Shen 👎
午 Wuu	巳 Si 👎
未 Wei	寅 Yin 👎
申 Shen	亥 Hai 👎
酉 You	申 Shen 👎
戌 Xu	巳 Si 👎
亥 Hai	寅 Yin 👎

3. 爐具放置點之評估 Evaluations of stove locations:

爐具放置點 Locations for Stoves	佳 Best 👍	中等 Medium ✔	差 Worst 👎	爐具放置點 Locations for Stoves	佳 Best 👍	中等 Medium ✔	差 Worst 👎
壬 Ren	👍			午 Wu			👎
丑 Chou		✔		坤 Kun			👎
甲 Jia	👍			酉 You			👎
辰 Chen		✔		乾 Chian			👎
丙 Bing	👍			癸 Gui	👍		
未 Wei		✔		寅 Yin		✔	
庚 Geng	👍			乙 Yi	👍		
戌 Xu		✔		巳 Si			👎
子 Zi			👎	丁 Ding	👍		
艮 Gen			👎	申 Shen		✔	
卯 Mao			👎	辛 Xin	👍		
巽 Xun			👎	亥 Hai		✔	

Chapter 7 Toilets & Bathrooms 廁所與浴室

1. 一般注意事項 General Feng Shui Rules

(1) A toilet bowl should not face the North.

(2) A toilet bowl should not face to the main door.

(3) The NE and SW are not recommended for installing the toilets.

(4) The toilets and the bathrooms should have good ventilation.

(5) The toilets should not be put in the center of your house.

(6) The ground of the toilets should not be higher than that of the house.

(7) The toilets should not face the kitchen.

2. 從房屋座向判斷廁所吉凶 To Feng Shui your toilets based on the sitting directions of your house

房屋座向 House Directions	廁所不利方位 Unfavorable toilet locations	房屋座向 House Directions	廁所不利方位 Unfavorable toilet locations	房屋座向 House Directions	廁所不利方位 Unfavorable toilet locations
壬 Ren	無 None	子 Zi	子、辰 Zi and Chen	癸 Gui	無 None
丑 Chou	酉、丑 You and Chou	艮 Gen	無 None	寅 Yin	午、戌 Wuu and Xu
甲 Jia	無 None	卯 Mao	卯、未 Mao and Wei	乙 Yi	無 None
辰 Chen	子、辰 Zi and Chen	巽 Xun	無 None	巳 Si	丑、酉 Chou and You
丙 Bing	無 None	午 Wuu	午、戌 Wuu and Xu	丁 Ding	無 None
未 Wei	卯、未 Mao and Wei	坤 Kun	無 None	申 Shen	子、辰 Zi and Chen
庚 Geng	無 None	酉 You	丑、酉 Chou and You	辛 Xin	無 None
戌 Xu	午、戌 Wuu and Wei	乾 Chian	無 None	亥 Hai	卯、未 Mao and Wei

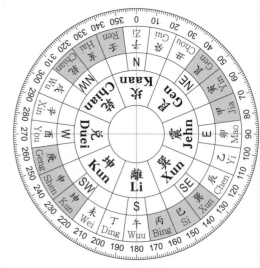

3. 從馬桶方位判斷吉凶 To Feng Shui your toilet bowels

馬桶方位 Toilet bowels	吉凶判斷 Good or bad		馬桶方位 Toilet bowels	吉凶判斷 Good or bad		馬桶方位 Toilet bowels	吉凶判斷 Good or bad	
壬 Ren	吉	Good	乙 Yi	吉	Good	坤 Kun	凶	Bad
子 Zi	凶	Bad	辰 Chen	中等	Fair	申 Shen	中等	Fair
癸 Gui	吉	Good	巽 Xun	中等	Fair	庚 Geng	吉	Good
丑 Chou	中等	Fair	巳 Si	中等	Fair	酉 You	凶	Bad
艮 Gen	凶	Bad	丙 Bing	吉	Good	辛 Xin	吉	Good
寅 Yin	中等	Fair	午 Wuu	凶	Bad	戌 Xu	中等	Fair
甲 Jia	吉	Good	丁 Ding	吉	Good	乾 Chian	凶	Bad
卯 Mao	凶	Bad	未 Wei	中等	Fair	亥 Hai	中等	Fair

Chapter 8 Windows and Lighting 窗戶與照明

1. Windows are not recommended to be located at the diagonal lines of a house. It would cause the family to lose money.

2. Arch-shaped windows are not recommended.

3. Avoid triangle-shaped windows.

4. French windows are not recommended in a house or in the back of an office desk with the exception of a business space.

5. Windows of an office should not be transparent.

6. Windows located in the back of an office desk should be curtained.

7. Avoid having two windows on the same wall.

8. Sunshade screens should be installed on the south-facing windows.

9. Round-shaped windows should be avoided.

10. Windows in the back of a house should not face the main door.

11. Bathrooms should have windows.

12. Avoid having windows in the back of a bed.

13. Pendant lights are suitable to be used in living rooms or dining rooms.

14. Round bulbs in various styles are appropriate for bedrooms, but pendant lights should not be installed above the beds.

15. Lighting should not be behind a bed.

16. Hanging lights are suitable to be placed above the dining tables.

17. A table lamp or reading lamp is recommended to be placed on a desk.

18. Avoid installing fluorescent lamps above the altar.

19. Hang fluorescent lamps horizontally at the entrance. Avoid hanging fluorescent lamps vertically at the entrance as it would look like a sword.

20. Offices usually use recessed ceiling light fixtures.

Chapter 9 Altar 神壇

建議神壇之方位 Locations Tips for Altar

屋座向 House Directions	建議神壇之方位 Locations Tips for Altar
壬 Ren	壬、子、艮、寅、辰、未、申、庚 Ren, Zi, Gen, Yin, Chen, Wei, Shen, Geng
子 Zi	壬、子、癸、丑、辰、巽 Ren, Zi, Gui, Chou, Chen, Xun
癸 Gui	癸、辰、申 Gui, Chen, Shen
丑 Chou	乙、巳、酉 Yi, Si, You
艮 Gen	辰、坤、戌 Chen, Kun, Xu
寅 Yin	丁、坤 Ding, Kun
甲 Jia	丑、卯、乙、申、乾、亥 Chou, Mao, Yi, Shen, Chian, Hai
卯 Mao	癸、甲、卯、乙、巽、未、申、亥 Gui, Jia, Mao, Yi, Xun, Wei, Shen, Hai
乙 Yi	壬、子、卯、乙、巳、坤、戌、亥 Ren, Zi, Mao, Yi, Si, Kun, Xu, Hai
辰 Chen	辰、午 Chen, Wuu

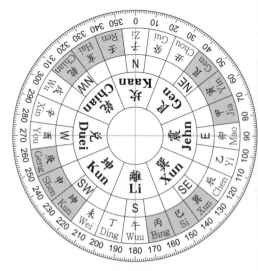

屋座向 House Directions	建議神壇之方位 Locations Tips for Altar
巽 Xun	壬、子、寅、辰、丙、午、未、酉、戌、乾 Ren, Zi, Yin, Chen, Bing, Wuu, Wei, You, Xu, Chian, Hai
巳 Si	壬、丑、酉、乾 Ren, Chou, You, Chian
丙 Bing	艮、甲、丙、午、丁、未、坤、申、酉、辛 Gen, Jia, Bing, Wuu, Ding, Wei, Kun, Shen, You, Xin
午 Wuu	艮、寅、乙、巽、丙、午、丁、未、坤、申、庚 Gen, Yin, Yi, Xun, Bing, Wuu, Ding, Wei, Kun, Shen, Geng
丁 Ding	丑、艮、寅、甲、巳、丙、午、丁、未、坤、申、酉 Chou, Gen, Yin, Jia, Si, Bing, Wuu, Ding, Wei, Kun, Shen, You
未 Wei	卯、午、申 Mao, Wuu, Shen
坤 Kun	乙、辰、申 Yi, Chen, Shen
申 Shen	癸、乙、坤、申 Gui, Yi, Kun, Shen
庚 Geng	癸、巽、丁、未、申、乾、亥 Gui, Xun, Ding, Wei, Shen, Chian, Hih
酉 You	丑、寅、巳、丁、未、坤 Chou, Yin, Si, Ding, Wei, Kun
辛 Xin	艮、巽、丙、丁、未 Gen, Xun, Bing, Ding, Wei
戌 Xu	子、甲、巳、午、申、庚、酉、辛、戌 Zi, Jia, Si, Wuu, Shen, Geng, You, Xin, Xu
乾 Chian	子、甲、丙、丁、坤、庚、酉、辛、乾 Zi, Jia, Bing, Ding, Kun, Geng, You, Xin, Xu
亥 Hai	壬、子、甲、卯、未、坤、庚、酉、辛、戌 Ren, Zi, Jia, Mao, Wei, Kun, Geng, You, Xin, Xu

神壇設置注意事項 6 things to avoid when setting up an altar at home

(1) Avoid setting up an altar under the stairways.

(2) The altar should not face the toilets.

(3) The altar should not be put next to a toilet or a bathroom.

(4) The altar should not be set under the beams as it might bring bad luck to kids.

(5) Altar statues should not be set at "Wei".

(6) Altar statues should not face the "knife edge", meaning corners, sharp edges or pointed objects projecting to your house across the street.

神壇離地的建議高度 Suggestions for the height of an altar				
102- 112.5 cm	123.3-124.1cm	144.7-155.5cm	166.2-176.9cm	187.7-198.4cm
209.2-219.9cm	230.7-241.3cm	252.0-262.8cm	273.4-284.2cm	292.0-305.6cm

神像不可設置於下列特殊年份與煞位 Altar statues should not be set in the following years and on the Jupiter direction.

年份 Zodiac Year	煞位 Unfavorable Statue setting
子 Zi	座午向子 Wuu faces to Zi
丑 Chou	座未向亥 Wei faces to Hai
寅 Yin	座未向丑 Wei faces to Chou
卯 Mao	座庚酉辛向甲卯乙 Site Geng,You,Xin face to Jia,Mao,Yi
辰 Chen	座亥向艮 Hai faces to Gen
巳 Si	座亥向巳 Hai faces to Si
午 Wuu	座壬子癸向丙午丁 Site Ren,Zi,Gui face to Bing,Wuu,Ding.
未 Wei	座亥向未 Hai faces to Wei
申 Shen	座丑向申 Chou faces to Shen
酉 You	座甲卯乙向庚酉辛 Site Jia,Mao,Yi face to Geng,You,Xin
戌 Xu	座辰向戌 Chen faces to Xu
亥 Hai	座巳向亥 Si faces to Hai

神像不可設置於屋煞位 Altar should not be set on goblin side.

屋座向 House Directions	屋煞位 Unlucky Feng Shui Directions
西北 Northwest	東南/東北 Southeast / Northeast
北 North	南/西北/東 South / Northwest / East
東北 Northeast	西南/南/北 Southwest / South / North
東 East	西/東北/南 West / Northeast / South
東南 Southeast	西北/西/東北 Northwest / West / Northeast
南 South	北/西北 North / Northwest
西南 Southwest	東北/西北/西 Northeast / Northwest / West
西 West	東/西 East / West

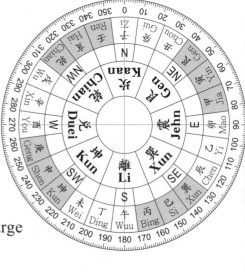

Chapter 10 Stairways 樓梯

1. Stairways should not be located in the center of a house with the exception of restaurants or public spaces.

2. Avoid having two stairways in a house except for large public spaces such as department stores and restaurants.

3. It is recommended that the number of the steps on a staircase is in odd numbers.

4. For safety reasons, the stairs of a staircase should not be too steep. (The height between the stairs must be moderate and the width not too narrow).

5. Avoid placing a kitchen under the stairways.

6. Putting a bed under the stairways is not recommended.

7. An altar is not allowed under the stairways.

8. It is not recommended to have exterior stairs.

9. A stairway facing outside is not auspicious.

10. A stairway installed at the same location that represents the zodiac symbol of the house owner should be avoided.

11. A stairway should not be on the "Ren", "Gui", "Chian" and west sides.

12. A stairway should not start from the locations that contradict the zodiac symbols of the family members.

13. The stairway should not face any doors.

14. Stoves should not be under the staircase.

15. Never put a bed under the stairs.

16. Avoid stairways on the "goblin" spot.

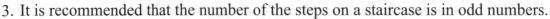

Chapter 11 Office 辦公室

辦公室/辦公桌注意事項 Feng Shui Rules for Office and Desks

(1) Avoid installing French windows behind an executive's desk.

(2) A ceiling with an opening in an office is not auspicious.

(3) The office desks should not face the corner.

(4) The office desks should not be under the beams.

(5) The office doors should not face the door of a toilet.

(6) A walkway between the office desks should be avoided.

(7) The office desk should not face the front door.

(8) The office desks should stay away from the corner of a triangle.

(9) The office desks should not face a fish bowl.

辦公桌之安置 Desk arrangement

辦公室的門在東方 The door of the office on the East

辦公桌方位 Desk location	判斷 Good or bad	辦公桌方位 Desk location	判斷 Good or bad	辦公桌方位 Desk location	判斷 Good or bad
壬方 Ren	不吉 No good	子方 ZI	極佳 Excellent	癸方 Gui	佳 Good
丑方 Chou	極佳 Excellent	艮方 Gen	不吉 No good	寅方 Yin	不吉 No good
甲方 Jia	吉 Good	卯方 Mao	不吉 No good	乙方 Yi	不吉 No good
辰方 Chen	不吉 No good	巽方 Xun	中等 Fair	巳方 Sih	不吉 No good
丙方 Bing	吉 Good	午方 Wuu	中等 Fair	丁方 Ding	不吉 No good
未方 Weih	吉 Good	坤方 Kun	不吉 No good	申方 Shen	不吉 No good
庚方 Geng	吉 Good	酉方 You	極佳 Excellent	辛方 Xin	極佳 Excellent
戌方 Syu	不吉 No good	乾方 Chian	不吉 No good	亥方 Haih	不吉 No good

辦公室的門在西方 The door of the office on the West

辦公桌方位 Desk location	判斷 Good or bad	辦公桌方位 Desk location	判斷 Good or bad	辦公桌方位 Desk location	判斷 Good or bad
壬方 Ren	極佳 Excellent	子方 ZI	吉 Good	癸方 Gui	極佳 Excellent
丑方 Chou	極佳 Excellent	艮方 Gen	吉 Good	寅方 Yin	吉 Good
甲方 Jia	吉 Good	卯方 Mao	吉 Good	乙方 Yi	吉 Good
辰方 Chen	吉 Good	巽方 Xun	極佳 Excellent	巳方 Sih	吉 Good
丙方 Bing	吉 Good	午方 Wuu	不吉 No good	丁方 Ding	極差 Very bad
未方 Weih	極佳 Excellent	坤方 Kun	吉 Good	申方 Shen	吉 Good
庚方 Geng	極佳 Excellent	酉方 You	極佳 Excellent	辛方 Xin	極佳 Excellent
戌方 Syu	吉 Good	乾方 Chian	吉 Good	亥方 Haih	吉 Good

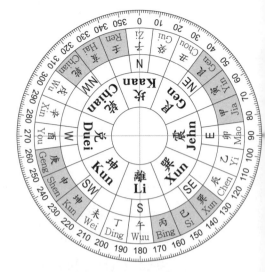

辦公室的門在南方 The door of the office on the South

辦公桌方位 Desk location	判斷 Good or bad	辦公桌方位 Desk location	判斷 Good or bad	辦公桌方位 Desk location	判斷 Good or bad
壬方 Ren	吉 Good	子方 ZI	吉 Good	癸方 Gui	吉 Good
丑方 Chou	中等 Fair	艮方 Gen	不吉 No good	寅方 Yin	不吉 No good
甲方 Jia	不吉 No good	卯方 Mao	吉 Good	乙方 Yi	吉 Good
辰方 Chen	極差 Very bad	巽方 Xun	不吉 No good	巳方 Sih	不吉 No good
丙方 Bing	吉 Good	午方 Wuu	極差 Very bad	丁方 Ding	極差 Very bad
未方 Weih	極佳 Excellent	坤方 Kun	吉 Good	申方 Shen	極佳 Excellent
庚方 Geng	吉 Good	酉方 You	吉 Good	辛方 Xin	吉 Good
戌方 Syu	吉 Good	乾方 Chian	吉 Good	亥方 Haih	吉 Good

辦公室的門在北方 The door of the office on the North

辦公桌方位 Desk location	判斷 Good or bad	辦公桌方位 Desk location	判斷 Good or bad	辦公桌方位 Desk location	判斷 Good or bad
壬方 Ren	極佳 Excellent	子方 ZI	極佳 Excellent	癸方 Gui	吉 Good
丑方 Chou	不吉 No good	艮方 Gen	吉 Good	寅方 Yin	不吉 No good
甲方 Jia	極佳 Excellent	卯方 Mao	極佳 Excellent	乙方 Yi	吉 Good
辰方 Chen	極佳 Excellent	巽方 Xun	極佳 Excellent	巳方 Sih	吉 Good
丙方 Bing	極差 Very bad	午方 Wuu	極差 Very bad	丁方 Ding	不吉 No good
未方 Weih	吉 Good	坤方 Kun	不吉 No good	申方 Shen	極佳 Excellent
庚方 Geng	極佳 Excellent	酉方 You	極佳 Excellent	辛方 Xin	極佳 Excellent
戌方 Syu	極佳 Excellent	乾方 Chian	不吉 No good	亥方 Haih	不吉 No good

辦公室的門在東北方 The door of the office on the Northeast

辦公桌方位 Desk location	判斷 Good or bad	辦公桌方位 Desk location	判斷 Good or bad	辦公桌方位 Desk location	判斷 Good or bad
壬方 Ren	吉 Good	子方 ZI	吉 Good	癸方 Gui	極佳 Excellent
丑方 Chou	吉 Good	艮方 Gen	吉 Good	寅方 Yin	吉 Good
甲方 Jia	不吉 No good	卯方 Mao	吉 Good	乙方 Yi	吉 Good
辰方 Chen	吉 Good	巽方 Xun	吉 Good	巳方 Sih	吉 Good
丙方 Bing	吉 Good	午方 Wuu	吉 Good	丁方 Ding	吉 Good
未方 Weih	吉 Good	坤方 Kun	極差 Very bad	申方 Shen	極差 Very bad
庚方 Geng	不吉 No good	酉方 You	吉 Good	辛方 Xin	吉 Good
戌方 Syu	不吉 No good	乾方 Chian	吉 Good	亥方 Haih	吉 Good

辦公室的門在西南方 The door of the office on the Southwest

辦公桌方位 Desk location	判斷 Good or bad	辦公桌方位 Desk location	判斷 Good or bad	辦公桌方位 Desk location	判斷 Good or bad
壬方 Ren	不吉 No good	子方 ZI	極佳 Excellent	癸方 Gui	極佳 Excellent
丑方 Chou	不吉 No good	艮方 Gen	吉 Good	寅方 Yin	吉 Good
甲方 Jia	吉 Good	卯方 Mao	中等 Fair	乙方 Yi	吉 Good
辰方 Chen	極佳 Excellent	巽方 Xun	不吉 No good	巳方 Sih	不吉 No good
丙方 Bing	中等 Fair	午方 Wuu	中等 Fair	丁方 Ding	中等 Fair
未方 Weih	極佳 Excellent	坤方 Kun	極佳 Excellent	申方 Shen	極佳 Excellent
庚方 Geng	不吉 No good	酉方 You	不吉 No good	辛方 Xin	不吉 No good
戌方 Syu	中等 Fair	乾方 Chian	中等 Fair	亥方 Haih	中等 Fair

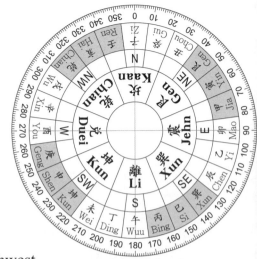

辦公室的門在西北方 The door of the office on the Northwest

辦公桌方位 Desk location	判斷 Good or bad	辦公桌方位 Desk location	判斷 Good or bad	辦公桌方位 Desk location	判斷 Good or bad
壬方 Ren	吉 Good	子方 ZI	不吉 No good	癸方 Gui	極差 Very bad
丑方 Chou	不吉 No good	艮方 Gen	不吉 No good	寅方 Yin	不吉 No good
甲方 Jia	不吉 No good	卯方 Mao	不吉 No good	乙方 Yi	不吉 No good
辰方 Chen	不吉 No good	巽方 Xun	不吉 No good	巳方 Sih	不吉 No good
丙方 Bing	極差 Very bad	午方 Wuu	極差 Very bad	丁方 Ding	極差 Very bad
未方 Weih	極差 Very bad	坤方 Kun	極差 Very bad	申方 Shen	極差 Very bad
庚方 Geng	極差 Very bad	酉方 You	極差 Very bad	辛方 Xin	不吉 No good
戌方 Syu	不吉 No good	乾方 Chian	中等 Fair	亥方 Haih	中等 Fair

辦公室的門在東南方 The door of the office on the Southeast

辦公桌方位 Desk location	判斷 Good or bad	辦公桌方位 Desk location	判斷 Good or bad	辦公桌方位 Desk location	判斷 Good or bad
壬方 Ren	不吉 No good	子方 ZI	不吉 No good	癸方 Gui	不吉 No good
丑方 Chou	中等 Fair	艮方 Gen	中等 Fair	寅方 Yin	極佳 Excellent
甲方 Jia	極差 Very bad	卯方 Mao	極差 Very bad	乙方 Yi	極差 Very bad
辰方 Chen	極差 Very bad	巽方 Xun	極差 Very bad	巳方 Sih	極差 Very bad
丙方 Bing	極差 Very bad	午方 Wuu	極差 Very bad	丁方 Ding	吉 Good
未方 Weih	中等 Fair	坤方 Kun	中等 Fair	申方 Shen	極差 Very bad
庚方 Geng	極差 Very bad	酉方 You	極差 Very bad	辛方 Xin	極差 Very bad
戌方 Syu	極差 Very bad	乾方 Chian	極差 Very bad	亥方 Haih	極差 Very bad

Chapter 12 Feng Shui Wealth Area & Study Luck Area
財位與文昌位

The "Feng Shui money area" is vital for inviting wealth to your home whereas the "Study area" is linked to family members' school performances.

屋座向 House Directions		財位 Wealth area		文昌位 Study area	
卦名 Gua Name	方位 Locations	卦名 Gua Name	方位 Locations	卦名 Gua Name	方位 Locations
坎 Kaan	北 North	坎 Kaan	北 North	艮 Gen	東北 Northeast
坤 Kun	西南 Southwest	坤 Kun	西南 Southwest	兌 Duei	西 West
震 Jehn	東 East	中 central	中 central	乾 Chian	西北 Northwest
巽 Xun	東南 Southeast	巽 Xun	東南 Southeast	中 Central	中 Central
乾 Chian	西北 Northwest	兌 Duei	西 West	震 Jehn	東 East
兌 Duei	西 West	乾/巽 Chian/Xun	西北/東南 Northwest/ Southeast	坤 Kun	西南 Southwest
艮 Gen	東北 Northeast	中 Central	中 central	坎 Kaan	北 North
離 Li	南 South	北 North	東北 Kaan	離 Li	南 South

PS：Wealth areas should be well-lit and clean enough to sit, sleep and place a potted plant. Money areas should not be dark, empty or dirty.

Chapter 13 Fish and Fish Tanks 魚與魚缸

1. Regarding the five elements, fish represents "fire". Here are a few examples of Feng Shui fish Gold fish, Catfish, Blood Parrot, Variegated carp, Red Dragon etc.
2. A landscape painting can be hung above the fish bowl.

3. It is recommended that a fish bowl be put in the dark place of a house.

4. Avoid placing a fish tank besides the window.

5. Keeping at least one black fish in the fish tank can counteract bad lucks.

6. It is advised to have a round or rectangle-shaped fish tank. Stay away from square or other shapes.

7. It is suggested that you use a fish bowl made of glass.

8. A fish bowl should not directly face the door.

9. Putting real crystal stones in a fish bowl in which the magnetic fields will help keep the water clean.

10. Different shapes of fish tanks stand for different elements. Round stands for metal, rectangle-wood, triangle-fire, square-earth and hexagonal-water.

形狀 Shape	○ 圓形 Round	▢ 長方形 Rectangle	△ 三角形 Triangle	□ 正方形 Square	⬡ 六角形 Hexagonal
五行 Five Elements	金 Metal	木 Wood	水 Fire	火 Earth	土 Water

11. It is suggested that the height of a fish bowl not exceed the heat of a person.

12. The height of a fish bowl should not be lower than the foot of a man.

13. A fish bowl placed on the directions of "Zi", "Wuu", "Mao" or "You" of a house is prone to attracting love affairs.

14. Do not put a fish tank in the kitchen.

15. A fish bowl should not be placed in the unlucky areas of a house as it might bring bad luck such as accidents to the elderly in the house.

16. The worst location to place a fish bowl is "Hai" position.

17. The dimensions of a Feng Shui fish bowl are suggested as -

16.1 ~ 26.8cm,   37.5 ~ 48.3cm,   59 ~ 69.8cm,   80.5 ~ 91.2cm,
102 ~ 112.6cm,   123.3 ~ 124.1cm,   144.7 ~ 155.5cm,   166.2 ~ 176.9cm,
187.7 ~ 198.4cm,   209.2 ~ 219.9cm,   230.7 ~ 241.3cm,   250.0 ~ 262.8cm,
273.4 ~ 284.2cm,   295.0 ~ 305.6cm

18. The good locations for a Feng Shui fish tank are listed as follows.

屋座向 House Directions	魚缸位置建議 Location suggestions for placing a fish bowel
壬子坤申乙辰 Ren Zi Kun Shen Yi Chen	艮寅丙辛戌 Gen Yin Bing Xin Syu
甲卯乾亥丁未 Jia Mao Chian Haih Ding Weih	巽巳戌庚酉癸丑 Xun Sih Syu Geng You Gui Chou
庚酉巽巳癸丑 Geng You Xun Sih Gui Chou	乾亥甲卯丁未 Chian Haih Jia Mao Ding Weih
丙午艮寅辛戌 Bing Wuu Gen Yin Xin Syu	坤申壬子乙辰 Kun Shen Ren Zi Yi Chen

☯ Feng Shui Common Sense

Q1: What is an "unlucky location"? Please explain.

A1:

It is inevitable for people to have back luck or experiences that things are not going their way. In general, we all attribute them to bad lucks. Some locations in our houses are not suitable for setting anything. We called them "unlucky locations".

The simplest way to find the "unlucky locations" in our house is to start from our house direction. For insistence, our house is on "Chian" (the middle of northwest) so the "unlucky direction" is on "Xun"(the middle of southeast) and so on.

Q2: Are there any differences in unlucky directions?

A2:

Unlucky locations such as "Guan Sha Wei", also called "Wu Huang Wei" are impacting people's luck in a given year. Therefore if this location of a house is under repair, it will bring about serious diseases to the families. It should not be neglected as it concerns the health of the families.

Unlucky locations such as "Sha Wei" are also called as "Killing location". Although it is not as bad as "Guan Sha Wei 關煞位", it still will cause people to suffer money loss and bad luck. The negative impact is not so serious as the "Guan Sha Wei 五黃位", but it still cannot be overlooked.

Here are the so-called 3 malignant locations (Jie Sha, Jai Sha and Suai Sha) that will bring you disasters. Please make sure that these locations be free from construction work in the following years.

Year of Yin, Wuu and Syu do not repair or remodel the northern area of the house.
Year of Shen, Zi and Chen do not repair or remodel the southern area of the house.
Year of Haih, Mao and Wei do not repair or remodel the western area of the house.
Year of Si, You and Chou do not repair or remodel the eastern area of the house.

Chapter 14 Storage rooms 儲藏室

1. A storage room represents "earth" in the five elements.
2. The areas of "Ren", "Gui", "Jia", "Yi", "Si", "Bing", "Ding", "Geng", "Xin" and "Hai" are suitable for placing a storage room.
3. Avoid the following locations for storages-"Zi", "Gen", "Mao", "Xun", "Wuu", "Kun", "You" and "Chian".
4. The door of a storage room should not face another door.

Chapter 15 Rockworks 假山

Rockworks are often seen in a villa. It is for pleasure and enjoyment. The rockworks should not be placed in front of a house even though it is on a lucky location.

假山位置吉凶 Feng Shui Rockworks locations:

位置 Locations	吉凶 Good or bad	位置 Locations	吉凶 Good or bad	位置 Locations	吉凶 Good or bad
壬方 Ren	吉 Good	子方 Zi	不吉 No good	癸方 Gui	吉 Good
丑方 Chou	差 Bad	艮方 Gen	差 Bad	寅方 Yin	極差 Very bad
甲方 Jia	差 Bad	卯方 Mao	極差 Very bad	乙方 Yi	差 Bad
辰方 Chen	差 Bad	巽方 Xun	差 Bad	巳方 Sih	差 Bad
丙方 Bing	差 Bad	午方 Wuu	差 Bad	丁方 Ding	差 Bad
未方 Weih	差 Bad	坤方 Kun	差 Bad	申方 Shen	差 Bad
庚方 Geng	吉 Good	酉方 You	差 Bad	辛方 Xin	吉 Good
戌方 Syu	吉 Good	乾方 Chian	吉 Good	亥方 Haih	吉 Good

Chapter 16　Ponds 池塘

In general, it is advised not to have a pond in the garden unless it is more than 100 meters away from the house.

池塘位置吉凶 Feng Shui pond locations

位置 Locations	吉凶 Good or bad	位置 Locations	吉凶 Good or bad	位置 Locations	吉凶 Good or bad
壬方 Ren	不吉 No Good	子方 Zi	吉 Good	癸方 Gui	差 Good
丑方 Chou	極差 Very bad	艮方 Gen	極差 Very bad	寅方 Yin	極差 Very bad
甲方 Jia	吉 Good	卯方 Mao	不吉 No Good	乙方 Yi	吉 Good
辰方 Chen	吉 Good	巽方 Xun	差 Bad	巳方 Sih	吉 Good
丙方 Bing	不吉 No Good	午方 Wuu	極差 Very bad	丁方 Ding	不吉 No Good
未方 Weih	不吉 No Good	坤方 Kun	不吉 No Good	申方 Shen	不吉 No Good
庚方 Geng	吉 Good	酉方 You	極差 Very bad	辛方 Xin	吉 Good
戌方 Syu	吉 Good	乾方 Chian	不吉 No Good	亥方 Haih	吉 Good

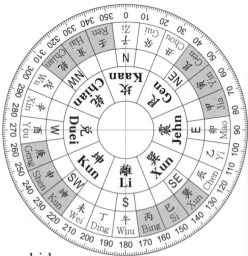

Chapter 17 Plants 植物

In Feng Shui, plants are divided into two categories, Yin and Yang. Basic rules of thumbs are to avoid "Yin plants" and stick to "Yang plants".

1. 陽樹 Yang Plants are azalea, date, chrysanthemum, orchid, peony, Chinese evergreen, pine, elm, persimmon, cypress, plum tree, cherry, common petunia, peach, maple, bougainvillea, cockscomb, Chinese parasol tree, bamboo and wolf berry.

2. 陰樹 Yin Plants include willow, blackwood, banana, grapes, plantain, papaya, pear, nanamu palm and banana.

⚠ Cautions

1. Avoid planting a Chinese parasol tree, a peach tree or a mulberry tree in front of a house.

2. Having too many plum trees around the house is unlucky.

3. Bamboos that are planted on the NW of a clinic are unlucky to the doctor.

4. It is necessary to keep all the plants well pruned.

Chapter 18 Other ornaments（decorations）其他裝飾品

1. 緞帶花 Satin flowers：It is advisable not to decorate the areas of "Zi", "Wuu", "Mao" or "You" with satin flowers as these artificial flowers are prone to attracting extramarital affairs.

2. 馬 Horses：When decorating with horses, avoid the number 5. It is recommended to put them on the south or northwest of the house. The lucky number for horses is eight.

3. 獅子 Lions：You should decorate lions in pairs and place them on each side of the front door facing outside.

4. 烏龜 Tortoises：

Wood tortoises – all directions are good.

Stone tortoises – Southwest and Northeast are preferable.

Copper tortoises – West and Northwest are the best.

Pottery tortoises – North is the most suitable.

5. 吊飾 Hanging ornaments : It is advisable not to hang ornaments in the areas of "Wei", "Shen", "Chou" or "Yin" as it might cause the inhabitants to have migraines.

6. 刀劍 Swords or knifes : It is suggested that you always keep swords out of the bedrooms, never take off the scabbards and hang them in the living room.

7. 龍 Dragons : Decorating your living room with a dragon brings happiness.

8. 沙發 Couches should not be set under any beams.

9. 鋼琴 A piano should be placed on the left side of a house.

10. 家電產品 Home appliances such as dryers, microwaves, conventional ovens, induction cookers and dehumidifiers should be carefully placed to avoid health problems.

☯ Feng Shui Q&A

Q: Some fishermen like to have turtle shells and lobster shells hung on the living room wall. Please advise the proper locations to hang these animal specimens in the house.

A:

In principle, animal specimens are not allowed to be placed in the house mainly because nobody knows if their souls are still inside.

Chapter 19 Basement 地下室

地下室品質之改善 Ideas to improve your basement Feng Shui:

Due to the exorbitant prices of real estate properties in urban areas, basements are always used for other purposes.

Here are some ideas that'll help you to improve the basement Feng Shui:

(1) Moisture : Use dehumidifiers to reduce moisture.

(2) Ventilation : Use fans to increase air flow.

(3) Lighting : Add lights to make the basement brighter.

(4) Evergreen plants can be introduced to increase fresh air.

(5) It is not suggested that an altar be installed in the basement.

不利的地下室/地下室不宜在 Unlucky directions for a basement	
(1)	東北方、西南方 NE, SW
(2)	屋中央 at the center of a house
(3)	臥室之下方 rightly under a sleeping room

適宜之地下室方位 Available directions for a basement		
(1)	北方 North	壬癸方 Ren, Gui
(2)	東方 East	甲乙方 Jia, Yi
(3)	南方 Sorth	丙丁方 Bing, Ding
(4)	西方 West	庚辛方 Geng, Xin
(5)	西北方 Northwest	乾方 Chian
(6)	東南方 Southeast	巽方 Xun

Chapter 20 Wells 水井

Wells in traditional Feng Shui concepts mean "faucets" in the modern sense although the two are completely different. We have to reinterpret these concepts too.

Preferable locations for wells are "Ren", "Gui", "Jia", "Yi", "Si", "Geng", "Xin" and

"Hai".

🔥Attentions:

1. Stones piled up beside a well should not be allowed.

2. Garbage beside a well is not permitted.

3. Avoid a big tree standing beside a well and casting a shade on the well.

4. A well should not be next to rest rooms.

5. A well should not be located in the front, middle or the back of a house.

Chapter 21 Feng Shui tips for house and environment
居家環境

1. A house should not be constructed on land that was used to be a temple, grave or a place that had fire accidents, a garbage dump, a low-lying land or a wet land.

2. A house should be not located on a dangerous route.

3. A house should not have low grounds both on the right and the left sides.

4. A house should not have parallel roads on either side.

5. A house should not have parallel rivers on either side.

6. Avoid "Y" or "T" shaped-road in front of a house.

7. Avoid a crossover bridge near your house.

8. Your altar should not face the corner of a building across the street.

9. A house should not directly face any roads on the directions of Zi, Wuu, Mao or You.

10. A house located in the neighborhood of a garbage dump is not auspicious.

11. Avoid a house facing the gap of two buildings across the street.

12. An electric tower located on the "Kun" of the house is good for the son in-law.

13. An electric tower located on the "Shen" of the house is good for the brothers.

14. An electric tower located on the "Bing",

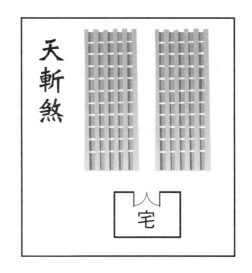

天斬煞

宅

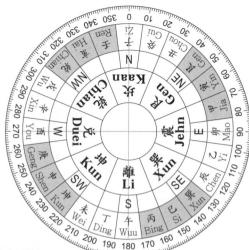

"Ding", "Xin", "Xun" and "Gen" would be beneficial to the students preparing for exams.

15. A ceremonial arch should not be taller than your front door.

16. Avoid a house with a bamboo field in the front.

17. A house should not be located on a cul-de-sac.

18. A house should not have a small stream running through the garden.

19. A house should not directly face a cross road.

20. A house door should not face the door of a temple.

21. Others：The followings are the examples of objects that, if within 20 meters of your house, would impact health and attract misfortunes for the family members. Chimneys, cross signs, sharp objects, building gap, wells, public toilets, garbage dumps, graves, temple's sharp roof, towers, churches, entrance of a parking lot, fire departments, morgues, cross-over bridges etc.

👍 The solution is to put a convex mirror on the wall of the house to reflect the outside vicious energy away.

Chapter 22 Protrusions and Hollowness
屋之凸出與凹入

Protrusions 屋之凸出：

屋座向 House Directions	凸出處 Protrusions	吉 Good 👍	普通 Fair ◎	不吉 No Good 👎
北方 North	壬方 Ren	👍		
	子方 Zi	👍		
	癸方 Gui	👍		
東北方 Northeast	丑方 Chou			👎
	艮方 Gen			👎
	寅方 Yin			👎
東方 East	甲方 Jia	👍		
	卯方 Mao		◎	
	乙方 Yi	👍		
東南方 Southeast	辰方 Chen		◎	
	巽方 Xun			👎
	巳方 Sih		◎	
南方 South	丙方 Bing	👍		
	午方 Wuu		◎	
	丁方 Ding	👍		
西南方 Southwest	未方 Weih			👎
	坤方 Kun			👎
	申方 Shen			👎
西方 West	庚方 Geng		◎	
	酉方 You		◎	
	辛方 Xin		◎	
西北方 Northwest	戌方 Syu		◎	
	乾方 Chian			👎
	亥方 Haih	👍		

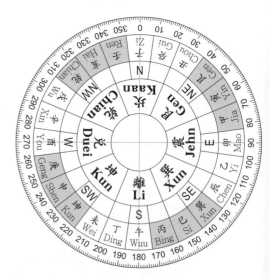

Hollowness 屋之凹入：

屋座向 House Directions	凹入處 Hollowness	不吉 No Good 👎	大凶 Very bad 👎👎👎
北方 North	壬方 Ren		👎👎👎
	子方 Zi		👎👎👎
	癸方 Gui		👎👎👎
東北方 Northeast	丑方 Chou	👎	
	艮方 Gen	👎	
	寅方 Yin	👎	
東方 East	甲方 Jia	👎	
	卯方 Mao	👎	
	乙方 Yi	👎	
東南方 Southeast	辰方 Chen	👎	
	巽方 Xun	👎	
	巳方 Sih	👎	
南方 South	丙方 Bing	👎	
	午方 Wuu	👎	
	丁方 Ding	👎	
西南方 Southwest	未方 Weih	👎	
	坤方 Kun	👎	
	申方 Shen	👎	
西方 West	庚方 Geng	👎	
	酉方 You		👎👎👎
	辛方 Xin		👎👎👎
西北方 Northwest	戌方 Syu	👎	
	乾方 Chian	👎	
	亥方 Haih	👎	

Chapter 23 Fence 圍牆

1. A fence should be neat and complete, uneven height is not auspicious.

2. The construction of a fence should not be finished before that of the house.

3. A fence should not have windows.

4. Any cracks in the northeast of a fence are not auspicious.

5. A fence should not be too high or too low.

6. A fence should not be too close to the house. The suggested minimal distance is 1/2 meter.

7. Avoid building a fence that is taller than the main door.

8. A fence should not have a back door.

9. A round-shaped fence is fortunate.

10. A fence should not be covered with vines.

11. Wire netting over the fence is not good.

12. Avoid using stone slates to build a fence.

Chapter 24 T-Shaped Road 路沖

Chinese believe that a house or the main door directly facing an alley, a gap, a road (T-shaped road) is extremely inauspicious and could attract misfortunes, diseases, poverty, car accidents and petty people.

👍化解方法 Feng Shui Cure:

1. Use tall, dense and big yang trees to block the negative energy or redirect and reflect the malignant energy back with a convex mirror or Shanghai zhen.

2. If a business space is facing a T-Shaped road, the automatic doors and the vast number of people coming in and out already serve as a Feng Shui cure.

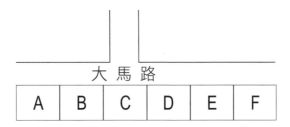

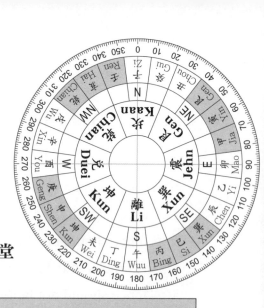

Chapter 25 Temple and Church 廟宇與教堂

廟宇 / 教堂 位置 Temple/Church				👍👍👍：大吉 VeryGood ○ ： 吉　Good × ：不吉 No Good				
屋座向 House Directions	東 E	東南 SE	南 S	西南 SW	西 W	西北 NW	北 N	東北 NE
壬子癸 North	×	×	×	○	×	×	○	×
丑艮寅 Northeast	×	×	×	○	×	○	×	○
甲卯乙 East	○	×	×	×	×	👍👍👍	×	×
辰巽巳 Southeast	×	👍👍👍	×	○	×	×	×	×
丙午丁 South	×	×	👍👍👍	×	×	×	×	👍👍👍
未坤申 Southwest	○	×	×	○	×	×	×	×
庚酉辛 West	×	👍👍👍	○	×	×	○	×	×
戌乾亥 Northwest	×	×	×	×	○	○	○	×

Chapter 26　Bridge 橋

Bridge (trestle, viaduct, flyover and overpass)

屋座向 House Directions	橋的位置 Location of Bridge								○ : 吉　Good ✕ :不吉 No Good	
	東 E	東南 SE	南 S	西南 SW	西 W	西北 NW	北 N	東北 NE
北方 North	✕	✕	✕	○	✕	✕	○	✕
東北方 Northeast	✕	✕	✕	✕	✕	○	✕	✕
東方 East	○	✕	✕	✕	✕	✕	✕	✕
東南方 Southeast	✕	✕	✕	○	✕	✕	✕	✕
南方 South	✕	○	○	✕	✕	✕	✕	○
西南方 Southwest	○	✕	✕	✕	✕	✕	✕	✕
西方 West	✕	○	✕	✕	✕	○	✕	✕
西北方 Northwest	✕	✕	✕	✕	○	✕	○	✕

Chapter 27 Sickness 疾病

The following is a list of health problems that are caused by bad feng shui. Please be cautious and consult a doctor when necessary.

1. House owners with Feng Shui fate of "Xun" and "Jehn" living in houses on the sides of "Chian" and "Duei" may easily get sick.

2. A house on Kun（SW）side faces a temple. The family members can have health problems easily.

3. Stoves face the door of a bedroom.

4. Stoves on Zi, Wuu, Mao and You might cause heart attacks.

5. Stoves on Chou and Yin might develop rheumatism.

6. Stoves on Wuu might attract eyes problems.

7. Stoves on Wei and Shen might cause digestion problems.

8. Stoves on You might cause lung problems.

9. Toilets located on Zi might cause heart attacks.

10. Toilets located on Chou, Gen and Mao might cause rheumatism.

11. A toilet located on Xun might cause digestion problems.

12. Toilets located on Wuu might cause eyes or heart problems.

13. Toilets located on Kun might be linked to allergies.

14. Toilets located on Shen might cause digestion problems.

15. Toilets located on You might attract lung problem.

16. Toilets located on Chian might be linked to apoplexy.

17. Toilets located on Hai might cause lung problems.

18. If the sitting directions of the toilets offend the zodiac signs of the house owner, he or she might have health problems.

生肖 Zodiac Symbol	被沖犯之徵兆 Symptoms
鼠 Rat	心、血、腎 Heart, Blood, Kidney
牛 Ox	風濕、疲勞 Rheumatism, Fatigue
虎 Tiger	疲勞、風濕 Fatigue, Rheumatism
兔 Hare	歇斯底里 Hysteria

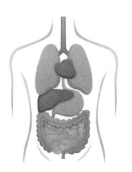

生肖 Zodiac Symbol	被沖犯之徵兆 Symptoms	
龍 Dragon	皮膚、胃、消化	Skin, Stomach, Digestion
蛇 Snake	喉、感冒	Throat, catch a cold
馬 Horse	眼、頭	Eye, Head
羊 Sheep	消化	Digestion
猴 Monkey	消化	Digestion
雞 Chicken	肺	Lung
狗 Dog	神經質、腎	Nervous breakdown, Kidney
豬 Pig	神經質、腎	Nervous breakdown, Kidney

Chapter 28 Disagreement 不和諧

房屋座向 House Directions		爐‧電咖啡壺等 Stoves, Electric Coffee pots etc.	不和諧的放置處 Inappropriate Locations
坎 Kaan	北 N	丙午丁 Bing ,Wuu, Ding	南 South
坤 Kun	西南 SW	艮丑寅 Gen, Chou , Yin	東北 Northeast
震 Jehn	東 E	庚酉辛 Geng ,You , Xin	西 West
巽 Xun	東南 SE	戌乾亥 Syu, Chian, Haih	西北 Northwest
乾 Chian	西北 NW	辰巽巳 Chen, Xun, Sih	南 Southeast
兌 Duei	西 W	甲卯乙 Jia, Mao, Yi	東 East
艮 Gen	東北 NE	未坤申 Weih, Kun, Shen	西南 Southwest
離 Li	南 S	壬子癸 Ren, Zi, Gui	北 North

Chapter 29 Corner house 邊間屋 (三角窗)

1. A corner house located on the SW of an intersection is not good.

2. A corner house located on the east of an intersection is not good.

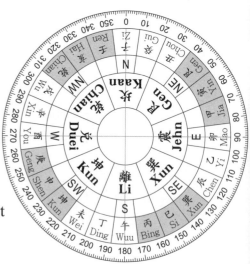

3. A corner house located on the convex of a crossroad is not auspicious.

4. The door of a corner house facing the "cross" of an intersection is unlucky.

5. A corner house is best for business purpose only.（not good for people.）

6. The 1st FL of a corner house is not suitable to live.

Chapter 30 Kylin（a Chinese unicorn） 麒麟

A Kylin (Chinese unicorn) was an auspicious and mythical animal in ancient China. It is said that Kylin would drive wicked things away (i.e. white tiger) for people.

The White tiger shows up in different spots in a house every zodiac year. If a Kylin is put on the spot where the white tiger shows, it can help to reduce the malignant energy in the house. Kylin are generally in pairs and placed on the white tiger spot of a certain zodiac year and faces directly the house door.

Zodiac year 年份		White Tiger stays白虎(放置麒麟的地方)
鼠 Mouse	子 Zi	西南 Southwest
牛 Ox	丑 Chou	西　West
虎 Tiger	寅 Yin	西北 Northwest
兔 Hare	卯 Mao	西北 Northwest

Zodiac year 年份		White Tiger stays 白虎(放置麒麟的地方)
龍 Dragon	辰 Chen	北 North
蛇 Snake	巳 Sih	東北 Northeast
馬 Horse	午 Wuu	東北 Northeast
羊 Sheep	未 Weih	東 East
猴 Monkey	申 Shen	東南 Southeast
雞 Chicken	酉 You	東南 Southeast
狗 Dog	戌 Syu	南 South
豬 Pig	亥 Haih	西南 Southwest

Chapter 31 Extramarital affairs 婚外情

容易發生婚外情的情況 The following situations are prone to attracting extramarital affairs:

1. Water faucets face the stove.

2. The door of the bedroom faces the main door.

3. The sitting direction of a house on the Zi, Wuu, Mao or You and the house has a drain on the Zi, Wuu, Mao or You might attract extramarital affairs.

4. Toilet bowls installed on Wei, Mao or Zi might draw love affairs.

5. Vine plants in front of a house door.

6. A well in front of a house.

7. Stoves installed on You or Chou.

8. House sitting on Shen, Zi or Chen with a drain on You.

9. House sitting on Yin, Wuu or Xu with a drain on Mao.

10. House located on Si, You and Chou with a drain on Wuu.

11. House located on Hai, Mao or Wei with a drain on Zi.

12. House sitting on Zi, Wuu, Mao or You with a T-shaped road and the zodiac symbols of the family members happen to be Rat, Horse, Rabbit and Rooster.

13. The house door faces an electric pole.

14. The sunken corner of a house on You, Bing, Wuu and Ding.

15. The master of a family with feng shui fate- 9 Li lives in a house located on Kaan.

16. A house sits on Kun(SW) or Kaan(N) and is located on the cross of an intersection.

17. The zodiac symbols of the family same as direction of stairways.

18. Fish tanks are placed on Zi, Wuu, Mao or You of a house.

19. Houses located on the following hexagrams.

卦位 Hexagram		度數 Degrees
節卦	Jier	106.875~112.50
歸妹卦	Gui Mei	118.125~123.75
需卦	Shiu	151.875~157.50
姤卦	Gou	185.625~191.25
訟卦	Soong	230.625~236.25
坎卦	Kaan	258.75~264.375

PS : Hanging a painting of peony flowers on the wall in the living room serves as a Feng Shui cure to reduce the severity of love affairs. (Red peonies help to reduce the severity of love affairs and green peonies can attract money.)

Chapter 32 Miscellaneous 雜項

1. Avoid having a garbage dump on the NW.（But a dust bin on Hai is auspicious.）

2. A house without the back door is not fortunate. (The daughter in-law and the mother in-law might not live in harmony.)

3. If the rear lane of a house is not wide enough, the daughter in-law and the mother in-law tend to have confrontations.

4. Mirrors facing the merchandise could increase sales.

5. Shops located vertically to the railway station could

improve sales.

6. A skylight must be moderate in size.

7. A skylight should not be located in the center or on the NE（Gen）and SW（Kun）sides and should not be above a well or the kitchen.

8. A corner house is best for business only.（not good for families.）

9. The diagonal line of a house should not have doors or windows. The family could run into money problems.

10. The Southwest of a house should not have an extended room.

11. It is not fortunate to have kitchen faucets that can be seen from the main door.

12. Avoid arched windows or doors in a house. Avoid having potted bamboos in front of a house especially for a clinic.

13. A pavilion connecting with the house is not auspicious.

14. A cross-shaped building might have more natural light but it might prevent the inhabitants from living in harmony.

15. Stairs connecting the house to the road bring bad luck to money.

16. A house facing an inverted road（a curve road in convex shape）is extremely vicious.

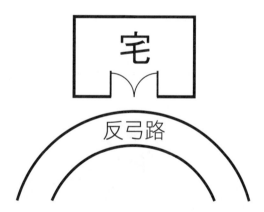

17. A house facing the cross point on SW or NE of an intersections is extremely unfortunate.

18. Avoid putting potted plants in a bedroom.

19. An overpass, flyover or road with the curved side facing the house is positive.

20. It is auspicious to have a round-shaped building.

21. Many sharp objects on the south of a house could attract fire accidents.

22. A house located at the end of Y shaped-road is extremely inauspicious because it looks like a pair of scissors.

23. A house in lateral shape because of the road extension might cause the family to have asthma.

24. Avoid raising any chickens or birds in the backyard of a house as it could cause the house owner to lose money.

25. A house next to an overpass is inauspicious.

26. Stoves placed on the malignant locations will cause disagreement.

27. Dolls should not be put besides the television set as the family members would be hurt by bad people.

28. The television set should not face the door of a bedroom.

Chapter 33 Popular traditional Feng Shui good luck charms
常用納福添財制煞用品

1) 鬥魚 Putting a paradise fish (fighting fish) in a small glass and on the lucky location of a house or individual lucky location would attract money.

2) 竹葉青 Placing Several Chinese evergreen plants in a vase on the lucky location of the house or individual lucky location would attract money.

3) 葫蘆 A calabash, gourd : If a house is facing a gas station, the gourd can be used to counteract the wicked energy. A gourd can also be placed under the beam of a house to inactivate the evils.

4) 珠簾 Beaded curtains：If two bedrooms face each other, the residents will not live in harmony but beaded curtains can serve as a Feng Shui cure.

5) 騏麟 Chinese unicorn：If you can see the back door from the front door or you have the front windows face directly to the back windows or you have the main door directly faces a long lane, the Chinese unicorn can serve as a Feng Shui cure.

6) 山海鎮 Shan Hai Zhen： It is served to correct the following situation: a dead end of a road; a cul-de-sac; a T-shaped road; a house directly facing the walls of a building; a house next to a road curve; a house facing a sharp object.

7) 三腳蟾蜍 A three-legged toad is used to bring in wealth, treasures and is usually put on individual lucky spot.

8) 貔貅 Fortune animals, a mythical animal. They are usually in a pair (male& female) and are used to attract wealth and are put on personal lucky location with their heads facing outside.

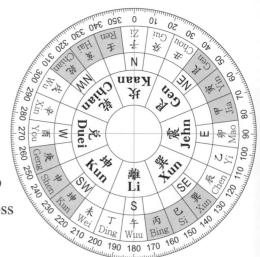

9) 乾坤八卦圖 Chian-Kun-Ba-Gua-Tu:The map will attract blessing, drive away misfortunes and bring in wealth. Examples : it can mitigate vicious spirits from vine trees outside, ease the pressure from the gap of two buildings and curtain walls of a building across the streets.

10) 石敢當 Shi-Gan-Dung : A stone tablet of 4'8"× 1'2"×4" H×W×T with Chinese characters"石敢當" written on top can ward off evil spirits. Examples: it will mitigate negative energy brought by arrow"sha", electric poles and bad energy from an object like the shape of pair of scissors.

11) 凸透鏡 A convex mirror is frequently used to reflect any evil spirits back such as negative energy from the ridge of a roof or from any objects such as bows and arrowed shapes and electric poles.

☯ Feng Shui Common Sense

Unlucky location (Jia Sha 夾煞) : The gap between two buildings.

"Jia Sha" happens when the building you're in has a bigger or taller building adjacent to it. The pressure from the bigger building tends to cause the residents of the smaller building to have bad luck in general or financial troubles.

易經難字註釋彙總
(Hard words of I-Ching in phonetic symbols and explanation)

1. 坤卦：牝 ㄆㄧㄣ ㄟ (pin)，雌牛。

2. 屯卦：邅 ㄓㄢ (zhan)，難以進行的樣子。

3. 訟卦：逋 ㄅㄨ (pu)，逃亡。

       掇 ㄉㄨㄛˊ (duo)，摘取。

       鞶 ㄆㄢˊ (pan)，束衣帶 (鞶帶：官服)。

4. 履卦：愬 ㄙㄨㄟ (su)，驚恐。

5. 謙卦：撝 ㄏㄨㄟ (hui) ＝揮，把內在能力表現出來。

6. 豫卦：盱 ㄒㄩ (syu)，張眼看。

7. 噬嗑卦：胏 ㄗˇ (zih)，帶有骨頭的乾肉。

8. 賁卦：賁 ㄅㄧ ㄟ (bi)，裝飾。

9. 无妄卦：菑 ㄗ (zih)，開墾荒地。

         畬 ㄩˊ (yu)，已墾植三年的熟田。

10.大畜卦：豶 ㄈㄣˊ (fen)，閹割過的豬。

11.大過卦：稊 ㄊㄧˊ (ti)，新嫩葉。

12.坎卦：洊 ㄐㄧㄢ ㄟ (jian)，一再地。

      窞 ㄉㄢ ㄟ (dan)，深坑。

      簋 ㄍㄨㄟˇ (gui)，古時的碗。

      牖 ㄧㄡˇ (you)，窗戶。

      纆 ㄇㄛ ㄟ (mo)，繩索。

13.離卦：昃 ㄗㄜ ㄟ (ze)，太陽西下。

14.咸卦：脢 ㄇㄟˊ (mei)，背脊肉。

      騰 ㄊㄥˊ (teng)，騰揚。

15.晉卦：鼫 ㄕˊ (shih)，齧ㄋㄧㄝ ㄟ鼠。

16.家人卦：嗃 ㄏㄜ ㄟ (he)，嚴酷。

17.損卦：遄 ㄔㄨㄢˊ (chuan)，迅速地。

18.夬卦：頄 ㄑㄧㄡˊ (ciu)，臉。

19.姤卦：柅 ㄋㄧˇ (ni)，古時剎車之木條。

      蹢 ㄉㄧˊ 躅 ㄓㄨˊ (di zhu)，來回走。

20.萃卦：齎 ㄐㄧ 咨 ㄗ (ji zih)，嗟嘆。

21.困卦：覿 ㄉㄧˊ (di)，相見。

      蒺 ㄐㄧˊ 藜 ㄌㄧˊ (ji Li)，海邊沙地之草有刺。

梘ㄋㄧㄝˋ 脆ㄨˋ (nie wu)，動搖不安。

22.井卦：繘ㄩˋ (yu)，取井水之繩。

鮒ㄈㄨˋ (fu)，小鯽魚。

渫ㄒㄧㄝˋ (xie)，掏出污泥。

甃ㄓㄡˋ (jhou)，以磚修井壁。

洌ㄌㄧㄝˋ (lie)，清澈的。

23.鼎卦：餗ㄙㄨˋ (su)，鼎中食物。

24.震卦：虩ㄒㄧˋ (xi)，驚恐的樣子。

鬯ㄔㄤˋ (chang)，古代祭祀用之香酒。

矍ㄐㄩㄝˊ (jue)，驚恐四方觀望的樣子。

25.漸卦：衎ㄎㄢˋ (kan)，快樂。

桷ㄐㄩㄝˊ (jue)，承屋瓦的方木。

26.歸妹卦：愆ㄑㄧㄢ (qian)，延誤。

刲ㄎㄨㄟ (kui)，宰殺。

27.豐卦：蔀ㄅㄨˋ (bu)，遮蔽。

闃ㄑㄩˋ (cyu)，靜寂的。

28.中孚卦：靡ㄇㄧˇ (mi)， 共同。

29.既濟卦：茀ㄈㄨˊ (fu)，飾物。

繻ㄒㄩ (syu)，彩帛。

袽ㄖㄨˊ (ru)，破舊衣物。

30.未濟卦：汔ㄑㄧˋ (ci)， 接近，幾乎。

參考文獻 (Reference Literature)

1. 方易經啟示錄 – 孫映達、楊亦鳴

2. 白話易經 – 吳豐隆

3. 白話易經 – 孫振聲

4. 易理精微 – 郭熙謀

5. 易經禪釋 – 巫山定夫

6. 易經占卜 – 楊智宇

7. 易經通俗講座 – 馮斌

8. 易經新詮 – 胡俊熊

9. 周易卜卦全集 – 徐伯鵬

10. 實用易經 – 張汝誠

11. 周易精解 – 楊維傑

12. Book of Changes – Chinese Text Project Translated by James Legge

國家圖書館出版品預行編目(CIP)資料

DIY：I-Ching & Modern Feng Shui：易經與現代風水 / 吳治逸作. -- 初版. --
臺中市：鑫富樂文教, 2016.09
面；　公分
中英對照
ISBN 978-986-93065-1-5(平裝)

1.易占　2.堪輿

292.1　　　　　　　　　　　　　　　　　　　　　105013876

DIY：I-Ching & Modern Feng Shui
——易經與現代風水　English Version

Writer：Roger Wu / 吳治逸
編輯審訂：Peter Liao、郝定慧、林大田
美術設計：楊易達
插畫：林大田、廖曉纓
圖表繪製：鑫富樂文教編輯部

發行人：林淑鈺
出版發行：Xin Fu Yue Culture & Education Co., Ltd.　鑫富樂文教事業有限公司
地址：No.77, Nanyang St., South Dist 40244,Taichung, Taiwan
　　　台中市南區南陽街77號1樓
電話：(04)2260-9293
傳真：(04)2260-7762
總經銷：Red Ants Books Co ., Ltd　紅螞蟻圖書有限公司
地址：114台北市內湖區舊宗路二段121巷19號
電話：(02)2795-3656
傳真：(02)2795-4100
email：red0511@ms51.hinet.net

2016年9月2日 初版一刷
定　價◎新台幣580元
（缺頁或破損的書，請寄回更換）

有著作權·侵害必究 Printed in Taiwan
ISBN 978-986-93065-1-5
公司網站：www.happybookp.com
回饋意見：joycelin@happybookp.com